THE
ROMANTICS
AND
VICTORIANS

THE PAGEANT OF LITERATURE

THE ROMANTICS AND VICTORIANS

Revised Edition

Sister Francis Camilla, S.L.
Webster College, Webster Groves, Missouri

John F. Ennis
King's College, Wilkes-Barre, Pennsylvania

New York   THE MACMILLAN COMPANY

© Copyright The Macmillan Company 1961, 1966

All rights reserved. No part of this book may be reproduced or utilized in any form or by any means, electronic or mechanical, including photocopying, recording or by any information storage and retrieval system, without permission in writing from the Publisher.

The Macmillan Company, New York
Collier-Macmillan Canada, Ltd., Toronto, Ontario
Printed in the United States of America

CONTENTS

THE TRANSITION FROM NEOCLASSICISM TO ROMANTICISM	1
THOMAS GRAY	6
Elegy Written in a Country Churchyard	6
Ode on the Death of a Favorite Cat	12
ROBERT BURNS	14
A Red, Red Rose	14
Ae Fond Kiss	15
John Anderson My Jo	16
My Heart's in the Highlands	17
Is There for Honest Poverty	18
To a Mouse	20
To a Louse	22
WILLIAM BLAKE	26
from Songs of Innocence	
Introduction	26
The Lamb	28
The Chimney Sweeper	29
The Little Black Boy	30
from Songs of Experience	
The Tiger	32
The Clod and the Pebble	33
The Chimney Sweeper	34
THE EARLY ROMANTICS	36
WILLIAM WORDSWORTH	40
Lines Written in Early Spring	40
Three Years She Grew	42
She Dwelt Among the Untrodden Ways	43
I Travelled Among Unknown Men	44
The Solitary Reaper	45
My Heart Leaps Up	46
I Wandered Lonely as a Cloud	47
Tintern Abbey	48
Composed Upon Westminster Bridge	53
London, 1802	54
Ode: Intimations of Immortality	55

vi • Contents

SAMUEL TAYLOR COLERIDGE	63
Kubla Khan	64
Christabel	66
The Rime of the Ancient Mariner	78
THE LATE ROMANTICS	102
GEORGE GORDON, LORD BYRON	106
She Walks in Beauty	106
The Destruction of Sennacherib	107
from Childe Harold's Pilgrimage	109
Sonnet on Chillon	120
Stanzas for Music	121
So We'll Go No More A-Roving	122
JOHN KEATS	123
On First Looking into Chapman's Homer	123
When I Have Fears	124
Proem from Endymion	125
La Belle Dame Sans Merci	127
The Eve of St. Agnes	129
Ode on a Grecian Urn	144
To Autumn	146
Ode to a Nightingale	148
PERCY BYSSHE SHELLEY	152
Ozymandias	152
Song to the Men of England	153
Ode to the West Wind	155
To a Skylark	159
Mutability	163
Stanzas	164
A Lament	166
from Adonais	167
ROMANTIC PROSE WRITERS	175
CHARLES LAMB	178
Dream Children: A Reverie	178
A Dissertation Upon Roast Pig	183
WILLIAM HAZLITT	193
On Going A Journey	193
THOMAS DE QUINCEY	205
On the Knocking at the Gate in Macbeth	205

VICTORIAN PROSE WRITERS	212
THOMAS BABINGTON MACAULAY	218
London Coffeehouses	218
London Streets	223
THOMAS CARLYLE	227
Storming the Bastille	228
Captains of Industry	234
MATTHEW ARNOLD	242
Sweetness and Light	243
JOHN HENRY, CARDINAL NEWMAN	251
Knowledge Viewed in Relation to Professional Skill	251
Literature	259
ROBERT LOUIS STEVENSON	263
Markheim	263
VICTORIAN POETS	283
ALFRED, LORD TENNYSON	288
Ulysses	288
Flower in the Crannied Wall	292
The Lady of Shalott	292
Morte D'Arthur	299
Crossing the Bar	307
ROBERT BROWNING	309
Cavalier Tunes	310
"How They Brought the Good News from Ghent to Aix"	312
The Last Ride Together	315
My Last Duchess	320
Prospice	322
ELIZABETH BARRETT BROWNING	324
from Sonnets from the Portuguese	
I thought once how Theocritus had sung	324
Go from me. Yet I feel that I shall stand	325
If thou must love me, let it be for naught	326
I lived with visions for my company	327
How do I love thee? let me count the ways	328
MATTHEW ARNOLD	329
Self-Dependence	329
Requiescat	331
Shakespeare	332
The Buried Life	333
Dover Beach	337

FRANCIS THOMPSON	340
Envoy	340
The Hound of Heaven	341
THOMAS HARDY	348
Summer Schemes	348
In Time of "The Breaking of Nations"	349
The Man He Killed	350
Drummer Hodge	351
The Darkling Thrush	352
ABOUT THE AUTHORS	355
GLOSSARY OF LITERARY TERMS	366

THE TRANSITION FROM NEOCLASSICISM TO ROMANTICISM

Variously called "The Age of Reason," "The Augustan Age," and "The Neoclassical Age," the eighteenth century was a period that, in the minds of many Englishmen, rivaled the glory of Rome under Caesar Augustus. It was a decorative age, rich in all the material luxuries needed by a wealthy aristocracy and a rising middle class to satisfy their desire for leisure and for tasteful ornamentation and display. The formal gardens where they strolled and conversed were intricately geometrical in design; the elegant town houses and stately country manors where they lived were furnished with the decorative work of the outstanding furniture designers and pottery makers of the period—Chippendale, Hepplewhite, and Wedgwood.

Writers of the period, led by Alexander Pope, Samuel Johnson, and John Dryden, emphasized balance and proportion and attempted to adhere strictly to the theories and rules of the classical writers. In this period of Neoclassicism, literature's function was to appeal to the mind rather than to the heart. Clarity and restraint, aided by wit and disciplined reasonableness, were the desired ends. It was an age of great prose. In poetry, the strict and symmetrical heroic couplet was the predominant verse form; the lyric was put aside in favor of satiric and philosophic verse.

The spirit of this Age of Reason fostered an attempt to force the world of man into neat, formal patterns—of thought, of speech, and of behavior. However, there was a strong undercurrent against such formalization of man, against "Nature methodized." It is true that the desire to be orderly and factual which was highly emphasized by the Neoclassical writers is part of man. But there is another desire in every person, a desire to be imaginative and unrestrained and to express personal emotions freely and warmly. This aspect of man's nature began to be reemphasized about the middle of the eighteenth century even as Neoclassicism was flourishing. It continued to grow quietly throughout the century until it finally burst into full bloom at the beginning of the nineteenth century. It was known as Romanticism.

It is easy to point out the excesses of the eighteenth century in its pursuit of a formal elegance, but it must be remembered that the concept of reasonableness it stressed did bring a critical spirit to all facets of human life. This same critical spirit was responsible, in part, for the development of the Romantic Movement. The revolt against Neoclassical principles of art began early in the eighteenth century. Interestingly enough, it was not the artificiality in literature that was first attacked but the neatly plotted formal gardens. In an essay in *The Spectator,* Joseph Addison pointed out the advantages of aiming at a certain rudeness in gardens since nature is distinguished by "rough, careless strokes."

It was not long, however, before writers began to criticize their contemporaries for the overemphasis on symmetry and polish in much of the art and literature of the period, which too often led to mere affectation and surface sparkle. Critics complained about the artificial conventions of Neoclassical literature. The heroic couplet appeared too confined for the wider issues of the day; the rules which governed drama were seen as too limiting. More important, writers began to treat themes not emphasized by the Neoclassical writers. They explored country life instead of the city and court life that interested the early eighteenth-century writers; they emphasized the beauty and mystery of nature and the pleasures and joys afforded by a return to simplicity; they demonstrated a humanitarian concern for the poor and downtrodden and a renewed confidence in the worth of the individual man. In short, they echoed the revolutions in philosophy, religion, industry, and government that were taking place in England and in Europe. A new spirit was dawning.

Both the philosophical and religious revolutions emphasized feeling and a new kind of social awareness. Jean Jacques Rousseau, the French thinker, stressed the basic goodness and benevolence of man's nature. The artificial elements in society were to be rejected in favor of the goodness of nature and the intuitive promptings of the heart. These impulses of the heart were fired further by the new evangelical religious sects which attempted to bring to the people a more intense religious experience than seemed to be available in the established religions. Speaking especially to the lower classes, the leaders of these sects preached a religion based on emotionalism and pious feelings rather than on reason and dogma.

The Industrial Revolution was responsible for vast social problems. Predominantly an agricultural country before the advent of the machine, England was changing from a country of pleasant farm lands and cottage workers to an industrial giant. The farm workers were leaving the small farms; machine-made goods were replacing the hand work of the peasants. As the farm laborers and cottage workers left the land and came to the sprawling, crowded cities, the pattern of social life changed. The graciousness of eighteenth-century London was on its way to being lost in the factory smoke of the newly emerging industrial age.

Two other great revolutions outside England contributed to the growing disillusionment with the rule of reason and right order. Condemned by most Englishmen, the American Revolution in 1776 nevertheless demonstrated the desire of man for "life, liberty, and the pursuit of happiness." The forces which led the founders of America to break with

England called into question the most basic element of English political and social thought—the right of the individual to have a voice in the process of government.

In 1789 the violent and bloody French Revolution was launched. Begun as a revolt against an outworn social order which cared too little for the common man, it soon evolved into something much larger, more symbolic. Soon its battle cry of "liberty, equality, fraternity" was heard all across Europe, announcing the end of an absolute monarchy with its arbitrary class distinctions and privileges. Within England, conflicting feelings and emotions were aroused. However, both those who saw the French Revolution as a threat to an established mode of life and those who cheered it as the dawn of a new world of justice and peace knew that it foreshadowed deep changes in all the works of men; that the world could never be the same.

The first fruits of these wide-ranging changes influenced English thought and were reflected in the literature of the period. Much of the change is reflected in the transition from the Neoclassical to the Romantic tradition and is very clearly seen in the poetry of Thomas Gray, Robert Burns, and William Blake, three great poets of the latter half of the eighteenth century. Their poetry represents a new intensity of feeling, a renewed awareness of the power of emotion, a rebirth of the sense of wonder, a greater freedom in both subject matter and form, and a genuine concern for the individual and for personal experience.

The work of Thomas Gray, coming in the mid-eighteenth century, is a mixture of Neoclassicism and the new Romanticism which was quietly developing. A classicist by training, Gray slowly and carefully refined and ordered each stanza he wrote. His concern for symmetry and correctness in form and his desire to teach a moral show a sympathy with the Neoclassical ideals. However, his interest in the past, his feeling for the common man, his underlying note of personal melancholy were signs of the coming Romanticism.

Robert Burns produced during his short lifetime some of the most intense lyrics in English literature, poems markedly different from those of the eighteenth century. This Scottish peasant who wrote many of his impassioned lyrics and poems of humanity in the Scots dialect was hailed as a natural song bird, a poet who sang the joys of his natural feelings.

Although Burns broke with the restrictive forms of Neoclassical poetry, he did not do so by instinct but by much studying of Scottish literary tradition and the oral heritage of Scottish folklore and song. He prefigures the Romantic Age by his use of language which spoke of and to the common man, by his love of nature, by his humanitarian interests, by his exaltation of the humble Scottish peasant, and by the intense personal feeling in his poetry. His poetry soared into regions the Neoclassical poets never dared enter.

William Blake, of all the early Romantics, broke most definitely with the Neoclassical writers and stands as one of the most original new poets. Neoclassicists had been particularly opposed to the metaphysical poets of the seventeenth century and their religious fervor and intensity. Blake, on the other hand, tried in his poetry to depict the soul. This attempt, using highly symbolic images in deceptively simple language, makes many of his poems difficult to interpret.

In his companion volumes, *Songs of Innocence* and *Songs of Experience,* Blake describes the "two contrary states of the human soul." In *Songs of Innocence,* he celebrates the joys of childhood, seeing the child not as an immature adult but as a distinct and different being. In clear and simple language he shows childhood as a condition of happiness, unity, and self-enjoyment. In *Songs of Experience,* he introduces the disruptive influence of doubt and the failure of love in the face of poverty, disease, war, and the repression of certain segments of society by the forces of Church and State.

Thomas Gray

(1716–1771)

Thomas Gray published fewer than 1000 lines of poetry during his lifetime, but that handful of poems exerted a powerful influence on his contemporaries. His careful craftsmanship, his use of classical allusions to carry tone and feeling, and his propriety in demonstrating the best of good manners mark him as a Neoclassicist. However, as one of the principal "graveyard poets," a group of eighteenth-century writers who wrote long, dark poems about life, death, immortality, and the value of country life, Gray exhibited the melancholic strain characteristic of the growing Romanticism.

His "Elegy Written in a Country Churchyard" stands as one of the best-known and most enduring poems in the English language. Its alternately rhymed four-line stanzas present universal feelings to which each man responds. In its quiet evocation of mood, in its pictorial re-creation of the idyllic life of the simple villagers, and in its concentration on the worth of the individual man, the poem remains a unique human achievement.

ELEGY WRITTEN IN A COUNTRY CHURCHYARD

The curfew tolls the knell of parting day,
    The lowing herd wind slowly o'er the lea,
The plowman homeward plods his weary way,
    And leaves the world to darkness and to me.

Now fades the glimmering landscape on the sight,   5
    And all the air a solemn stillness holds,
Save where the beetle wheels his droning flight,
    And drowsy tinklings lull the distant folds;

Elegy Written in a Country Churchyard

Save that from yonder ivy-mantled tower
    The moping owl does to the moon complain   10
Of such, as wandering near her secret bower,
    Molest her ancient solitary reign.

Beneath those rugged elms, that yew-tree's shade,
    Where heaves the turf in many a moldering heap,
Each in his narrow cell forever laid,   15
    The rude forefathers of the hamlet sleep.

The breezy call of incense-breathing Morn,
    The swallow twittering from the straw-built shed,
The cock's shrill clarion, or the echoing horn,
    No more shall rouse them from their lowly bed.   20

For them no more the blazing hearth shall burn,
    Or busy housewife ply her evening care;
No children run to lisp their sire's return,
    Or climb his knees the envied kiss to share.

Oft did the harvest to their sickle yield,   25
    Their furrow oft the stubborn glebe [1] has broke;
How jocund did they drive their team afield!
    How bowed the woods beneath their sturdy stroke!

Let not Ambition mock their useful toil,
    Their homely joys, and destiny obscure;   30
Nor Grandeur hear, with a disdainful smile,
    The short and simple annals of the poor.

The boast of heraldry, the pomp of power,
    And all that beauty, all that wealth e'er gave,
Awaits alike the inevitable hour: 35
    The paths of glory lead but to the grave.

---

[1] **glebe:** sod

Nor you, ye proud, impute to these the fault,
    If Memory o'er their tomb no trophies raise,
Where through the long-drawn aisle and fretted vault
    The pealing anthem swells the note of praise.   40

Can storied urn or animated bust
    Back to its mansion call the fleeting breath?
Can Honor's voice provoke the silent dust,
    Or Flattery soothe the dull cold ear of Death?

Perhaps in this neglected spot is laid   45
    Some heart once pregnant with celestial fire;
Hands that the rod of empire might have swayed,
    Or waked to ecstasy the living lyre.

But Knowledge to their eyes her ample page
    Rich with the spoils of time did ne'er unroll;   50
Chill Penury repressed their noble rage,
    And froze the genial current of the soul.

Full many a gem of purest ray serene
    The dark unfathomed caves of ocean bear;
Full many a flower is born to blush unseen,   55
    And waste its sweetness on the desert air.

Some village Hampden [2] that with dauntless breast
    The little tyrant of his fields withstood;
Some mute inglorious Milton here may rest,
    Some Cromwell guiltless of his country's blood.   60

The applause of listening senates to command,
    The threats of pain and ruin to despise,
To scatter plenty o'er a smiling land,
    And read their history in a nation's eyes,

---

[2] **Hampden:** a country landowner who defied the tax levies of Charles I.

Their lot forbade; nor circumscribed alone 65
    Their growing virtues, but their crimes confined;
Forbade to wade through slaughter to a throne,
    And shut the gates of mercy on mankind,

The struggling pangs of conscious truth to hide,
    To quench the blushes of ingenuous shame, 70
Or heap the shrine of Luxury and Pride
    With incense kindled at the Muse's flame.

Far from the madding crowd's ignoble strife,
    Their sober wishes never learned to stray;
Along the cool sequestered vale of life 75
    They kept the noiseless tenor of their way.

Yet ev'n these bones from insult to protect
    Some frail memorial still erected nigh,
With uncouth rimes and shapeless sculpture decked,
    Implores the passing tribute of a sigh. 80

Their name, their years, spelt by the unlettered Muse,
    The place of fame and elegy supply;
And many a holy text around she strews,
    That teach the rustic moralist to die.

For who, to dumb Forgetfulness a prey, 85
    This pleasing anxious being e'er resigned,
Left the warm precincts of the cheerful day,
    Nor cast one longing, lingering look behind?

On some fond breast the parting soul relies,
    Some pious drops the closing eye requires; 90
Ev'n from the tomb the voice of Nature cries,
    Ev'n in our ashes live their wonted fires.

For thee,[3] who mindful of the unhonored dead
    Dost in these lines their artless tale relate;
If chance, by lonely Contemplation led,   95
    Some kindred spirit shall inquire thy fate,

Haply some hoary-headed swain may say,
    "Oft have we seen him at the peep of dawn
Brushing with hasty steps the dews away
    To meet the sun upon the upland lawn.   100

"There at the foot of yonder nodding beech
    That wreathes its old fantastic roots so high,
His listless length at noontide would he stretch,
    And pore upon the brook that babbles by.

"Hard by yon wood, now smiling as in scorn,   105
    Muttering his wayward fancies he would rove,
Now drooping, woeful wan, like one forlorn,
    Or crazed with care, or crossed in hopeless love.

"One morn I missed him on the customed hill,
    Along the heath, and near his favorite tree;   110
Another came; nor yet beside the rill,
    Nor up the lawn, nor at the wood was he;

"The next with dirges due in sad array
    Slow through the church-way path we saw him borne.
Approach and read (for thou canst read) the lay,   115
    Graved on the stone beneath yon aged thorn."

The Epitaph

Here rests his head upon the lap of Earth
    A youth to Fortune and to Fame unknown.
Fair Science frowned not on his humble birth,
    And Melancholy marked him for her own.   120

---
[3] **thee:** refers to the poet himself

Large was his bounty, and his soul sincere,
  Heaven did a recompense as largely send;
He gave to Misery all he had, a tear,
  He gained from Heaven ('twas all he wished) a friend.

No farther seek his merits to disclose,   125
  Or draw his frailties from their dread abode,
(There they alike in trembling hope repose),
  The bosom of his Father and his God.

For Discussion

1. The first three stanzas of the poem serve to set the scene and to evoke a mood. What is the scene? What is the mood evoked? How do the details of setting contribute to the mood? How do rhythm and choice of words in lines 7–8 contribute to this mood?
2. In lines 13–28 the poet depicts the life of the villagers. What were their pleasures? In lines 29–64, what answer does he give to those who scoff at the natural simplicity of the life of these people? Point out specific lines and stanzas which describe his attitude and the reasons for this attitude.
3. Note the dramatic contrast between lines 65–72 and lines 73–76. What is the narrator's attitude toward sophisticated society? Why does he feel that the life of the villagers is more worthwhile?
4. What purpose is served by the introduction of the "hoary-headed swain" as narrator in line 97? What effect does this have on the poem?
5. What themes in this poem show the change from Neoclassicism to Romanticism? Support your answer by pointing out specific lines.
6. Gray is a craftsman in the Neoclassical tradition, utilizing the sounds of language to create harmony of tone. Point out lines which show Gray's ability to create "sound" pictures consistent with the meaning.

ODE ON THE DEATH OF A FAVORITE CAT
Drowned in a Tub of Gold-Fishes

'Twas on a lofty vase's side,
Where China's gayest art had dyed
    The azure flowers, that blow;
Demurest of the tabby kind,
The pensive Selima reclined,   5
    Gazed on the lake below.

Her conscious tail her joy declared;
The fair round face, the snowy beard,
    The velvet of her paws,
Her coat, that with the tortoise vies,   10
Her ears of jet, and emerald eyes,
    She saw; and purred applause.

Still had she gazed; but 'midst the tide
Two angel forms were seen to glide,
    The genii of the stream;   15
Their scaly armor's Tyrian hue
Through richest purple to the view
    Betrayed a golden gleam.

The hapless nymph with wonder saw:
A whisker first and then a claw,   20
    With many an ardent wish,
She stretched in vain to reach the prize.
What female heart can gold despise?
    What cat's averse to fish?

Presumptuous maid! with looks intent   25
Again she stretched, again she bent,
    Nor knew the gulf between.
(Malignant Fate sat by, and smiled)
The slippery verge her feet beguiled,
    She tumbled headlong in.   30

Eight times emerging from the flood
She mewed to every watery god,
   Some speedy aid to send.
No dolphin came,[1] no nereid [2] stirred:
Nor cruel Tom, nor Susan heard.
   A favorite has no friend!

From hence, ye beauties, undeceived,
Know, one false step is ne'er retrieved,
   And be with caution bold.
Not all that tempts your wandering eyes
And heedless hearts, is lawful prize;
   Nor all, that glisters, gold.

---

[1] According to a legend, Arion, a Greek musician, thrown overboard by sailors, was rescued on the back of a dolphin.
[2] **nereid:** a sea nymph

For Discussion

1. An ode is a dignified lyric on a serious subject, using exalted language. How does the use of this form contribute to the humor of the poem?
2. Point out specific examples of the poet's use of exaggerated language which contribute to the humor of the poem.
3. What is the "message" of this poem? Does this "message" add to or detract from the humor of the poem? Explain.
4. "The pensive Selima" seems to have many female characteristics. For example, what causes her to purr applause? What importance does this have for the final stanza?

For Composition

1. In describing the scene in the country churchyard, Gray carefully selects connotative words which contribute to the mood he wishes to evoke. Decide on a mood you wish to convey and describe a specific place in terms of this mood.
2. In "Elegy Written in a Country Churchyard" the poet suggests that lack of education and opportunity kept the villagers from achieving fame and renown. In a short essay, discuss the effect that your own education has had on you and on your plans for the future.

Robert Burns

(1759–1796)

The poetry of Robert Burns is very personal and spontaneous, a fusion of intuition and art. Written in the Scots dialect, the poetry came straight from the soil of his beloved native land to reach the hearts of all men.

This impassioned lyric quality is best seen in his love poems, which are among the most famous in English literature. They are alive with the emotion of love—the exhilaration of falling in love; the agony of falling out of love. They range from the hyperbolic promises of the young lover to the serene beauty of mature love to the bitterness of lost love.

Burns had a deep love for the common man and for the ordinary things of nature. He wrote fiercely of the hypocrisy and insincerity he saw in people. A man of the people himself, Burns re-creates for each of us the joy of being human.

A RED, RED ROSE

Oh, my luve is like a red, red rose,
    That's newly sprung in June;
Oh, my luve is like the melodie,
    That's sweetly played in tune.

As fair art thou, my bonie lass,   5
    So deep in luve am I;
And I will luve thee still, my dear,
    Till a' the seas gang [1] dry.

---

[1] **gang:** go

Till a' the seas gang dry, my dear,
    And the rocks melt wi' the sun!   10
And I will luve thee still, my dear,
    While the sands o' life shall run.

And fare thee weel, my only luve,
    And fare thee weel a while!
And I will come again, my luve,   15
    Tho' it were ten thousand mile!

For Discussion

1. Two outstanding qualities of this poem are its simplicity and spontaneity. Support this statement by pointing out specific lines. Try to show how the poem would be less spontaneous if it were less carefully constructed.
2. Is the speaker in this poem young or old? Consider carefully the language clues, particularly the frequent use of hyperbole. Is the frequent use of hyperbole in keeping with the character of the speaker? Is he sincere?
3. Note the similes the speaker uses to describe his love. What do they imply of her characteristics?

AE FOND KISS

Ae fond kiss, and then we sever!
Ae farewell, and then forever!
Deep in heart-wrung tears I'll pledge thee,
Warring sighs and groans I'll wage thee.
Who shall say that Fortune grieves him,   5
While the star of hope she leaves him?
Me, nae cheerfu' twinkle lights me,
Dark despair around benights me.

I'll ne'er blame my partial fancy:
Naething could resist my Nancy!   10
But to see her was to love her,
Love but her, and love for ever.

Had we never loved sae kindly,
Had we never loved sae blindly,
Never met—or never parted— 15
We had ne'er been broken-hearted.

Fare thee weel, thou first and fairest!
Fare thee weel, thou best and dearest!
Thine be ilka joy and treasure,
Peace, Enjoyment, Love, and Pleasure! 20
Ae fond kiss, and then we sever!
Ae farewell, alas, for ever!
Deep in heart-wrung tears I'll pledge thee,
Warring sighs and groans I'll wage thee.

For Discussion

1. Why does the speaker call Nancy the "best and dearest"? What perhaps has he understood about life from his love for this "first and fairest"?
2. The first four lines of the poem and the last four lines are, with one change, identical. How does the change in wording change the emotion and contribute to the impact of the poem?
3. Lines 13–16 are simple yet highly intense. What elements contribute to their power and intensity? What other lines show the poet's particular ability to choose words for their sound as well as for their meaning?

JOHN ANDERSON MY JO

John Anderson my jo,[1] John,
    When we were first acquent,
Your locks were like the raven,
    Your bonie brow was brent;[2]
But now your brow is beld,[3] John, 5
    Your locks are like the snaw;
But blessings on your frosty pow,
    John Anderson my jo.

[1] **jo:** sweetheart   [2] **brent:** smooth   [3] **beld:** bald

John Anderson my jo, John,
    We clamb the hill thegither;
And mony a canty [4] day, John,
    We've had wi' ane anither.
Now we maun [5] totter down, John,
    And hand in hand we'll go,
And sleep thegither at the foot,
    John Anderson my jo.

[4] **canty:** happy   [5] **maun:** must

For Discussion

1. What is the attitude of the speaker toward John Anderson? Show how the poem deals not only with their present life but also with the past and the future.
2. Substitute modern English words for the dialect in the poem. Does the music of the poem gain or lose by this substitution? Discuss.
3. How does the poet avoid sentimentality in this poem? How would the effect of the poem be altered if the poet had described the lives of the speaker and John Anderson in general terms, instead of particularizing the various stages?
4. The metaphor of the journey is frequently used by writers to represent man's life. Explain the effectiveness of the hill metaphor, showing how its use is consistent with the character of the people involved in the poem.

MY HEART'S IN THE HIGHLANDS

Farewell to the Highlands, farewell to the North,
The birth-place of valour, the country of worth;
Wherever I wander, wherever I rove,
The hills of the Highlands for ever I love.
My heart's in the Highlands, my heart is not here;
My heart's in the Highlands a-chasing the deer;
A-chasing the wild deer, and following the roe,
My heart's in the Highlands, wherever I go.

Farewell to the mountains high cover'd with snow;
Farewell to the straths and green valleys below;   10
Farewell to the forests and wild-hanging woods;
Farewell to the torrents and loud-pouring floods.
My heart's in the Highlands, my heart is not here;
My heart's in the Highlands a-chasing the deer;
A-chasing the wild deer, and following the roe,   15
My heart's in the Highlands, wherever I go.

For Discussion

1. What do the Highlands represent to the speaker of this poem? How does the music of the poem—the sound and the rhythm—help to convey his emotion?
2. This poem contains repetition of words and rhythm. What is the effect of this repetition? Consider particularly the relationship between sound and meaning.
3. The poem abounds in visual images. Point out the use of those images which give a very personal quality to a common emotion. How does the use of concrete particulars make the poem both personal and universal?

IS THERE FOR HONEST POVERTY

Is there for honest poverty,
    That hings his head, an' a' that?
The coward slave, we pass him by,
    We dare be poor for a' that!
        For a' that, an' a' that,   5
        Our toils obscure, an' a' that;
    The rank is but the guinea's stamp;
        The man's the gowd [1] for a' that.

What tho' on hamely fare we dine,
    Wear hodden-gray,[2] an' a' that?   10
    Gie fools their silks, and knaves their wine,

---

[1] **gowd:** gold   [2] **hodden-gray:** coarse cloth

A man's a man for a' that.
    For a' that, an' a' that,
      Their tinsel show, an' a' that;
    The honest man, tho' e'er sae poor,
      Is king o' men for a' that.

Ye see yon birkie,[3] ca'd "a lord,"
    Wha struts, an' stares, an' a' that?
Tho' hundreds worship at his word,
    He's but a cuif [4] for a' that.
    For a' that, an' a' that,
      His ribband, star, an' a' that,
    The man o' independent mind,
      He looks and laughs at a' that.

A prince can mak a belted knight,
    A marquis, duke, an' a' that;
But an honest man's aboon his might,
    Guid faith, he mauna fa' that!
    For a' that, an' a' that,
      Their dignities, an' a' that,
    The pith o' sense an' pride o' worth
      Are higher rank than a' that.

Then let us pray that come it may,
    As come it will for a' that,
That sense and worth o'er a' the earth
    May bear the gree,[5] an' a' that.
    For a' that, an' a' that,
      It's coming yet, for a' that,
    That man to man the warld o'er
      Shall brothers be for a' that.

---

[3] **birkie:** fine fellow   [4] **cuif:** blockhead   [5] **gree:** crown or laurel

For Discussion

1. This poem shows Burns's intense interest in and sympathy for the common man. Would this poem be as effective without the use of dialect? What precisely does the use of dialect do for the poem?
2. Are poor people often the "coward slaves" spoken of in the first stanza? Give reasons for your answer.
3. The first four stanzas of the poem move from particular incidents to generalizations about life. What is the purpose of the final stanza of the poem? Under what conditions can the world that Burns hopes for in this poem be realized? Do you think he is overly optimistic? Idealistic?
4. Why might this poem be called a poetic Declaration of Independence? Consider both the values which are praised and the faults which are condemned.

TO A MOUSE

On Turning Her Up in Her Nest with the Plough, November, 1785

Wee, sleekit,[1] cow'rin tim'rous beastie,
Oh, what a panic's in thy breastie!
Thou need na start awa sae hasty
    Wi' bickering brattle!
I wad be laith [2] to rin an' chase thee   5
    Wi' murdering pattle! [3]

I'm truly sorry man's dominion
Has broken Nature's social union,
An' justifies that ill opinion
    Which makes thee startle   10
At me, thy poor, earth-born companion,
    An' fellow mortal!

---
[1] **sleekit:** sleek
[2] **laith:** loath
[3] **pattle:** small spade

To a Mouse • 21

I doubt na, whyles, but thou may thieve:
What then? poor beastie, thou maun live!
A daimen icker [4] in a thrave   15
    'S a sma' request;
I'll get a blessin wi' the lave,[5]
    An' never miss 't!

Thy wee bit housie, too, in ruin!
Its silly wa's the win's are strewin!   20
An' naething, now, to big a new ane,
    O' foggage [6] green!
An' bleak December's win's ensuin',
    Baith snell [7] an' keen!

Thou saw the fields laid bare an' waste, 25
An' weary winter comin' fast,
An' cozie here, beneath the blast,
    Thou thought to dwell,
Till crash! the cruel coulter past
    Out thro' thy cell.   30

That wee bit heap o' leaves an' stibble
Has cost thee monie a weary nibble!
Now thou's turned out, for a' thy trouble,
    But house or hald,[8]
To thole [9] the winter's sleety dribble, 35
    An' cranreuch [10] cauld!

But, Mousie, thou art no thy lane [11]
In proving foresight may be vain:

[4] **daimen icker:** an ear of grain now and then
[5] **lave:** rest
[6] **foggage:** grass
[7] **snell:** sharp
[8] **but house or hald:** without house or possession
[9] **thole:** endure
[10] **cranreuch:** frost
[11] **no thy lane:** not alone

> The best-laid schemes o' mice an' men
>   Gang aft agley,[12]   40
> An' lea'e us nought but grief an' pain
>   For promised joy.
>
> Still thou art blest, compared wi' me!
> The present only toucheth thee:
> But, och! I backward cast my e'e,   45
>   On prospects drear!
> An' forward, tho' I canna see,
>   I guess an' fear!

[12] **gang aft agley:** often go astray

For Discussion

1. Show how the note of friendly compassion grows as the poem progresses. In what ways does the speaker identify himself with the mouse?
2. How does the pause at the end of the first four lines of each stanza emphasize the speaker's attitude in the last two lines?
3. The second stanza of the poem uses little dialect. Does this have any effect on the poem as a poem? Explain.
4. What is the speaker's feeling about the world as expressed in the last two stanzas? Compare this feeling with that expressed in "Is There for Honest Poverty."

TO A LOUSE

On Seeing One on a Lady's Bonnet at Church

> Ha! wh' are ye gaun, ye crowlin' ferlie![1]
> Your impudence protects you sairly;[2]
> I canna say but ye strunt[3] rarely,

[1] **crowlin' ferlie:** crawling wonder
[2] **sairly:** greatly
[3] **strunt:** strut

Owre gauze and lace;
Though faith! I fear ye dine but sparely
    On sic a place.

Ye ugly, creepin', blastit wonner,
Detested, shunned by saunt an' sinner!
How dare ye set your fit upon her,
    Sae fine a lady?
Gae somewhere else, and seek your dinner
    On some poor body.

Swith, in some beggar's haffet squattle; [4]
There ye may creep, and sprawl, and sprattle [5]
Wi' ither kindred jumping cattle,
    In shoals and nations;
Where horn nor bane [6] ne'er dare unsettle
    Your thick plantations.

Now haud ye there,[7] ye're out o' sight,
Below the fatt'rels,[8] snug an' tight;
Na, faith ye yet! ye'll no be right
    Till ye've got on it,
The very tapmost tow'ring height
    O' Miss's bonnet.

My sooth! right bauld ye set your nose out,
As plump and gray as onie grozet; [9]
O for some rank mercurial rozet,[10]
    Or fell red smeddum! [11]

---

[4] **Swith, in some beggar's haffet squattle:** quick, sprawl in some beggar's head
[5] **sprattle:** struggle
[6] **horn nor bane:** comb nor poison
[7] **haud ye there:** stay where you are
[8] **fatt'rels:** ribbon ends
[9] **grozet:** gooseberry
[10] **rozet:** rosin
[11] **smeddum:** powder

24 • ROBERT BURNS

> I'd gie you sic a hearty dose o't,
>   Wad dress your droddum! [12]   30
> I wad na been surprised to spy
> You on an auld wife's flainen toy; [13]
> Or aiblins some bit duddie boy,[14]
>   On's wyliecoat; [15]
> But Miss's fine Lunardi! [16] fie,   35
>   How daur ye do 't?
>
> O Jenny, dinna toss your head,
> An' set your beauties a' abread! [17]
> Ye little ken what cursèd speed
>   The blastie's makin'!   40
> Thae winks and finger ends, I dread,
>   Are notice takin'!
>
> O wad some Pow'r the giftie gie us
> To see oursels as ithers see us!
> It wad frae mony a blunder free us,   45
>   And foolish notion:
> What airs in dress an' gait wad lea'e us,
>   And e'en devotion!

[12] **Wad dress your droddum:** would put an end to you
[13] **flainen toy:** flannel cap
[14] **Or aiblins some bit duddie boy:** or perhaps on some little ragged boy
[15] **wyliecoat:** flannel vest
[16] **Lunardi:** a type of bonnet
[17] **abread:** abroad

For Discussion

1. What tone does the speaker use in addressing the insect? What basic contrast explains the humor in the situation? Point out specific words and phrases which indicate the tone of the entire poem.
2. This poem abounds in bright, descriptive touches. Point out particularly apt examples.

3. To what conclusion does this seemingly casual poem point? Is the last stanza solemnly didactic or wryly ironic? Support your answer with references to the poem.
4. Compare the mood of this poem with that of "To a Mouse."

For Composition

1. In imitation of the lyrics of Burns, try to write a short lyric in which you attempt to convey some deep-felt emotion. Remember that the great lyrics show emotion through the medium of experience.
2. The poetry of Robert Burns has always had a great appeal for the average man. Write a theme in which you discuss particular works, showing why they would appeal especially to the unsophisticated man.

William Blake ROMANTIC

(1757–1827)

The poetry of William Blake has its own particular blend of the earthly and the unearthly set in language which is highly symbolic yet deceptively simple. As a poet Blake fulfills the basic tenet of Romanticism—the rebirth of wonder and of the imagination. Moreover, his poetry shows a new awareness of and a sympathy for the individual.

Blake wrote about nature, the streets of London, the people who crowded the city. In the *Songs of Innocence,* he expresses the wonder, the joy, and the happiness of the world of the child. His is the vision of the poet who has retained the sense of wonder, and he expresses this wonder in language which is childlike but not childish. *Songs of Experience* often shows the same dramatic situations as *Songs of Innocence,* but now darkened by a sense of age, of evil, of disease, and of the destructive influences of society. It is in his highly imaginative use of language, however, that Blake is the most original—and the most difficult—of all the pre-Romantics.

from SONGS OF INNOCENCE

INTRODUCTION

Piping down the valleys wild,
Piping songs of pleasant glee,
On a cloud I saw a child,
And he laughing said to me:

"Pipe a song about a Lamb!" 5
So I piped with merry cheer.
"Piper, pipe that song again."
So I piped: he wept to hear.

"Drop thy pipe, thy happy pipe;
Sing thy songs of happy cheer." 10
So I sung the same again,
While he wept with joy to hear.

"Piper, sit thee down and write
In a book, that all may read."
So he vanished from my sight, 15
And I plucked a hollow reed,

And I made a rural pen,
And I stained the water clear,
And I wrote my happy songs
Every child may joy to hear. 20

For Discussion

1. This poem is the first in the volume *Songs of Innocence*. How does the speaker suggest innocence and simplicity? How does he say he came to write his poems?
2. What does the Lamb mean to the child? What different significance could it have for the reader?
3. Why is the word "Songs" used instead of "Poems"? What is suggested about the quality the other works in the volume will possess?
4. Analyze the repetition of vowel sounds in this poem. What vowels predominate in the first two stanzas? What is the effect of the repetition?

THE LAMB

Little Lamb, who made thee?
Dost thou know who made thee?
Gave thee life, and bid thee feed,
By the stream and o'er the mead?
Gave thee clothing of delight,   5
Softest clothing, woolly, bright?
Gave thee such a tender voice,
Making all the vales rejoice?
   Little Lamb, who made thee?
   Dost thou know who made thee?   10

Little Lamb, I'll tell thee,
Little Lamb, I'll tell thee:
He is calléd by thy name,
For He calls Himself a Lamb.
He is meek, and He is mild;   15
He became a little child.
I a child, and thou a lamb,
We are calléd by His name.
   Little Lamb, God bless thee!
   Little Lamb, God bless thee!   20

For Discussion

1. What is the dramatic situation given in the first stanza? Point out words describing the Lamb which convey the impression of innocence.
2. How does the language of the speaker suggest his innocence and youth? How does the two-part structure of the poem underscore the innocence?
3. In what way does stanza 2 develop a relationship between the speaker, the Lamb, and the Maker? What is this relationship? Do you agree with some critics that the Lamb here represents Christ? Explain.

4. Why is Blake's simple, childlike language not childish? Point out lines that particularly demonstrate his ability to avoid that fault.

THE CHIMNEY SWEEPER

When my mother died I was very young,
And my father sold me while yet my tongue
Could scarcely cry ' 'weep! 'weep! 'weep!' 'weep!'
So your chimneys I sweep, and in soot I sleep.

There's little Tom Dacre, who cried when his head,   5
That curl'd like a lamb's back, was shav'd: so I said
'Hush, Tom! never mind it, for when your head's bare
You know that the soot cannot spoil your white hair.'

And so he was quiet, and that very night,
As Tom was a-sleeping, he had such a sight!—   10
That thousands of sweepers, Dick, Joe, Ned, and Jack,
Were all of them lock'd up in coffins of black.

And by came an Angel who had a bright key,
And he open'd the coffins and set them all free;
Then down a green plain leaping, laughing, they run,   15
And wash in a river, and shine in the sun.

Then naked and white, all their bags left behind,
They rise upon clouds and sport in the wind;
And the Angel told Tom, if he'd be a good boy,
He'd have God for his father, and never want joy.   20

And so Tom awoke; and we rose in the dark,
And got with our bags and our brushes to work.
Tho' the morning was cold, Tom was happy and warm;
So if all do their duty they need not fear harm.

For Discussion

1. During Blake's time, small boys would earn their living by climbing into chimneys to sweep out the soot. What other facts of the boy's background evoke the reader's sympathy?
2. Pay careful attention to the structure of the sentences. What does the use of connectives like "then," "for," and "and" indicate about the speaker and his attitude toward his lot in life?
3. Is the last line of the poem meant to be the moral or is it merely the final word of the speaker? What is the effect on the reader?
4. Compare this poem to the other poems from *Songs of Innocence*. What are the similarities? What are the differences? Why does the poem appear in *Songs of Innocence* rather than in *Songs of Experience*?

THE LITTLE BLACK BOY

My mother bore me in the southern wild,
And I am black, but O! my soul is white;
White as an angel is the English child,
But I am black, as if bereaved of light.

My mother taught me underneath a tree,　　　　　　5
And, sitting down before the heat of day,
She took me on her lap and kisséd me,
And, pointing to the east, began to say:

"Look on the rising sun,—there God does live,
And gives His light, and gives His heat away;　　　10
And flowers and trees and beasts and men receive
Comfort in morning, joy in the noonday.

"And we are put on earth a little space,
That we may learn to bear the beams of love;
And these black bodies and this sunburnt face   15
Is but a cloud, and like a shady grove.

"For when our souls have learned the heat to bear,
The cloud will vanish; we shall hear His voice,
Saying: 'Come out from the grove, My love and care,
And round My golden tent like lambs rejoice.' "   20

Thus did my mother say, and kisséd me;
And thus I say to little English boy.
When I from black and he from white cloud free,
And round the tent of God like lambs we joy,

I'll shade him from the heat, till he can bear   25
To lean in joy upon our Father's knee;
And then I'll stand and stroke his silver hair,
And be like him, and he will then love me.

For Discussion

1. The poem suggests an experience which has bewildered the speaker, the "little black boy." Can you suggest what the experience might have been? How does the boy react to his mother's words? What is the relation between the setting of the poem and the words of the mother?
2. What is the theme of this poem? How does this theme show another view of Blake as a romantic poet?
3. How would the poem be changed if the last two lines read:
   And then I'll kneel and watch him standing there,
   And look at him, and he will look at me.

from **SONGS OF EXPERIENCE**

THE TIGER

Tiger! Tiger! burning bright
In the forests of the night,
What immortal hand or eye
Could frame thy fearful symmetry?

In what distant deeps or skies   5
Burnt the fire of thine eyes?
On what wings dare he aspire?
What the hand dare seize the fire?

And what shoulder, and what art,
Could twist the sinews of thy heart?   10
And when thy heart began to beat,
What dread hand, and what dread feet?

What the hammer? what the chain?
In what furnace was thy brain?
What the anvil? what dread grasp   15
Dare its deadly terrors clasp?

When the stars threw down their spears,
And watered heaven with their tears,
Did he smile his work to see?
Did he who made the Lamb make thee?   20

Tiger! Tiger! burning bright
In the forests of the night,
What immortal hand or eye
Dare frame thy fearful symmetry?

For Discussion

1. In what way do the language and imagery of this poem differ from the language and imagery of its companion, "The Lamb"?
2. The speaker in "The Lamb" shows complete trust and faith. Is this same trust apparent in "The Tiger"? What causes are at work which might bring the speaker to question, but to receive no answers to his questions?
3. The speaker in this poem is both fearful of the tiger and struck by the beauty of the animal. Do you think the tiger might represent something other than pure evil? Discuss.
4. What is the difference between lines 3 and 4 and lines 23 and 24? What is the effect of that difference?
5. Compare the rhythm of "The Tiger" with that of "The Lamb." How does rhythm contribute to the effect of each poem?

THE CLOD AND THE PEBBLE

"Love seeketh not itself to please,
Nor for itself hath any care,
But for another gives its ease,
And builds a Heaven in Hell's despair."

So sung a little Clod of Clay, 5
Trodden with the cattle's feet,
But a Pebble of the brook
Warbled out these meters meet:

"Love seeketh only self to please,
To bind another to its delight, 10
Joys in another's loss of ease,
And builds a Hell in Heaven's despite."

For Discussion

1. In this poem the voices of the clod and the pebble portray two kinds of love, two views of life. What is the difference between the two? What comment is made by the narrator in the second stanza?
2. In this poem the symbols are taken from nature. Is the poem concerned only with nature and the world of inanimate things? Explain.
3. Notice the parallel structuring of the first and third stanzas. What is the effect of the structure on the meaning of the poem?

THE CHIMNEY SWEEPER

A little black thing among the snow,
Crying ' 'weep! 'weep!' in notes of woe!
'Where are thy father and mother, say?'—
'They are both gone up to the Church to pray.

'Because I was happy upon the heath, 5
And smil'd among the winter's snow,
They clothèd me in the clothes of death,
And taught me to sing the notes of woe.

'And because I am happy and dance and sing,
They think they have done me no injury, 10
And are gone to praise God and His Priest and King,
Who make up a Heaven of our misery.'

For Discussion

1. The phrase " 'weep! 'weep!" is used in both "The Chimney Sweeper" poems. How does the use in this poem differ from the use in the poem from *Songs of Innocence* (see page 29).

The Chimney Sweeper • 35

2. Who is the speaker in the first two lines? Does he differ from the speaker in line 3?
3. Indicate the contrasts in this poem. How do these contrasts contribute to the effectiveness of the poem?
4. What does this poem say about the harm good people do? Is the harm done actively or passively? Discuss.

For Composition

1. Write a short critical paper in which you discuss Blake's use of contrast as a poetic device. Consider not only his use of contrasting symbols such as the lamb and the tiger but also his use of contrast in language.
2. Blake's imagination led him to see the ordinary things of life in a new and different way. Think about some of the ordinary things of life—sleeping, eating, day, night, colors, clocks, sitting—and see if they remain ordinary when you think about them. Explore, in a short paper, one of these ordinary phenomena in an imaginative and unusual way.

THE EARLY ROMANTICS

In 1798, William Wordsworth and Samuel Taylor Coleridge published a small volume of poetry called *Lyrical Ballads,* an "experiment" which was to prove a landmark in English poetry. The very title marked it as a revolutionary book which clearly broke with the Neoclassical tradition and formally ushered in the Romantic Period.

The world which witnessed this event was very different from the world of the formal and elegant eighteenth century. The skepticism of the eighteenth century and the doctrines of Rousseau had questioned the long-held Judaeo-Christian view of the world. Writers sought through imagination rather than reason to establish an order in the inner world of the individual; through creativity, rather than adherence to rules, they tried to perceive the universe, apprehend God, and determine man's role in life. Theirs was the commitment of the individual man to honor and liberty and the desire to make for himself a better world.

The poets and prose writers who wrote during the first three decades of the nineteenth century were vigorous individuals, each responding in his own way to the world about him, each embodying a unique poetic response to the promptings of feeling, thought, intuition, and imagination. It is, therefore, very difficult to set up large categories and neatly classify the writers. However, although they varied in response, all of the Romantics did share certain basic beliefs and attitudes which appear in various combinations in the different writers.

The Romantic writers reacted against the strict rules of the Neoclassicists. Believing in a greater spontaneity of expression, they disregarded the strict rules of the eighteenth century regarding meter and rhyme. They made use of the forms of lyric poetry, which they felt best expressed the ideas they wished to convey. They saw the source of poetry in a personal emotion deeply felt. Poets described imaginatively their feelings in moments of crisis and intensity. They found wonder in nature and in reality and expressed this love of life in their poetry. The Romantics sang of the common man living his simple life close to nature. Setting high ideals for themselves, they often expressed the loneliness and melancholy which comes of not reaching a goal. They rebelled against tyrannical authority which stifled man and robbed him of his freedom. The fabled past, particularly the medieval period, furnished the Romantics with materials for stories of terror, mystery, and enchantment and provided the ballad form and the old oral folk tradition for models. Above all else, the Romantics prized the imagination and intuition as the sources of truth, the way by which man could reconcile the opposing forces in nature and life.

The credo of the Romantic poets was stated in the "Preface" to the Second Edition of the *Lyrical Ballads,* published in 1800. Poetry, Wordsworth declared, should be written in the language of the common man and should be about incidents and situations from common life. He opposed the lifeless and stilted language of poetic diction, defining the poet as "a man speaking to man." However, it was the job of the poet to take these everyday situations and "throw over them a certain coloring of imagination, whereby ordinary things should be presented to the mind in an unusual aspect." It was hoped that the poetry presented in the volume would be "well adapted to interest mankind permanently, and not unimportant in the quality . . . of its moral relations."

In the writing of *Lyrical Ballads,* Coleridge and Wordsworth each responded in his own way. Wordsworth started with ordinary events and showed the wonder to be found in them. His was the world of birds, trees, flowers, and, above all, the common man; but he enlarged the beauty of the natural scene to show what he believed was the essential oneness of the universe. Coleridge wrote about incidents that were both eerie and supernatural. However, his strange and mysterious landscapes become so real that readers are willing to believe temporarily that this world of imagination is true and solid.

William Wordsworth's view of the world was shaped by his studies, by his association with his sister Dorothy and with Coleridge, and, above all, by his life in the beautiful Lake District of northern England. An early supporter and defender of the French Revolution, he was deeply disillusioned when the promised freedom became a tyranny worse than that which it had replaced.

He believed that man truly becomes man only when he is in communion with nature, for nature enables him to "see into the life of things." Wordsworth, therefore, believed that rustic life was to be preferred to life in the cities; for "in that condition the essential passions of the heart find a better soil in which they can attain their maturity . . . and the passions of man are incorporated with the beautiful and permanent forms of nature." In his personal life, however, this champion of the common man found it difficult to communicate with the common men he met.

If Wordsworth was the supreme poet of nature and the champion of the common man, he was also the poet of remembrance and self-reflection. Time and again in his poetry, he stressed the need for contemplation, for looking back at those pleasurable moments which give "life and food/ For future years." Poetry for Wordsworth was "the spontaneous overflow of powerful emotion . . . recollected in tranquillity." It is his ability to communicate the thoughts and feelings of a "man speaking to men" that gives Wordsworth his high place as a lyric poet.

Samuel Taylor Coleridge, although he agreed with Wordsworth that nature is a moral teacher, explored instead the landscapes of his own imagination and the unknown and scarcely touched world of man's inner being. Coleridge wrote highly symbolic poetry; and his language, far from the supposed language of ordinary men, was carefully and artistically chosen to give reality to the worlds of symbol and imagination.

The work done by Coleridge in literary criticism is as significant today as is his poetry. According to his theory of literature, a work of art—a poem or a play— grows organically like a flower or tree; it develops from within, assuming a form and shape innate to it and peculiarly its own. This theory explained for the first time why Shakespeare's plays are works of art even though the dramatist did not observe the unities of the ancient Greeks. Coleridge also stated the important principle that poetry is always a "reconciliation of opposite or discordant qualities," such as sameness with difference, the general with the specific, the strange with the familiar, and freedom with order.

Perhaps the most famous phrase in Coleridge's critical writings is found in his description of how a great work of art produces in readers a "willing suspension of disbelief which constitutes poetic faith." So attractive is such a work, Coleridge said, that even when it is a highly imaginary poem like "The Rime of the Ancient Mariner," the reader allows himself to believe for the time being that the story is true. It is such theories that have placed Coleridge high among the critics of English literature; it is the power of his imagination exploring the depths of man's being that makes him one of the most forceful and fascinating of poets.

William Wordsworth

(1770–1850)

William Wordsworth was a poet of two voices: one which he adopted when writing of the simple rustic life and one which expressed his more philosophical reflections. He is the poet who sought to speak to men from his own contemplation of the wonder of the life around him. The simplicity of his diction records the wonder he saw in nature and in the common man. He felt that the best things in a man are brought out when he is in close touch and harmony with nature, and it is nature that can bring man peace and contentment.

In the sonnet form, however, which he revived after it had been neglected by eighteenth century authors, and in some of his longer poems, such as the Immortality Ode and "Tintern Abbey," he departs from his own principle of using the simple language of everyday life and turns to a more elevated language—with magnificent results.

Wordsworth's simplicity and directness in describing natural scenery, his quiet meditative mood expressed with verbal beauty and power, and his concern for the common man make him not only "Nature's high priest" in English lyric poetry but also the man of feeling and sensitivity who wrote for all men.

LINES WRITTEN IN EARLY SPRING

I heard a thousand blended notes,
While in a grove I sate reclined,
In that sweet mood when pleasant thoughts
Bring sad thoughts to the mind.

Lines Written in Early Spring • 41

  To her fair works did Nature link   5
  The human soul that through me ran;
  And much it grieved my heart to think
  What man has made of man.

  Through primrose tufts, in that green bower,
  The periwinkle trailed its wreaths;   10
  And 't is my faith that every flower
  Enjoys the air it breathes.

  The birds around me hopped and played;
  Their thoughts I cannot measure;
  But the least motion which they made,   15
  It seemed a thrill of pleasure.

  The budding twigs spread out their fan
  To catch the breezy air;
  And I must think, do all I can,
  That there was pleasure there.   20

  If this belief from Heaven be sent,
  If such be Nature's holy plan,
  Have I not reason to lament
  What man has made of man?

For Discussion

1. The speaker in this poem is surrounded by the beauties of nature. Are his feelings centered only on the beauty he sees? What is the paradox expressed in lines 3 and 4?
2. What is the speaker's attitude toward nature? Does he view it as a friend? A consoler? A teacher? What is the "belief" referred to in line 21? What is "Nature's holy plan"?
3. What overtones do the following words and phrases convey: "sweet mood" (line 3); "grieved" (line 7); "made" (lines 8 and 24); "lament" (line 23)?
4. Note that the title of this poem is *"Lines* Written in Early Spring." How is the grammatical structure within each stanza related to the title of the poem? To the theme?

THREE YEARS SHE GREW

Three years she grew in sun and shower,
Then Nature said, "A lovelier flower
  On earth was never sown;
This child I to myself will take;
She shall be mine, and I will make   5
  A lady of my own.

"Myself will to my darling be
Both law and impulse: and with me
  The girl, in rock and plain,
In earth and heaven, in glade and bower,   10
Shall feel an overseeing power
  To kindle or restrain.

"She shall be sportive as the fawn
That wild with glee across the lawn,
  Or up the mountain springs;   15
And hers shall be the breathing balm,
And hers the silence and the calm
  Of mute insensate things.

"The floating clouds their state shall lend
To her; for her the willow bend;   20
  Nor shall she fail to see
Even in the motions of the storm
Grace that shall mold the maiden's form
  By silent sympathy.

"The stars of midnight shall be dear   25
To her; and she shall lean her ear
  In many a secret place
Where rivulets dance their wayward round,
And beauty born of murmuring sound
  Shall pass into her face.   30

"And vital feelings of delight
Shall rear her form to stately height,
   Her virgin bosom swell;
Such thoughts to Lucy I will give
While she and I together live   35
   Here in this happy dell."

Thus Nature spake—The work was done—
How soon my Lucy's race was run!
   She died, and left to me
This heath, this calm, and quiet scene;   40
The memory of what has been,
   And never more will be.

For Discussion

1. This and the two poems which follow it come from a group known as the "Lucy" poems. What is the relation of Lucy to nature?
2. How does this poem mingle the emotions of sadness and joy? How do the references to nature convey this feeling?
3. How does the last stanza convey the speaker's emotion?

SHE DWELT AMONG THE UNTRODDEN WAYS

She dwelt among the untrodden ways
   Beside the springs of Dove,[1]
A maid whom there were none to praise
   And very few to love:

A violet by a mossy stone   5
   Half hidden from the eye!
—Fair as a star, when only one
   Is shining in the sky.

[1] **Dove:** an English stream

She lived unknown, and few could know
    When Lucy ceased to be;⠀⠀⠀⠀⠀⠀⠀⠀10
But she is in her grave, and, oh,
    The difference to me!

For Discussion

1. This poem is a beautiful example of expression of intense feeling through simple language. Point out examples of words and phrases which are particularly effective in conveying the emotion of the speaker.
2. How would the poem be different if the following changes were made: "untraveled" for "untrodden" (line 1); "girl" for "maid" (line 3); "died" for "ceased to be" (line 10); "but what/A difference" for "and, oh/The difference" (lines 11–12)?

I TRAVELLED AMONG UNKNOWN MEN

I travelled among unknown men,
    In lands beyond the sea;
Nor, England! did I know till then
    What love I bore to thee.

'Tis past, that melancholy dream!⠀⠀⠀⠀⠀⠀⠀⠀5
    Nor will I quit thy shore
A second time; for still I seem
    To love thee more and more.

Among thy mountains did I feel
    The joy of my desire;⠀⠀⠀⠀⠀⠀⠀⠀10
And she I cherished turned her wheel
    Beside an English fire.

Thy mornings showed, thy nights concealed,
    The bowers where Lucy played;
And thine too is the last green field⠀⠀⠀⠀⠀⠀⠀⠀15
    That Lucy's eyes surveyed.

For Discussion

1. How does this poem differ from the two previous "Lucy" poems?
2. Show how the speaker in the poem deals with both an intimate personal emotion and a larger personal emotion. What is the relationship between the two?

THE SOLITARY REAPER

Behold her, single in the field,
Yon solitary Highland lass!
Reaping and singing by herself;
Stop here, or gently pass!
Alone she cuts and binds the grain   5
And sings a melancholy strain;
Oh listen! for the vale profound
Is overflowing with the sound.

No nightingale did ever chaunt
More welcome notes to weary bands   10
Of travellers in some shady haunt
Among Arabian sands:
A voice so thrilling ne'er was heard
In springtime from the cuckoo-bird
Breaking the silence of the seas   15
Among the farthest Hebrides.[1]

Will no one tell me what she sings?—
Perhaps the plaintive numbers flow
For old, unhappy, far-off things,
And battles long ago: 20
Or is it some more humble lay,
Familiar matter of today?
Some natural sorrow, loss, or pain,
That has been, and may be again?

[1] **Hebrides:** two groups of islands off the coast of Scotland

Whate'er the theme, the maiden sang 25
As if her song could have no ending;
I saw her singing at her work,
And o'er the sickle bending;—
I listened, motionless and still;
And, as I mounted up the hill, 30
The music in my heart I bore,
Long after it was heard no more.

For Discussion

1. Wordsworth defined poetry as "emotion recollected in tranquillity." How does this definition fit this poem?
2. What influence does the setting have on the meaning of the poem? If we accept line 17 at face value, what is the poem saying about the effect which sound by itself has in conveying emotion and feeling?
3. Give the literal meanings of the following words; then suggest their connotations in this poem: "solitary" (line 2); "strain" (line 6); "chaunt" (line 9); "plaintive" (line 18). In what way do the overtones of these words contribute to the total impression of the poem?
4. What Romantic characteristics does this poem display?

MY HEART LEAPS UP

My heart leaps up when I behold
   A rainbow in the sky:
So was it when my life began;
So is it now I am a man;
So be it when I shall grow old, 5
   Or let me die!
The child is father of the man;
And I could wish my days to be
Bound each to each by natural piety.

For Discussion

1. How are the first two lines typical of Romantic poetry in mood, subject matter, and diction?
2. What is it precisely that the child can teach adults? What relation does the poet see beween a love of nature and "natural piety"?
3. Compare the view of William Blake concerning children to that of Wordsworth. Are they alike or unlike? Explain.

I WANDERED LONELY AS A CLOUD

I wandered lonely as a cloud
That floats on high o'er vales and hills,
When all at once I saw a crowd,
A host, of golden daffodils;
Beside the lake, beneath the trees,   5
Fluttering and dancing in the breeze.

Continuous as the stars that shine
And twinkle on the Milky Way,
They stretched in never-ending line
Along the margin of a bay: 10
Ten thousand saw I at a glance,
Tossing their heads in sprightly dance.

The waves beside them danced; but they
Outdid the sparkling waves in glee:
A poet could not but be gay,   15
In such a jocund company:
I gazed—and gazed—but little thought
What wealth the show to me had brought:

For oft, when on my couch I lie
In vacant or in pensive mood,   20
They flash upon that inward eye
Which is the bliss of solitude;
And then my heart with pleasure fills,
And dances with the daffodils.

48 • WILLIAM WORDSWORTH

For Discussion

1. How do the visual images of the poem aid the reader in responding to the physical situation of the poet?
2. Is the speaker in this poem a lonely man or a contemplative man? In answering this question, pay attention to the diction of the poem.
3. What do lines 17 and 18 tell us about the nature of experience? How is this comment developed in the last stanza? How does the last stanza of the poem relate to Wordsworth's theory of poetry—"emotion recollected in tranquillity"?

LINES COMPOSED A FEW MILES ABOVE TINTERN ABBEY

On Revisiting the Banks of the Wye during a Tour, July 13, 1798

Five years have past; five summers, with the length
Of five long winters! and again I hear
These waters, rolling from their mountain springs
With a soft inland murmur.—Once again
Do I behold these steep and lofty cliffs,   5
That on a wild secluded scene impress
Thoughts of more deep seclusion; and connect
The landscape with the quiet of the sky.
The day is come when I again repose
Here, under this dark sycamore, and view   10
These plots of cottage-ground, these orchard-tufts,
Which at this season, with their unripe fruits,
Are clad in one green hue, and lose themselves
'Mid groves and copses. Once again I see
These hedgerows, hardly hedgerows, little lines   15
Of sportive wood run wild: these pastoral farms,
Green to the very door; and wreaths of smoke
Sent up, in silence, from among the trees!

appreciates nature when lost

Tintern Abbey • 49

With some uncertain notice, as might seem
Of vagrant dwellers in the houseless woods, 20
Or of some hermit's cave, where by his fire
The hermit sits alone.
              These beauteous forms,
Through a long absence, have not been to me
As is a landscape to a blind man's eye:
But oft, in lonely rooms, and 'mid the din 25
Of towns and cities, I have owed to them
In hours of weariness, sensations sweet,
Felt in the blood, and felt along the heart;
And passing even into my purer mind,
With tranquil restoration:—feelings too 30
Of unremembered pleasure: such, perhaps,
As have no slight or trivial influence
On that best portion of a good man's life,
His little, nameless, unremembered acts
Of kindness and of love. Nor less, I trust, 35
To them I may have owed another gift,
Of aspect more sublime; that blessed mood,
In which the burthen of the mystery,
In which the heavy and the weary weight
Of all this unintelligible world, 40
Is lightened:—that serene and blessed mood
In which the affections gently lead us on,—
Until, the breath of this corporeal frame
And even the motion of our human blood
Almost suspended, we are laid asleep 45
In body, and become a living soul:
While with an eye made quiet by thy power
Of harmony, and the deep power of joy,
We see into the life of things.
                   If this
Be but a vain belief, yet, oh! how oft— 50
In darkness and amid the many shapes
Of joyless daylight; when the fretful stir

Unprofitable, and the fever of the world,
Have hung upon the beatings of my heart—
How oft, in spirit, have I turned to thee,
O sylvan Wye! thou wanderer through the woods,
How often has my spirit turned to thee!

    And now, with gleams of half-extinguished thought,
With many recognitions dim and faint,
And somewhat of a sad perplexity,
The picture of the mind revives again;
While here I stand, not only with the sense
Of present pleasure, but with pleasing thoughts
That in this moment there is life and food
For future years. And so I dare to hope,
Though changed, no doubt, from what I was when first
I came among these hills; when like a roe
I bounded o'er the mountains, by the sides
Of the deep rivers, and the lonely streams,
Wherever nature led: more like a man
Flying from something that he dreads, than one
Who sought the thing he loved. For nature then
(The coarser pleasures of my boyish days,
And their glad animal movements all gone by)
To me was all in all.—I cannot paint
What then I was. The sounding cataract
Haunted me like a passion; the tall rock,
The mountain, and the deep and gloomy wood,
Their colors and their forms, were then to me
An appetite; a feeling and a love,
That had no need of a remoter charm,
By thought supplied, nor any interest
Unborrowed from the eye.—That time is past,
And all its aching joys are now no more,
And all its dizzy raptures. Not for this
Faint I, nor mourn nor murmur; other gifts
Have followed; for such loss, I would believe,
Abundant recompense. For I have learned

To look on nature, not as in the hour
Of thoughtless youth; but hearing oftentimes
The still, sad music of humanity,
Nor harsh nor grating, though of ample power
To chasten and subdue. And I have felt
A presence that disturbs me with the joy
Of elevated thoughts; a sense sublime,
Of something far more deeply interfused,
Whose dwelling is the light of setting suns,
And the round ocean and the living air,
And the blue sky, and in the mind of man;
A motion and a spirit, that impels
All thinking things, all objects of all thought,
And rolls through all things. Therefore am I still
A lover of the meadows and the woods,
And mountains; and of all that we behold
From this green earth; of all the mighty world
Of eye, and ear,—both what they half create,
And what perceive; well pleased to recognize
In nature and the language of the sense,
The anchor of my purest thoughts, the nurse,
The guide, the guardian of my heart, and soul
Of all my moral being.
     Nor perchance,
If I were not thus taught, should I the more
Suffer my genial spirits to decay:
For thou art with me here upon the banks
Of this fair river; thou my dearest friend,[1]
My dear, dear friend; and in thy voice I catch
The language of my former heart, and read
My former pleasures in the shooting lights
Of thy wild eyes. Oh! yet a little while
May I behold in thee what I was once,
My dear, dear sister! and this prayer I make,
Knowing that Nature never did betray

---

[1] **dearest friend:** his sister, Dorothy Wordsworth

The heart that loved her; 'tis her privilege,
Through all the years of this our life, to lead
From joy to joy: for she can so inform 125
The mind that is within us, so impress
With quietness and beauty, and so feed
With lofty thoughts, that neither evil tongues,
Rash judgments, nor the sneers of selfish men,
Nor greetings where no kindness is, nor all 130
The dreary intercourse of daily life
Shall e'er prevail against us, or disturb
Our cheerful faith, that all which we behold
Is full of blessings. Therefore let the moon
Shine on thee in thy solitary walk; 135
And let the misty mountain-winds be free
To blow against thee: and, in after years,
When these wild ecstasies shall be matured
Into a sober pleasure; when thy mind
Shall be a mansion for all lovely forms, 140
Thy memory be as a dwelling-place
For all sweet sounds and harmonies; oh! then,
If solitude, or fear, or pain, or grief,
Should be thy portion, with what healing thoughts
Of tender joy wilt thou remember me, 145
And these my exhortations! Nor, perchance—
If I should be where I no more can hear
Thy voice, nor catch from thy wild eyes these gleams
Of past existence—wilt thou then forget
That on the banks of this delightful stream 150
We stood together; and that I, so long
A worshipper of Nature, hither came
Unwearied in that service: rather say
With warmer love—oh! with far deeper zeal
Of holier love. Nor wilt thou then forget 155
That after many wanderings, many years
Of absence, these steep woods and lofty cliffs,
And this green pastoral landscape, were to me
More dear, both for themselves and for thy sake!

For Discussion

1. This poem is a poem of memory which shows how the principles learned in the past are relevant to the present and are "life and food" for the future. How is this idea of past and present established in the opening lines? In what way does the poet build up a picture of the setting? What is the attitude of the speaker toward the setting?
2. In what ways has nature been a source of comfort to the speaker (lines 23–57)? How do these lines reflect Wordsworth's poetic credo? What is the "best portion of a good man's life"?
3. What are the joys of nature which the speaker felt in his youth (lines 65–83)? How do the images that he uses reveal his feeling about nature at this time of his life?
4. In lines 84–111, the speaker describes the stages of the influence of nature in his growth from childhood to maturity. What are these stages? Why does the speaker think the third stage is the best? What is the presence which disturbs him (line 94)? How, in this poem, is nature a moral teacher?
5. In line 116, the speaker addresses his sister. Why is it important that she be there? What is his message to his sister as they stand on the banks of the River Wye? How does this message indicate the response that man should make to nature?
6. This poem is one of the great examples of contemplative poetry, both in content and in form. Identify the predominant meter of the poem. Can you suggest reasons why this verse form is most appropriate to this kind of poem?

COMPOSED UPON WESTMINSTER BRIDGE

Earth has not anything to show more fair:
Dull would he be of soul who could pass by
A sight so touching in its majesty:
This city now doth, like a garment, wear
The beauty of the morning; silent, bare, 5

Ships, towers, domes, theatres, and temples lie
Open unto the fields, and to the sky;
All bright and glittering in the smokeless air.
Never did sun more beautifully steep
In his first splendor, valley, rock, or hill;   10
Ne'er saw I, never felt, a calm so deep!
The river glideth at his own sweet will:
Dear God! the very houses seem asleep;
And all that mighty heart is lying still!

For Discussion

1. The speaker in this poem is looking at London early in the morning before the city is alive with its daily occupations. What qualities ordinarily found only in the country does he see in London at dawn? What emotions does the scene evoke for the speaker?
2. Identify the figure of speech in lines 4–5. What descriptive qualities does it convey? In your opinion, why is this particular figure of speech appropriate?
3. Read the poem aloud. How does the very sound of the words help to convey the feeling of the poem?
4. Chart the rhyme scheme of the sonnet. What type of sonnet is it—Italian or Shakespearean? How does the use of the sonnet form aid in discovering the meaning of the poem?

LONDON, 1802

Milton! thou should'st be living at this hour;
England hath need of thee: she is a fen
Of stagnant waters: altar, sword, and pen,
Fireside, the heroic wealth of hall and bower,
Have forfeited their ancient English dower   5
Of inward happiness. We are selfish men;
Oh! raise us up, return to us again;
And give us manners, virtue, freedom, power.

Thy soul was like a star, and dwelt apart;
Thou hadst a voice whose sound was like the sea: 10
Pure as the naked heavens, majestic, free,
So didst thou travel on life's common way,
In cheerful godliness; and yet thy heart
The lowliest duties on herself did lay.

For Discussion

1. This poem begins with an apostrophe to John Milton, the great Puritan poet. Why does England "need" Milton?
2. What is the poet saying in lines 3–6? What figure of speech is being used?
3. Discuss the figures of speech used in describing Milton. In what way are they appropriate to him?
4. Are the criticisms of England made in this poem of a material or spiritual nature? Explain.
5. What type of sonnet is this? In what way is this use of the sonnet form a change from the Elizabethan use?

ODE
INTIMATIONS OF IMMORTALITY
from RECOLLECTIONS OF EARLY CHILDHOOD

The child is father of the man;
And I could wish my days to be
Bound each to each by natural piety.

1

There was a time when meadow, grove, and stream,
The earth, and every common sight,
       To me did seem
      Apparelled in celestial light,
The glory and the freshness of a dream. 5
It is not now as it hath been of yore;—
        Turn wheresoe'er I may,
         By night or day,
The things which I have seen I now can see no more.

2

   The rainbow comes and goes,   10
   And lovely is the rose;
   The moon doth with delight
 Look round her when the heavens are bare;
    Waters on a starry night
    Are beautiful and fair;   15
  The sunshine is a glorious birth;
  But yet I know, where'er I go,
That there hath passed away a glory from the earth.

3

Now, while the birds thus sing a joyous song,
   And while the young lambs bound   20
    As to the tabor's [1] sound,
To me alone there came a thought of grief:
A timely utterance gave that thought relief,
    And I again am strong:
The cataracts blow their trumpets from the steep; 25
No more shall grief of mine the season wrong;
I hear the echoes through the mountains throng,
The winds come to me from the fields of sleep,
    And all the earth is gay;
     Land and sea   30
   Give themselves up to jollity,
    And with the heart of May
   Doth every beast keep holiday;—
    Thou child of joy,
Shout round me, let me hear thy shouts, thou happy
  shepherd-boy!   35

4

Ye blessèd creatures, I have heard the call
   Ye to each other make; I see
  The heavens laugh with you in your jubilee:

[1] **tabor:** a small drum

My heart is at your festival,
My head hath its coronal, 40
The fullness of your bliss, I feel—I feel it all.
    Oh evil day! if I were sullen
    While Earth herself is adorning,
        This sweet May-morning,
    And the children are culling 45
        On every side,
    In a thousand valleys far and wide,
    Fresh flowers; while the sun shines warm,
And the babe leaps up on his mother's arm:—
    I hear, I hear, with joy I hear! 50
    —But there's a tree, of many, one,
A single field which I have looked upon,
Both of them speak of something that is gone:
    The pansy at my feet
    Doth the same tale repeat: 55
Whither is fled the visionary gleam?
Where is it now, the glory and the dream?

5

Our birth is but a sleep and a forgetting:
The soul that rises with us, our life's star,
    Hath had elsewhere its setting, 60
        And cometh from afar:
    Not in entire forgetfulness,
    And not in utter nakedness,
But trailing clouds of glory do we come
    From God, who is our home: 65
Heaven lies about us in our infancy!
Shades of the prison-house begin to close
    Upon the growing boy,
But he beholds the light, and whence it flows;
    He sees it in his joy; 70
The youth, who daily farther from the east
    Must travel, still is Nature's priest,

>   And by the vision splendid
>   Is on his way attended;
> At length the man perceives it die away, 75
> And fade into the light of common day.

6

Earth fills her lap with pleasures of her own;
Yearnings she hath in her own natural kind,
And, even with something of a mother's mind,
>   And no unworthy aim, 80
>   The homely nurse doth all she can
To make her foster-child, her inmate man,
>   Forget the glories he hath known,
And that imperial palace whence he came.

7

Behold the child among his new-born blisses, 85
A six years' darling of a pigmy size!
See, where 'mid work of his own hand he lies,
Fretted by sallies of his mother's kisses,
With light upon him from his father's eyes!
See, at his feet, some little plan or chart, 90
Some fragment from his dream of human life,
Shaped by himself with newly-learnéd art;
>   A wedding or a festival,
>   A mourning or a funeral;
>   And this hath now his heart, 95
>   And unto this he frames his song:
>   Then will he fit his tongue
> To dialogues of business, love, or strife;
>   But it will not be long
>   Ere this be thrown aside, 100
>   And with new joy and pride
> The little actor cons another part;
> Filling from time to time his "humorous stage" [2]

---

[2] **"humorous stage"**: changeable stage; refers to an Elizabethan sonnet by Samuel David.

With all the persons, down to palsied Age,
That Life brings with her in her equipage;
    As if his whole vocation
    Were endless imitation.

8

Thou, whose exterior semblance doth belie
    Thy soul's immensity;
Thou best philosopher, who yet dost keep
Thy heritage, thou eye among the blind,
That, deaf and silent, read'st the eternal deep,
Haunted forever by the eternal mind,—
    Mighty prophet! Seer blest!
    On whom those truths do rest,
Which we are toiling all our lives to find,
In darkness lost, the darkness of the grave;
Thou, over whom thy immortality
Broods like the day, a master o'er a slave,
A presence which is not to be put by;
Thou little child, yet glorious in the might
Of heaven-born freedom on thy being's height,
Why with such earnest pains dost thou provoke
The years to bring the inevitable yoke,
Thus blindly with thy blessedness at strife?
Full soon thy soul shall have her earthly freight,
And custom lie upon thee with a weight,
Heavy as frost, and deep almost as life!

9

    Oh joy! that in our embers
    Is something that doth live,
    That nature yet remembers
    What was so fugitive!
The thought of our past years in me doth breed
Perpetual benediction: not indeed
For that which is most worthy to be blest—

Delight and liberty, the simple creed
Of childhood, whether busy or at rest,
With new-fledged hope still fluttering in his breast:—
    Not for these I raise
      The song of thanks and praise;   140
  But for those obstinate questionings
  Of sense and outward things,
  Fallings from us, vanishings;
  Blank misgivings of a creature
Moving about in worlds not realized,   145
High instincts before which our mortal nature
Did tremble like a guilty thing surprised:
    But for those first affections,
    Those shadowy recollections,
  Which, be they what they may,   150
Are yet the fountain light of all our day,
Are yet a master light of all our seeing;
  Uphold us, cherish, and have power to make
Our noisy years seem moments in the being
Of the eternal silence: truths that wake,   155
    To perish never;
Which neither listlessness, nor mad endeavor,
    Nor man nor boy,
Nor all that is at enmity with joy,
Can utterly abolish or destroy!   160
    Hence in a season of calm weather
    Though inland far we be,
Our souls have sight of that immortal sea
    Which brought us hither,
    Can in a moment travel thither,   165
And see the children sport upon the shore,
And hear the mighty waters rolling evermore.

10

Then sing, ye birds, sing, sing a joyous song!
    And let the young lambs bound
    As to the tabor's sound!   170

We in thought will join your throng,
    Ye that pipe and ye that play,
    Ye that through your hearts to-day
    Feel the gladness of the May!
What though the radiance which was once so bright 175
Be now forever taken from my sight,
    Though nothing can bring back the hour
Of splendor in the grass, of glory in the flower;
    We will grieve not, rather find
    Strength in what remains behind; 180
    In the primal sympathy
    Which having been must ever be;
    In the soothing thoughts that spring
    Out of human suffering;
    In the faith that looks through death, 185
In years that bring the philosophic mind.

11

And O ye fountains, meadows, hills, and groves,
Forebode not any severing of our loves!
Yet in my heart of hearts I feel your might;
I only have relinquished one delight 190
To live beneath your more habitual sway.
I love the brooks which down their channels fret,
Even more than when I tripped lightly as they;
The innocent brightness of a new-born day
    Is lovely yet; 195
The clouds that gather round the setting sun
Do take a sober coloring from an eye
That hath kept watch o'er man's mortality;
Another race hath been, and other palms are won.
Thanks to the human heart by which we live, 200
Thanks to its tenderness, its joys, and fears,
To me the meanest flower that blows can give
Thoughts that do often lie too deep for tears.

For Discussion

1. This is a poem of growth and growing, asking questions and receiving answers. The poem opens with the tone of the "once-upon-a-time" tale. Why is this tone appropriate for the first four stanzas? What regret does the speaker express?
2. Pay particular attention to the images in the opening stanzas. What sense appeal predominates? Explain the meaning of lines 56 and 57.
3. How does the poet use the light images in the fifth stanza?
4. What is the attitude of the speaker to childhood in stanza 8?
5. In stanzas 10–11, the speaker returns to the joy in nature he alluded to in stanza 1. What is the difference in his attitude? Why do you think his attitude has changed? What has he lost forever? What, however, has he gained? Consider his statements in stanzas 10–11 to support your answer.
6. Wordsworth believed that the love of nature leads to the love of man. How does he express this belief in stanzas 5–7 and 10–11? Is this belief valid? Is it realistic?
7. Is the diction of this poem consistent with its theme? Discuss the difference in diction between this poem and any one of Wordsworth's shorter poems.
8. Why could this poem not have been written during the Neoclassical period? Consider not only the attitude toward nature but also the basic theme of the poem.
9. What criticisms of civilization is the poet making? How does his choice of subject help him make these criticisms?

For Composition

1. Throughout the poetry of William Wordsworth we see a man alone communing with nature and learning to live with his fellow man. What is the value of solitary contemplation for living? Can a man in the twentieth century "afford" the luxury of contemplation? Write a theme on the value of solitude in your own life or on the need for contemplation in our present-day world.
2. Write a short paper setting forth your feelings on seeing a familiar scene in an unfamiliar light or on revisiting a favorite place. Or write a poem on the same subject.

Samuel Taylor Coleridge

(1772–1834)

Of all the Romantic poets, Samuel Taylor Coleridge was the most successful in creating a sense of awe and wonder in his work —and in ways that had never been seen before. For the characters and events which were products of his imagination, he built a world so compelling that readers were held and gave freely that "willing suspension of disbelief which constitutes poetic faith."

"Kubla Khan," with its wonderful music and its strange Oriental images, captures the imagination of readers, though the meaning of the poem has been the subject of much discussion. "Christabel," a much longer work which Coleridge never finished, is a story of terror and mystery set against the medieval background which the Romantics loved. This poem brought a new and melodious meter to poetry, a meter that was to have an important influence on such poets as Byron and Scott. "The Rime of the Ancient Mariner," with its startling imagery, its directness, and its wild imagination, was something entirely new in poetry. Beyond the plot of the poem were worlds of wonder for the reader to explore, worlds which bring to each person a new awareness of himself.

It is for his ability to make us believe in the products of his imagination and for his skill in creating verbal pictures of delight, wonder, and fear that Coleridge stands as one of the most compelling of poets.

KUBLA KHAN

or, a Vision in a Dream

In Xanadu did Kubla Khan [1]
A stately pleasure-dome decree:
Where Alph, the sacred river, ran
Through caverns measureless to man
    Down to a sunless sea.   5
So twice five miles of fertile ground
With walls and towers were girdled round:
And there were gardens bright with sinuous rills,
Where blossomed many an incense-bearing tree;
And here were forests ancient as the hills,   10
Enfolding sunny spots of greenery.

But oh! that deep romantic chasm which slanted
Down the green hill athwart a cedarn cover!
A savage place! as holy and enchanted
As e'er beneath a waning moon was haunted   15
By woman wailing for her demon-lover!
And from this chasm, with ceaseless turmoil seething,
As if this earth in fast thick pants were breathing,
A mighty fountain momently was forced:
Amid whose swift half-intermitted burst   20
Huge fragments vaulted like rebounding hail,
Or chaffy grain beneath the thresher's flail:
And 'mid these dancing rocks at once and ever
It flung up momently the sacred river.
Five miles meandering with a mazy motion   25
Through wood and dale the sacred river ran,
Then reached the caverns measureless to man,
And sank in tumult to a lifeless ocean:
And 'mid this tumult Kubla heard from far
Ancestral voices prophesying war!   30

---
[1] **Kubla Khan:** the founder of the Mongol dynasty in China in the 13th century.

  The shadow of the dome of pleasure
  Floated midway on the waves;
  Where was heard the mingled measure
  From the fountain and the caves.
It was a miracle of rare device,   35
A sunny pleasure-dome with caves of ice!

  A damsel with a dulcimer
  In a vision once I saw:
  It was an Abyssinian maid,
  And on her dulcimer she played,   40
  Singing of Mount Abora.
  Could I revive within me
  Her symphony and song,
   To such a deep delight 'twould win me,
That with music loud and long,   45
I would build that dome in air,
That sunny dome! those caves of ice!
And all who heard should see them there,
And all should cry, Beware! Beware!
His flashing eyes, his floating hair!   50
Weave a circle round him thrice,
And close your eyes with holy dread,
For he on honey-dew hath fed,
And drunk the milk of Paradise.

For Discussion

1. The beginning of this poem sets a specific scene. Point out the precise details in the opening lines. What is the purpose of this exactness of detail in the light of the dream quality of the rest of the poem?
2. It has been said that Coleridge achieved his effects in the first section by emphasis on the connotative rather than the denotative quality of the words. Do you agree? Support your answer by pointing to specific words and phrases. What is the mood evoked by the names used in this part?

3. Read the poem aloud to hear the musical quality, its effects, and overtones. Point out those words and details which mingle sound, mood, and meaning.
4. Note the use of combinations of opposites. How do these combinations relate to the total poem? How can terror and enchantment be mingled?
5. The poem shifts tone and rhythm at certain points. What effect is achieved by this? Analyze the different rhythms used in the various sections of the poem.
6. The poem is open to two interpretations, depending on the meaning given to the word "could" in line 42. According to one interpretation, Coleridge means that he would, through his imagination, create in poetry that dome in air, but he cannot; he is not able to do so. Others believe that the poet means that he can create as he desires, and they argue that the meter and swiftness of the poem reflect the confidence of the poet. With which interpretation do you agree? Explain.
7. Point out examples in the poem of similes and metaphors. What effect do they have in reinforcing the imaginative quality of the work?

CHRISTABEL

Part I

'Tis the middle of night by the castle clock,
And the owls have awakened the crowing cock,
Tu—whit!——Tu—whoo!
And hark, again! the crowing cock,
How drowsily it crew.   5

   Sir Leoline, the baron rich,
Hath a toothless mastiff bitch;
From her kennel beneath the rock
She maketh answer to the clock,
Four for the quarters, and twelve for the hour;   10
Ever and aye, by shine and shower,

Sixteen short howls, not over loud;
Some say, she sees my lady's shroud.

   Is the night chilly and dark?
The night is chilly, but not dark.　15
The thin gray cloud is spread on high;
It covers but not hides the sky.
The moon is behind, and at the full;
And yet she looks both small and dull.
The night is chill, the cloud is gray:　20
'Tis a month before the month of May,
And the spring comes slowly up this way.

   The lovely lady, Christabel,
Whom her father loves so well,
What makes her in the wood so late,　25
A furlong from the castle gate?
She had dreams all yesternight
Of her own bethrothéd knight;
And she in the midnight wood will pray
For the weal of her lover that's far away.　30

   She stole along, she nothing spoke,
The sighs she heaved were soft and low,
And naught was green upon the oak
But moss and rarest mistletoe:
She kneels beneath the huge oak tree,　35
And in silence prayeth she.

   The lady sprang up suddenly,
The lovely lady, Christabel!
It moaned as near, as near can be,
But what it is she cannot tell.—　40
On the other side it seems to be,
Of the huge, broad-breasted, old oak tree.

The night is chill; the forest bare;
Is it the wind that moaneth bleak?
There is not wind enough in the air 45
To move away the ringlet curl
From the lovely lady's cheek—
There is not wind enough to twirl
The one red leaf, the last of its clan,
That dances as often as dance it can, 50
Hanging so light, and hanging so high,
On the topmost twig that looks up at the sky.

   Hush, beating heart of Christabel!
Jesu, Maria, shield her well!
She folded her arms beneath her cloak, 55
And stole to the other side of the oak.
   What sees she there?

There she sees a damsel bright,
Drest in a silken robe of white,
That shadowy in the moonlight shone: 60
The neck that made that white robe wan,
Her stately neck, and arms were bare;
Her blue-veined feet unsandaled were,
And wildly glittered here and there
The gems entangled in her hair. 65
I guess, 'twas frightful there to see
A lady so richly clad as she—
Beautiful exceedingly!

   "Mary mother, save me now!"
Said Christabel, "And who art thou?" 70

   The lady strange made answer meet,
And her voice was faint and sweet:—
"Have pity on my sore distress,

I scarce can speak for weariness:
Stretch forth thy hand, and have no fear!" 75
Said Christabel, "How camest thou here?"
And the lady, whose voice was faint and sweet,
Did thus pursue her answer meet:—

"My sire is of a noble line,
And my name is Geraldine: 80
Five warriors seized me yestermorn,
Me, even me, a maid forlorn:
They choked my cries with force and fright,
And tied me on a palfrey white.
The palfrey was as fleet as wind, 85
And they rode furiously behind.
They spurred amain, their steeds were white:
And once we crossed the shade of night.
As sure as Heaven shall rescue me,
I have no thought what men they be; 90
Nor do I know how long it is
(For I have lain entranced, I wis)
Since one, the tallest of the five,
Took me from the palfrey's back,
A weary woman, scarce alive. 95
Some muttered words his comrades spoke:
He placed me underneath this oak;
He swore they would return with haste;
Whither they went I cannot tell—
I thought I heard, some minutes past, 100
Sounds as of a castle bell.
Stretch forth thy hand," thus ended she;
"And help a wretched maid to flee."

Then Christabel stretched forth her hand,
And comforted fair Geraldine: 105
"Oh well, bright dame! may you command
The service of Sir Leoline;

And gladly our stout chivalry
Will he send forth, and friends withal,
To guide and guard you safe and free 110
Home to your noble father's hall."

    She rose; and forth with steps they passed
That strove to be, and were not, fast.
Her gracious stars the lady blest,
And thus spake on sweet Christabel: 115
"All our household are at rest,
The hall as silent as the cell;
Sir Leoline is weak in health,
And may not well awakened be,
But we will move as if in stealth, 120
And I beseech your courtesy,
This night, to share your couch with me."

    They crossed the moat, and Christabel
Took the key that fitted well;
A little door she opened straight, 125
All in the middle of the gate;
The gate that was ironed within and without,
Where an army in battle array had marched out.
The lady sank, belike through pain,
And Christabel with might and main 130
Lifted her up, a weary weight,
Over the threshold of the gate:
Then the lady rose again,
And moved, as she were not in pain.

    So free from danger, free from fear, 135
They crossed the court: right glad they were.
And Christabel devoutly cried
To the lady by her side:
"Praise we the Virgin all divine
Who hath rescued thee from thy distress!" 140

"Alas, alas!" said Geraldine,
"I cannot speak for weariness."
So free from danger, free from fear,
They crossed the court: right glad they were.

    Outside her kennel the mastiff old 145
Lay fast asleep in moonshine cold.
The mastiff old did not awake,
Yet she an angry moan did make!
And what can ail the mastiff bitch?
Never till now she uttered yell 150
Beneath the eye of Christabel.
Perhaps it is the owlet's scritch:
For what can ail the mastiff bitch?

    They passed the hall, that echoes still
Pass as lightly as you will! 155
The brands were flat, the brands were dying,
Amid their own white ashes lying;
But when the lady passed, there came
A tongue of light, a fit of flame;
And Christabel saw the lady's eye, 160
And nothing else saw she thereby,
Save the boss of the shield of Sir Leoline tall,
Which hung in a murky old niche in the wall.
"Oh softly tread," said Christabel,
"My father seldom sleepeth well." 165

    Sweet Christabel her feet doth bare,
And jealous of the listening air
They steal their way from stair to stair,
Now in glimmer, and now in gloom,
And now they pass the baron's room, 170
As still as death, with stifled breath!
And now have reached her chamber door;
And now doth Geraldine press down
The rushes of the chamber floor.

The moon shines dim in the open air, 175
And not a moonbeam enters here.
But they without its light can see
The chamber carved so curiously,
Carved, with figures strange and sweet,
All made out of the carver's brain, 180
For a lady's chamber meet:
The lamp with twofold silver chain
Is fastened to an angel's feet.

The silver lamp burns dead and dim;
But Christabel the lamp will trim. 185
She trimmed the lamp, and made it bright,
And left it swinging to and fro,
While Geraldine, in wretched plight,
Sank down upon the floor below.

"O weary lady, Geraldine, 190
I pray you, drink this cordial wine!
It is a wine of virtuous powers;
My mother made it of wild flowers."

"And will your mother pity me,
Who am a maiden most forlorn?" 195
Christabel answered—"Woe is me!
She died the hour that I was born.
I have heard the gray-haired friar tell
How on her death-bed she did say,
That she should hear the castle-bell 200
Strike twelve upon my wedding-day.
O mother dear! that thou wert here!"
"I would," said Geraldine, "she were!"

But soon with altered voice, said she—
"Off, wandering mother! Peak and pine! 205
I have power to bid thee flee."

Alas! what ails poor Geraldine?
Why stares she with unsettled eye?
Can she the bodiless dead espy?
And why with hollow voice cries she, 210
"Off, woman, off! this hour is mine—
Though thou her guardian spirit be,
Off, woman, off! 'tis given to me."

    Then Christabel knelt by the lady's side,
And raised to heaven her eyes so blue— 215
"Alas!" said she, "this ghastly ride—
Dear lady! it hath 'wildered you!"
The lady wiped her moist cold brow,
And faintly said, " 'Tis over now!"

    Again the wild-flower wine she drank: 220
Her fair large eyes 'gan glitter bright,
And from the floor whereon she sank,
The lofty lady stood upright;
She was most beautiful to see,
Like a lady of a far countree. 225

And thus the lofty lady spake—
"All they, who live in the upper sky,
Do love you, holy Christabel!
And you love them, and for their sake
And for the good which me befell, 230
Even I in my degree will try,
Fair maiden, to requite you well.
But now unrobe yourself; for I
Must pray, ere yet in bed I lie."

    Quoth Christabel, "So let it be!" 235
And as the lady bade, did she.
Her gentle limbs did she undress,
And lay down in her loveliness.

But through her brain of weal and woe
So many thoughts moved to and fro, 240
That vain it were her lids to close;
So half-way from the bed she rose,
And on her elbow did recline
To look at the lady Geraldine.

Beneath the lamp the lady bowed, 245
And slowly rolled her eyes around;
Then drawing in her breath aloud,
Like one that shuddered, she unbound
The cincture from beneath her breast:
Her silken robe, and inner vest, 250
Dropt to her feet, and full in view,
Behold! her bosom and half her side—
A sight to dream of, not to tell!
Oh shield her! shield sweet Christabel!

Yet Geraldine nor speaks nor stirs; 255
Ah! what a stricken look was hers!
Deep from within she seems half-way
To lift some weight with sick assay,
And eyes the maid and seeks delay;
Then suddenly, as one defied, 260
Collects herself in scorn and pride,
And lay down by the maiden's side!—
And in her arms the maid she took,
      Ah well-a-day!
And with low voice and doleful look 265
These words did say:
"In the touch of this bosom there worketh a spell,
Which is lord of thy utterance, Christabel!
Thou knowest tonight, and wilt know tomorrow,
This mark of my shame, this seal of my sorrow; 270

But vainly thou warrest,
    For this is alone in
Thy power to declare,
    That in the dim forest
Thou heard'st a low moaning, 275
And found'st a bright lady, surpassingly fair:
And didst bring her home with thee in love and in charity,
To shield her and shelter her from the damp air."

The Conclusion to Part I

It was a lovely sight to see
The lady Christabel, when she 280
Was praying at the old oak tree.
    Amid the jagged shadows
    Of mossy leafless boughs,
    Kneeling in the moonlight
    To make her gentle vows; 285
Her slender palms together prest,
Heaving sometimes on her breast;
Her face resigned to bliss or bale—
Her face, oh call it fair not pale,
And both blue eyes more bright than clear, 290
Each about to have a tear.

With open eyes (ah woe is me!)
Asleep, and dreaming fearfully,
Fearfully dreaming, yet, I wis,
Dreaming that alone, which is— 295
O sorrow and shame! Can this be she,
The lady, who knelt at the old oak tree?
And lo! the worker of these harms,
That holds the maiden in her arms,
Seems to slumber still and mild, 300
As a mother with her child.

A star hath set, a star hath risen,
O Geraldine! since arms of thine
Have been the lovely lady's prison.
O Geraldine! one hour was thine— 305
Thou'st had thy will! By tairn¹ and rill,
The night-birds all that hour were still.
But now they are jubilant anew,
From cliff and tower, tu—whoo! tu—whoo!
Tu—whoo! tu—whoo! from wood and fell! 310

And see! the lady Christabel
Gathers herself from out her trance:
Her limbs relax, her countenance
Grows sad and soft; the smooth thin lids
Close o'er her eyes; and tears she sheds— 315
Large tears that leave the lashes bright!
And oft the while she seems to smile
As infants at a sudden light!

Yea, she doth smile, and she doth weep,
Like a youthful hermitess, 320
Beauteous in a wilderness,
Who, praying always, prays in sleep.
And, if she move unquietly,
Perchance, 'tis but the blood so free
Comes back and tingles in her feet. 325
No doubt she hath a vision sweet.
What if her guardian spirit 'twere?
What if she knew her mother near?
But this she knows, in joys and woes,
That saints will aid if men will call: 330
For the blue sky bends over all!

¹ **tairn:** a small mountain lake or pool

For Discussion

1. Point out examples in the opening lines which hint at mystery, terror, and evil. Show how these details also function to give an exact setting for the poem and help to create the haunting mood.
2. When Christabel is first introduced in the poem what details are given to point out her character? What might she represent?
3. Under what circumstances do Christabel and Geraldine meet? What dramatic contrast can be found between the setting and Geraldine's appearance?
4. What hints make the reader suspect that Geraldine is not who she says she is (lines 123–165)? Do you have any reason for believing she might not be quite human? Who or what do you think she is? Why must Geraldine always remain in the presence of Christabel?
5. Explain lines 204–214. To whom is Geraldine speaking? What do these lines tell of the battle between good and evil? Is this idea further developed in the Conclusion to Part I? Discuss.
6. Many of the elements in this poem are opposites—good and evil; light and dark; satanic nightmare and religious peace. Point out examples of each of these and discuss their contribution to the mood of the poem and to its meaning.
7. What use does Coleridge make of the elements of fear? Suspense? The supernatural? Do these elements aid in his securing from his readers their "willing suspension of disbelief"?

THE RIME OF THE ANCIENT MARINER

Argument

How a Ship, having first sailed to the Equator, was driven by Storms to the cold Country toward the South Pole; how the ancient Mariner cruelly and in contempt of the laws of hospitality killed a Seabird and how he was followed by many and strange Judgments: and in what manner he came back to his own Country.

Part I

<small>An ancient Mariner meeteth three Gallants bidden to a wedding-feast and detaineth one.</small>

It is an ancient Mariner,
And he stoppeth one of three.
"By thy long gray beard and glittering eye,
Now wherefore stopp'st thou me?

"The Bridegroom's doors are opened wide,   5
An I am next of kin;
The guests are met, the feast is set:
May'st hear the merry din."

He holds him with his skinny hand;
"There was a ship," quoth he.   10
"Hold off! unhand me, gray-beard loon!"
Eftsoons[1] his hand dropped he.

He holds him with his glittering eye—
The Wedding-Guest stood still,

<small>The Wedding-Guest is spellbound by the eye of the old seafaring man and constrained to hear his tale.</small>

And listens like a three years' child: 15
The Mariner hath his will.

The Wedding-Guest sat on a stone:
He cannot choose but hear;
And thus spake on that ancient man,
The bright-eyed Mariner.   20

---

[1] **Eftsoons:** quickly

The Rime of the Ancient Mariner • 79

"The ship was cheered, the harbor cleared,
Merrily did we drop
Below the kirk,[2] below the hill,
Below the lighthouse top.

The Mariner tells how the ship sailed southward with a good wind and fair weather, till it reached the Line.

"The sun came up upon the left, 25
Out of the sea came he
And he shone bright, and on the right
Went down into the sea.

"Higher and higher every day,
Till over the mast at noon—" 30
The Wedding-Guest here beat his breast,
For he heard the loud bassoon.

The Wedding-Guest heareth the bridal music; but the Mariner continueth his tale.

The bride hath paced into the hall,
Red as a rose is she;
Nodding their heads before her goes 35
The merry minstrelsy.

The Wedding-Guest he beat his breast,
Yet he cannot choose but hear;
And thus spake on that ancient man,
The bright-eyed Mariner. 40

The ship driven by a storm toward the South Pole.

"And now the Storm-blast came, and he
Was tyrannous and strong.
He struck with his o'ertaking wings,
And chased us south along.

"With sloping masts and dipping prow, 45
As who pursued with yell and blow
Still treads the shadow of his foe,
And forward bends his head,
The ship drove fast, loud roared the blast,
And southward aye we fled. 50

[2] **kirk:** church

"And now there came both mist and snow,
And it grew wondrous cold;
And ice, mast-high, came floating by,
As green as emerald.

The land of ice, and of fearful sounds, where no living thing was to be seen.

"And through the drifts [3] the snowy clifts [4]   55
Did send a dismal sheen;
Nor shapes of men nor beasts we ken—
The ice was all between.

"The ice was here, the ice was there,
The ice was all around   60
It cracked and growled, and roared and howled
Like noises in a swound! [5]

Till a great sea bird, called the Albatross, came through the snow-fog, and was received with great joy and hospitality.

"At length did cross an Albatross,
Thorough the fog it came;
As if it had been a Christian soul,   65
We hailed it in God's name.

"It ate the food it ne'er had eat,
And round and round it flew.
The ice did split with a thunder fit;
The helmsman steered us through!   70

And lo! the Albatross proveth a bird of good omen, and followeth the ship as it returned northward through fog and floating ice.

"And a good south wind sprung up behind;
The Albatross did follow,
And every day, for food or play,
Came to the mariners' hollo!

"In mist or cloud, on mast or shroud,[6]   75
It perched for vespers [7] nine;
Whiles all the night, through fog-smoke white,
Glimmered the white moonshine."

---

[3] **drifts:** mist   [4] **clifts:** icebergs   [5] **swound:** dream   [6] **shroud:** rope
[7] **vespers:** evening prayers

The Rime of the Ancient Mariner • 81

<small>The ancient Mariner inhospitably killeth the pious bird of good omen.</small>

"God save thee, ancient Mariner!
From the fiends, that plague thee thus!—
Why look'st thou so?"—"With my crossbow
I shot the Albatross!"

Part II

"The Sun now rose upon the right,
Out of the sea came he,
Still hid in mist, and on the left
Went down into the sea.

"And the good south wind still blew behind,
But no sweet bird did follow,
Nor any day for food or play
Came to the mariners' hollo!

<small>His shipmates cry out against the ancient Mariner for killing the bird of good luck.</small>

"And I had done a hellish thing,
And it would work 'em woe;
For all averred, I had killed the bird
That made the breeze to blow.
Ah wretch! said they, the bird to slay,
That made the breeze to blow!

<small>But when the fog cleared off, they justify the same, and thus make themselves accomplices in the crime.</small>

"Nor dim nor red, like God's own head,
The glorious Sun uprist;
Then all averred, I had killed the bird
That brought the fog and mist.
'Twas right, said they, such birds to slay,
That bring the fog and mist.

<small>The fair breeze continues; the ship enters the Pacific Ocean, and sails northward, even till it reaches the Line.</small>

"The fair breeze blew, the white foam flew,
The furrow [8] followed free;
We were the first that ever burst
Into that silent sea.

[8] **furrow:** wake

82 • Samuel Taylor Coleridge

The ship hath been suddenly becalmed.

"Down dropped the breeze, the sails dropped
    down,
'Twas sad as sad could be;
And we did speak only to break
The silence of the sea!   110

"All in a hot and copper sky,
The bloody Sun, at noon,
Right up above the mast did stand,
No bigger than the Moon.

"Day after day, day after day,   115
We stuck, nor breath nor motion;
As idle as a painted ship
Upon a painted ocean.

And the Albatross begins to be avenged.

"Water, water, everywhere,
And all the boards did shrink;   120
Water, water, everywhere,
Nor any drop to drink.

"The very deep did rot: O Christ!
That ever this should be!
Yea, slimy things did crawl with legs   125
Upon the slimy sea.

A Spirit had followed them; one of the invisible inhabitants of this planet, neither departed souls nor angels. . . . They are very numerous, and there is no climate or element without one or more.

"About, about, in reel and rout
The death fires danced at night;
The water, like a witch's oils,
Burnt green and blue and white.   130

"And some in dreams assurèd were
Of the Spirit that plagued us so;
Nine fathom deep he had followed us
From the land of mist and snow.

The Rime of the Ancient Mariner • 83

"And every tongue, through utter drought,   135
Was withered at the root;
We could not speak, no more than if
We had been choked with soot.

The shipmates, in their sore distress, would fain throw the whole guilt on the ancient Mariner; in sign whereof they hang the dead sea bird around his neck.

"Ah! welladay! what evil looks
Had I from old and young!   140
Instead of the cross, the Albatross
About my neck was hung.

Part III

"There passed a weary time. Each throat
Was parched, and glazed each eye.
A weary time! a weary time!   145
How glazed each weary eye,
When looking westward, I beheld
A something in the sky.

The ancient Mariner beholdeth a sign in the element afar off.

"At first it seemed a little speck,
And then it seemed a mist;   150
It moved and moved, and took at last
A certain shape, I wist.

"A speck, a mist, a shape, I wist!
And still it neared and neared:
As if it dodged a water sprite,   155
It plunged and tacked and veered.

At its nearer approach, it seemeth him to be a ship; and at a dear ransom he freeth his speech from the bonds of thirst.

"With throats unslaked, with black lips baked,
We could nor laugh nor wail;
Through utter drought all dumb we stood!
I bit my arm, I sucked the blood,   160
And cried, A sail! A sail!

A flash of joy;

"With throats unslaked, with black lips baked,
Agape they heard me call:
Gramercy! they for joy did grin,
And all at once their breath drew in,   165
As they were drinking all.

And horror follows. For can it be a ship that comes onward without wind or tide?

"See! see! (I cried) she tacks no more!
Hither to work us weal;
Without a breeze, without a tide,
She steadies with upright keel!   170

"The western wave was all aflame.
The day was well-nigh done!
Almost upon the western wave
Rested the broad bright Sun;
When that strange shape drove suddenly   175
Betwixt us and the Sun.

It seemeth him but the skeleton of a ship.

"And straight the Sun was flecked with bars,
(Heaven's Mother send us grace!)
As if through a dungeon grate he peered
With broad and burning face.   180

"Alas! (thought I, and my heart beat loud)
How fast she nears and nears!
Are those her sails that glance in the Sun,
Like restless gossameres?

And its ribs are seen as bars on the face of the setting Sun. The Specter-Woman and her Death-mate, and no other on board the skeleton ship.

"Are those her ribs through which the Sun   185
Did peer, as through a grate?
And is that Woman all her crew?
Is that a Death? and are there two?
Is Death that woman's mate?

"Her lips were red, her looks were free,[9]   190
Her locks were yellow as gold:

[9] **free:** wild

The Rime of the Ancient Mariner • 85

Like vessel, like crew!

Her skin was as white as leprosy,
The nightmare Life-in-Death was she,
Who thicks man's blood with cold.

Death and Life-in-Death have diced for the ship's crew, and she (the latter) winneth the ancient Mariner.

"The naked hulk alongside came,   195
And the twain were casting dice;
'The game is done! I've won! I've won!'
Quoth she, and whistles thrice.

No twilight within the courts of the Sun.

"The Sun's rim dips; the stars rush out:
At one stride comes the dark;   200
With far-heard whisper, o'er the sea,
Off shot the specter bark.

At the rising of the Moon,

"We listened and looked sideways up!
Fear at my heart, as at a cup,
My lifeblood seemed to sip!   205
The stars were dim, and thick the night,
The steersman's face by his lamp gleamed white;
From the sails the dew did drip—
Till clomb above the eastern bar
The hornèd Moon, with one bright star   210
Within the nether tip.

One after another,

"One after one, by the star-dogged Moon,
Too quick for groan or sigh,
Each turned his face with a ghastly pang,
And cursed me with his eye.   215

His shipmates drop down dead.

"Four times fifty living men,
(And I heard nor sigh nor groan)
With heavy thump, a lifeless lump,
They dropped down one by one.

But Life-in-Death begins her work on the ancient Mariner.

"The souls did from their bodies fly—   220
They fled to bliss or woe!

And every soul, it passed me by,
Like the whizz of my crossbow!"

Part IV

The Wedding-Guest feareth that a Spirit is talking to him;

"I fear thee, ancient Mariner!
I fear thy skinny hand! 225
And thou art long, and lank, and brown,
As is the ribbed sea sand.

But the ancient Mariner assureth him of his bodily life, and proceedeth to relate his horrible penance.

"I fear thee and thy glittering eye,
And thy skinny hand, so brown."—
"Fear not, fear not, thou Wedding-Guest! 230
This body dropped not down.

"Alone, alone, all, all alone,
Alone on a wide, wide sea!
And never a saint took pity on
My soul in agony. 235

He despiseth the creatures of the calm,

"The many men, so beautiful!
And they all dead did lie:
And a thousand thousand slimy things
Lived on; and so did I.

And envieth that they should live, and so many lie dead.

"I looked upon the rotting sea, 240
And drew my eyes away;
I looked upon the rotting deck,
And there the dead men lay.

"I looked to heaven, and tried to pray;
But or ever a prayer had gusht, 245
A wicked whisper came, and made
My heart as dry as dust.

"I closed my lids, and kept them close,
And the balls like pulses beat;

The Rime of the Ancient Mariner • 87

For the sky and the sea, and the sea and the sky   250
Lay like a load on my weary eye,
And the dead were at my feet.

<small>But the curse liveth for him in the eye of the dead men.</small>

"The cold sweat melted from their limbs,
Nor rot nor reek did they;
The look with which they looked on me   255
Had never passed away.

<small>In his loneliness and fixedness he yearneth towards the journeying Moon, and the stars that still sojourn, yet still move onward; and everywhere the blue sky belongs to them, and is their appointed rest, and their native country and their own natural homes, which they enter unannounced, as lords that are certainly expected, and yet there is silent joy at their arrival.</small>

"An orphan's curse would drag to hell
A spirit from on high;
But oh! more horrible than that
Is a curse in a dead man's eye!   260
Seven days, seven nights, I saw that curse,
And yet I could not die.

"The moving Moon went up the sky,
And nowhere did abide;
Softly she was going up,   265
And a star or two beside—

"Her beams bemocked the sultry main,
Like April hoar-frost spread;
But where the ship's huge shadow lay,
The charmèd water burnt alway   270
A still and awful red.

<small>By the light of the Moon he beholdeth God's creatures of the great calm.</small>

"Beyond the shadow of the ship,
I watched the water snakes:
They moved in tracks of shining white,
And when they reared, the elfish light   275
Fell off in hoary flakes.

"Within the shadow of the ship
I watched their rich attire:

>Blue, glossy green, and velvet black,
>They coiled and swam; and every track
>Was a flash of golden fire.

Their beauty and their happiness. He blesseth them in his heart.

>"Oh happy living things! no tongue
>Their beauty might declare:
>A spring of love gushed from my heart,
>And I blessed them unaware;
>Sure my kind saint took pity on me,
>And I blessed them unaware.

The spell begins to break.

>"The selfsame moment I could pray;
>And from my neck so free
>The Albatross fell off, and sank
>Like lead into the sea.

Part V

>"O sleep! it is a gentle thing,
>Beloved from pole to pole!
>To Mary Queen the praise be given!
>She sent the gentle sleep from Heaven,
>That slid into my soul.

By grace of the holy Mother, the ancient Mariner is refreshed with rain.

>"The silly [10] buckets on the deck,
>That had so long remained,
>I dreamt that they were filled with dew;
>And when I awoke, it rained.

>"My lips were wet, my throat was cold,
>My garments all were dank;
>Sure I had drunken in my dreams,
>And still my body drank.

>"I moved, and could not feel my limbs;
>I was so light—almost
>I thought that I had died in sleep,
>And was a blessèd ghost.

---

[10] **silly:** empty

The Rime of the Ancient Mariner • 89

He heareth sounds and seeth strange sights and commotions in the sky and the elements.

"And soon I heard a roaring wind:
It did not come anear; 310
But with its sound it shook the sails,
That were so thin and sere.

"The upper air burst into life!
And a hundred fire-flags sheen,[11]
To and fro they were hurried about! 315
And to and fro, and in and out,
The wan stars danced between.

"And the coming wind did roar more loud,
And the sails did sigh like sedge;[12]
And the rain poured down from one black
    cloud; 320
The Moon was at its edge.

"The thick black cloud was cleft, and still
The Moon was at its side:
Like waters shot from some high crag,
The lightning fell with never a jag, 325
A river steep and wide.

"The loud wind never reached the ship,
Yet now the ship moved on!

The bodies of the ship's crew are inspired, and the ship moves on;

Beneath the lightning and the Moon
The dead men gave a groan. 330

"They groaned, they stirred, they all uprose,
Nor spake, nor moved their eyes;
It had been strange, even in a dream,
To have seen those dead men rise.

"The helmsman steered, the ship moved on; 335
Yet never a breeze upblew;

[11] **sheen:** lightning   [12] **sedge:** tall rushes

The mariners all 'gan work the ropes,
Where they were wont to do;
They raised their limbs like lifeless tools—
We were a ghastly crew.　　　　　　　　340

"The body of my brother's son
Stood by me, knee to knee:
The body and I pulled at one rope,
But he said nought to me."

But not by the souls of the men, nor by demons of earth or middle air, but by a blessed troop of angelic spirits sent down by the invocation of the guardian saint.

"I fear thee, ancient Mariner!"　　　　345
"Be calm, thou Wedding-Guest!
'Twas not those souls that fled in pain,
Which to their corses came again,
But a troop of spirits blest:

"For when it dawned—they dropped their
　　　arms,　　　　　　　　　　　　　350
And clustered round the mast;
Sweet sounds rose slowly through their mouths,
And from their bodies passed.

"Around, around, flew each sweet sound,
Then darted to the Sun;　　　　　　　355
Slowly the sounds came back again,
Now mixed, now one by one.

"Sometimes a-dropping from the sky
I heard the skylark sing;
Sometimes all little birds that are,　　　360
How they seemed to fill the sea and air
With their sweet jargoning! [13]

[13] **jargoning:** confused sounds

"And now 'twas like all instruments,
Now like a lonely flute;
And now it is an angel's song, 365
That makes the heavens be mute.

"It ceased; yet still the sails made on
A pleasant noise till noon,
A noise like of a hidden brook
In the leafy month of June, 370
That to the sleeping woods all night
Singeth a quiet tune.

"Till noon we quietly sailed on,
Yet never a breeze did breathe:
Slowly and smoothly went the ship, 375
Moved onward from beneath.

The lonesome Spirit from the South Pole carries on the ship as far as the Line, in obedience to the angelic troop, but still requireth vengeance.

"Under the keel nine fathom deep,
From the land of mist and snow,
The spirit slid; and it was he
That made the ship to go. 380
The sails at noon left off their tune,
And the ship stood still also.

"The Sun, right up above the mast,
Had fixed her to the ocean;
But in a minute she 'gan stir, 385
With a short uneasy motion—
Backwards and forwards half her length
With a short uneasy motion.

"Then like a pawing horse let go,
She made a sudden bound: 390
It flung the blood into my head,
And I fell down in a swound.

The Polar Spirit's fellow demons, the invisible habitants of the element, take part in his wrong; and two of them relate, one to the other, that penance long and heavy for the ancient Mariner hath been accorded to the Polar Spirit, who returneth southward.

"How long in that same fit I lay,
I have not to declare;
But ere my living life returned, 395
I heard, and in my soul discerned,
Two voices in the air.

" 'Is it he?' quoth one, 'Is this the man?
By Him who died on cross,
With his cruel bow he laid full low 400
The harmless Albatross.

" 'The spirit who bideth by himself
In the land of mist and snow,
He loved the bird that loved the man
Who shot him with his bow.' 405

"The other was a softer voice,
As soft as honey-dew:
Quoth he, 'The man hath penance done,
And penance more will do.'

Part VI

First Voice

" 'But tell me, tell me! speak again, 410
Thy soft response renewing—
What makes that ship drive on so fast?
What is the ocean doing?'

Second Voice

" 'Still as a slave before his lord,
The ocean hath no blast; 415
His great bright eye most silently
Up to the Moon is cast—

" 'If he may know which way to go;
For she guides him smooth or grim.

The Rime of the Ancient Mariner • 93

See, brother, see! how graciously 420
She looketh down on him.'

First Voice

The Mariner hath been cast into a trance; for the angelic power causeth the vessel to drive northward faster than human life could endure.

" 'But why drives on that ship so fast,
Without or wave or wind?'

Second Voice

" 'The air is cut away before,
And closes from behind. 425

" 'Fly, brother, fly! more high, more high!
Or we shall be belated:
For slow and slow that ship will go,
When the Mariner's trance is abated.'

The supernatural motion is retarded; the Mariner awakes, and his penance begins anew.

"I woke, and we were sailing on 430
As in a gentle weather:
'Twas night, calm night, the Moon was high;
The dead men stood together.

"All stood together on the deck,
For a charnel dungeon [14] fitter: 435
All fixed on me their stony eyes,
That in the Moon did glitter.

"The pang, the curse, with which they died,
Had never passed away:
I could not draw my eyes from theirs, 440
Nor turn them up to pray.

The curse is finally expiated.

"And now this spell was snapped: once more
I viewed the ocean green,
And looked far forth, yet little saw
Of what had else been seen— 445

---

[14] **dungeon:** burial vault

"Like one, that on a lonesome road
Doth walk in fear and dread,
And having once turned round, walks on,
And turns no more his head;
Because he knows, a frightful fiend   450
Doth close behind him tread.

"But soon there breathed a wind on me,
Nor sound nor motion made:
Its path was not upon the sea,
In ripple or in shade.   455

"It raised my hair, it fanned my cheek
Like a meadow gale of spring—
It mingled strangely with my fears,
Yet it felt like a welcoming,

"Swiftly, swiftly flew the ship,   460
Yet she sailed softly too:
Sweetly, sweetly blew the breeze—
On me alone it blew.

And the ancient Mariner beholdeth his native country.

"Oh! dream of joy! is this indeed
The lighthouse top I see?   465
Is this the hill? Is this the kirk?
Is this mine own countree?

"We drifted o'er the harbor bar,
And I with sobs did pray—
O let me be awake, my God!   470
Or let me sleep alway.

"The harbor bay was clear as glass,
So smoothly it was strewn!
And on the bay the moonlight lay,
And the shadow of the Moon.   475

The Rime of the Ancient Mariner • 95

"The rock shone bright, the kirk no less,
That stands above the rock:
The moonlight steeped in silentness
The steady weathercock.

The angelic spirits leave the dead bodies

"And the bay was white with silent light   480
Till, rising from the same,
Full many shapes, that shadows were,
In crimson colours came.

"A little distance from the prow
Those crimson shadows were: 485
I turned my eyes upon the deck—
Oh, Christ, what saw I there!

"Each corse lay flat, lifeless and flat,·
And, by the holy rood!
And appear in their own forms of light.
A man all light, a seraph-man,   490
On every corse there stood.

"This seraph-band, each waved his hand:
It was a heavenly sight!
They stood as signals to the land,
Each one a lovely light: 495

"This seraph-band, each waved his hand;
No voice did they impart—
No voice; but oh! the silence sank
Like music on my heart.

"But soon I heard the dash of oars,   500
I heard the Pilot's cheer;
My head was turned perforce away,
And I saw a boat appear.

"The Pilot and the Pilot's boy,
I heard them coming fast: 505
Dear Lord in Heaven! it was a joy
The dead men could not blast.

"I saw a third—I heard his voice:
It is the Hermit good!
He singeth loud his godly hymns   510
That he makes in the wood.
He'll shrieve my soul, he'll wash away
The Albatross's blood.

Part VII

<small>The Hermit of the Wood,</small>

"This Hermit good lives in that wood
Which slopes down to the sea.   515
How loudly his sweet voice he rears!
He loves to talk with marineres
That come from a far countree.

"He kneels at morn, and noon, and eve—
He hath a cushion plump: 520
It is the moss that wholly hides
The rotted old oak-stump.

"The skiff boat neared: I heard them talk,
'Why, this is strange, I trow! [15]
Where are those lights so many and fair,   525
That signal made but now?

<small>Approacheth the ship with wonder.</small>

" 'Strange, by my faith!' the Hermit said—
'And they answered not our cheer! [16]
The planks look warped! and see those sails,
How thin they are and sere!   530
I never saw aught like to them,
Unless perchance it were

[15] **trow:** think   [16] **cheer:** call

" 'Brown skeletons of leaves that lag
My forest brook along,
When the ivy-tod [17] is heavy with snow,   535
And the owlet whoops to the wolf below,
That eats the she-wolf's young.'

" 'Dear Lord! it hath a fiendish look'—
(The Pilot made reply)
'I am afeared'—'Push on, push on!'   540
Said the Hermit cheerily.

"The boat came closer to the ship,
But I nor spake nor stirred;
The boat came close beneath the ship,
And straight a sound was heard.   545

The ship suddenly sinketh.

"Under the water it rumbled on,
Still louder and more dread:
It reached the ship, it split the bay;
The ship went down like lead.

The ancient Mariner is saved in the Pilot's boat.

"Stunned by that loud and dreadful sound,   550
Which sky and ocean smote,
Like one that hath been seven days drowned
My body lay afloat;
But swift as dreams, myself I found
Within the Pilot's boat.   555

"Upon the whirl, where sank the ship,
The boat spun round and round;
And all was still, save that the hill
Was telling of the sound.

"I moved my lips—the Pilot shrieked   560
And fell down in a fit;

---

[17] **ivy-tod:** bush

The holy Hermit raised his eyes,
And prayed where he did sit.

"I took the oars: the Pilot's boy, 565
Who now doth crazy go,
Laughed loud and long, and all the while
His eyes went to and fro.
'Ha! ha!' quoth he, 'full plain I see,
The Devil knows how to row.'

"And now, all in my own countree, 570
I stood on the firm land!
The Hermit stepped forth from the boat,
And scarcely he could stand.

The ancient Mariner earnestly entreateth the Hermit to shrieve him; and the penance of life falls on him.

" 'O shrieve me, shrieve me, holy man!'
The Hermit crossed his brow. 575
'Say quick,' quoth he, 'I bid thee say—
What manner of man art thou?'

"Forthwith this frame of mine was wrenched
With a woeful agony,
Which forced me to begin my tale; 580
And then it left me free.

And ever and anon throughout his future life an agony constraineth him to travel from land to land,

"Since then, at an uncertain hour,
That agony returns;
And till my ghastly tale is told,
This heart within me burns. 585

"I pass, like night, from land to land;
I have strange power of speech;
That moment that his face I see
I know the man that must hear me:
To him my tale I teach. 590

"What loud uproar bursts from that door!
The wedding-guests are there;
But in the garden-bower the bride
And bride-maids singing are;
And hark the little vesper bell, 595
Which biddeth me to prayer!

"O Wedding-Guest! this soul hath been
Alone on a wide, wide sea:
So lonely 'twas, that God himself
Scarce seemèd there to be. 600

"O sweeter than the marriage-feast,
'Tis sweeter far to me,
To walk together to the kirk
With a goodly company!—

"To walk together to the kirk, 605
And all together pray,
While each to his great Father bends,
Old men, and babes, and loving friends,
And youths and maidens gay!

"Farewell, farewell! but this I tell 610
To thee, thou Wedding-Guest!
He prayeth well, who loveth well
Both man and bird and beast.

And to teach by his own example love and reverence to all things that God made and loveth.

"He prayeth best, who loveth best
All things both great and small; 615
For the dear God who loveth us,
He made and loveth all."

The Mariner, whose eye is bright,
Whose beard with age is hoar,
Is gone: and now the Wedding-Guest 620
Turned from the bridegroom's door.

> He went like one that hath been stunned,
> And is of sense forlorn:
> A sadder and a wiser man,
> He rose the morrow morn. 625

For Discussion

1. Summarize the action of the poem, the order of events, and the setting for each event. Remember always that the setting given in the first two stanzas and returned to at the end of the poem must be kept in mind while reading the poem. What is the relationship between the sound of the wedding feast and the story told by the Mariner? Why do we not know the name of the Mariner or that of the Wedding Guest?
2. Note the description of the coming of the Albatross, the central symbol of the poem. What is the meaning of the simile in lines 65–66? How does this description dramatically affect the last line of Part I?
3. What possible motive could the Mariner have had to kill the Albatross? Was this a crime against God? Against nature? Against the "oneness in nature"? Explain.
4. What was the initial reaction of the other mariners to the killing of the Albatross? Why did they change their attitude? Do they become accomplices in the Mariner's crime?
5. Why is the appearance of the specter ship ironic? How is Death-in-Life described? Who receives the more terrible punishment, the Mariner or the other seamen? Since the action of the poem takes place when the Mariner was young, does his youth further aggravate the tortures he must bear alone? Discuss.
6. What action on the part of the Mariner leads to his relief? Does this give a possible clue to the probable motive for his killing the Albatross? What had to be reborn in the Mariner?
7. Part V is a good example of Coleridge's ability to mingle the real and the unreal. How does he gain the reader's "willing suspension of disbelief" in this section?

The Rime of the Ancient Mariner • 101

8. What information is given by the dialogue between the two voices? What happens further to torment the Mariner? How is the spell finally broken?
9. What is the relationship between the specific details of the Mariner's native country and the description of the world of the voyage? How is the Hermit contrasted to the Mariner?
10. Notice that the Albatross is not mentioned in Part VII. What possible reasons can you give for this?
11. Coleridge said that this poem had too much moral. What is the direct statement of the moral? What are other possible meanings for this seemingly didactic statement?
12. Most first readers of this poem remember vivid scenes and sections of the poem created by Coleridge's imagination and his power over words. Pick out examples of particularly striking scenes and discuss the reasons for their effectiveness.
13. The poem abounds in contrasting images and in single images used in several ways. Discuss the function of the following in the total meaning of the poem: water; sun and moon; natural and supernatural.
14. Point out examples of archaic words and phrases. What effect do they have on the tone of the poem? Compare the diction used in the poem to that of the gloss.

For Composition

1. Retell the first meeting of Christabel and Geraldine from the point of view of Geraldine. Work to achieve both the sense and mood of the original setting and the quality of suspense.
2. Imagine yourself as the Wedding Guest who rises the next morning a sadder but wiser man. Write a diary entry in which you try to come to terms with the experience of the Mariner's story—the reasons that it affected you so deeply.

THE LATE ROMANTICS

Firmly established by the poetry of Wordsworth and Coleridge, the Romantic Movement was continued and strengthened by three young poets of major significance in English literature: George Gordon, Lord Byron; John Keats; and Percy Bysshe Shelley. To many of their countrymen, Byron, Keats, and Shelley were revolutionary nonconformists, not only in the freedom of expression they sought, but more important, in the freedom of thought they insisted upon. Their voices came at a time when many in England felt that dissent in any form must be held in check to safeguard the nation and to prevent a revolution similar to that which had shaken France. These young writers had not known the elation at the prospect of egalitarianism inspired by the French Revolution; nor had they experienced the disillusionment engendered by the Reign of Terror that had so quickly muddied the effects of the Revolution. And although England had defeated Napoleon at Trafalgar and Waterloo, battles sacred to English nationalism, the country was tasting bitter fruits of victory. Problems in unemployment caused by returning veterans, crises in agriculture and manufacturing, and pressing social problems were causing deep stresses in English life—factors which contributed to the prevailing conservatism that feared the fresh voices of the Romantic poets.

The Late Romantics • 103

Although these three poets, Byron, Keats, and Shelley, are usually grouped together, they are more different than alike. Sharing certain beliefs, each one came to a different way of expressing his thoughts and ideas; each one built his own system of values.

All three shared a violent hatred of tyranny and authoritarian repression of the human spirit. In *Childe Harold*, Byron scoffed with skeptical irreverence at the rejoicing over the defeat of Napoleon, seeing his defeat as merely the triumph of tyrannous kings and forces of reaction. Keats feared the suppression of the spirit of man, weighed down by the drabness of a life without beauty or joy. Shelley wrote poems of outrage against the repressive measures brought against the working man; King Ozymandias stands as the symbol of the vanity of the tyrant.

Like Wordsworth, all three poets shared a love of nature. However, they differed strongly in their attitudes toward it. Byron delighted in the vastness, energy, and spectacle of the mountains, valleys, and oceans. To Keats, nature was alive with beauty for the five senses, which he would explore for its richness, its color, and its glow. Shelley sought in nature a mirror for his own feelings and emotions.

The volume and quality of work presented by these poets show the range of subject and thought of the Romantics. They held the belief that poetry should be representative of all human life, that it should explore the imagination and spirit of men. They sang of the past, the beauty of nature in all its forms, the oppression of the common man, the beauty of art and poetry, the joys of love, the depth of melancholy, the need for feeling and imagination—all the joys and sorrows to which man is heir.

In his own day George Gordon, Lord Byron, was considered *the* Romantic poet by most European critics. A legend in his own time, he was catapulted to fame by the publication of *Childe Harold's Pilgrimage*. Here was a new voice speaking in easy and fluent verse with impulsive defiance, with the exuberant energy of the individual. For many,

Byron himself was the Byronic hero, that man who was, in Macaulay's words, "proud, moody, cynical, with defiance on his brow, and misery in his heart, a scorner of his kind, implacable in revenge, yet capable of deep and strong emotion."

Byron's poetry often seems a blend of Neoclassical form and Romantic themes. He was concerned with correctness of form; and his use of satire and his admiration for the heroic couplet show his debt to Pope, a poet he greatly admired. His language, for the most part, belongs to the older school of the Neoclassicists. However, in his strong presentation of his individual feelings, in his love for the wild and energetic forces in nature, in his love of freedom, and in his commitment to the value of the individual, he is one of the most outspoken Romantics.

John Keats sought for permanence in beauty—in art, in literature, and in nature. The opening lines of the "Proem" from *Endymion* are a poetic statement of this creed of beauty:

> A Thing of beauty is a joy for ever:
> Its loveliness increases . . .

For him beauty gave meaning to life, and he expressed this beauty with intensity and sensitivity. His poetry enchants the senses with its richness of imagery and its luxuriousness of tone.

Both his poetry and his letters reveal a deep concern with the role of the poet and the art of poetry. For Keats, the poet should be a man who has no identity himself because he is "everything and nothing." The poet must have what Keats termed "Negative Capability," the ability to be in "uncertainties, Mysteries, doubts, without any irritable reaching after fact & reason." The poet should not seek to find neat answers to the deep questions of life; he must let his mind and imagination entertain all kinds of ideas. Poetry, the making of a work of art, is "a wording of [man's] highest thoughts." Throughout his poetry, we see a deep concern with the basic relation of art to life and to living.

Keats is a craftsman concerned with form, diction, and imagery; his odes stand among the finest in English. He possessed a sense of the complexity of life and of the pain in pleasure and the pleasure in pain. He could perceive the essence of a particular moment. These qualities, and his attempt to reach a vision of reality through the senses and imagination, make him esteemed not only as a Romantic but as a poet of truly universal appeal.

Percy Bysshe Shelley during his own lifetime was a center of conflicting critical opinions and has remained so. A supreme idealist and an extreme heretic, he sought in nature to find his dream of an ideal world which would begin again the "world's great age." A believer in the perfectibility of man, he had an all-embracing enthusiasm for humanity and fought against tyranny and oppression in any form. He saw his role as poet to be that of a seer, a "legislator" who would "quicken a new birth" among men.

Although Shelley denounced the evils he readily found in the world, he offered little in the way of concrete remedies for these defects. As he saw his idealistic world being rejected, he often gave way to melancholy and self-pity. He himself expressed this best in "Adonais": "thy hopes are gone before; from all things here/ They have departed."

The imagery and language of Shelley's poetry are much more abstract than that of either Byron or Keats. A "scorner of the ground," Shelley soared into a world of mist, illusion, and the ideal. Often his poems lack a strong sense of structure and demand careful reading and attention, and often we feel rather than see his world, responding to the music of words and images which convey the emotional quality and intensity of the situation.

George Gordon, Lord Byron

(1788–1824)

Paradoxically, Byron, the most famous Romantic in his own day, was the least Romantic of the five major poets. In his life he seemed to be the epitome of the Romantic, flamboyant, self-assertive, and long-suffering; but in his art he often demonstrated a close affinity to the Neoclassicists in his love of form.

His reactions to nature and to life were direct, certainly not as complicated as those of the poet-philosopher, Wordsworth. Byron delighted in the energy and sweep of nature. His references to nature are of nature as turbulent and vast. In a sense, his own great liberal sense of freedom reflected the free energy he deeply admired in nature. He hated tyranny as the force which would subdue and crush the individual.

Much of Byron's poetry is a projection of himself, a fact which causes difficulty in separating the work and the artist. The dramatic performance in *Childe Harold's Pilgrimage,* particularly in Cantos III and IV, is essentially that of Byron, the man and the poet. He becomes the individual at war with society, ranging the world and expressing his own personality in fierce, natural, and impetuous speech.

SHE WALKS IN BEAUTY

She walks in beauty, like the night
    Of cloudless climes and starry skies;
And all that's best of dark and bright
    Meet in her aspect and her eyes;
Thus mellowed to that tender light   5
    Which heaven to gaudy day denies.

One shade the more, one ray the less,
    Had half impaired the nameless grace
Which waves in every raven tress,
    Or softly lightens o'er her face;   10
Where thoughts serenely sweet express
    How pure, how dear, their dwelling-place.

And on that cheek, and o'er that brow,
    So soft, so calm, yet eloquent,
The smiles that win, the tints that glow,   15
    But tell of days in goodness spent,
A mind at peace with all below,
    A heart whose love is innocent!

For Discussion

1. Examine the title given to this poem. Is it to be read literally or figuratively? Are there physical elements in the description of the lady which develop the image of the night? What are the non-material details which develop the image?
2. In addition to the basic night image, there are images of light and day. Do these images work in opposition to the night image? Do they strengthen the night image?
3. What exactly is the speaker in the poem praising about the lady?

THE DESTRUCTION OF SENNACHERIB

The Assyrian [1] came down like the wolf on the fold,
And his cohorts were gleaming in purple and gold;
And the sheen of their spears was like stars on the sea,
When the blue wave rolls nightly on deep Galilee.

Like the leaves of the forest when summer is green,   5
That host with their banners at sunset were seen;

---

[1] **Assyrian:** King Sennacherib who invaded Palestine in the 7th century B.C.

Like the leaves of the forest when autumn hath blown,
That host on the morrow lay withered and strown.

For the Angel of Death spread his wings on the blast,
And breathed in the face of the foe as he passed;
And the eyes of the sleepers waxed deadly and chill,
And their hearts but once heaved, and forever grew still!

And there lay the steed with his nostril all wide,
But through it there rolled not the breath of his pride;
And the foam of his gasping lay white on the turf,
And cold as the spray of the rock-beating surf.

And there lay the rider distorted and pale,
With the dew on his brow, and the rust on his mail;
And the tents were all silent, the banners alone,
The lances unlifted, the trumpet unblown.

And the widows of Ashur are loud in their wail,
And the idols are broke in the temple of Baal;
And the might of the Gentile, unsmote by the sword,
Hath melted like snow in the glance of the Lord!

For Discussion

1. This poem makes great use of contrast expressed in concrete objects. Compare the picture given in the first stanza to that given in the last stanza. How does each stanza work? What is the effect of juxtaposing these stanzas? Compare the similes used in each stanza.
2. Note the function of the horse and the rider in the fourth and fifth stanzas. What is the purpose of the grisly description? What larger meanings are conveyed by the use of such words as "banners," "lances," "trumpet," in lines 19 and 20.
3. Stanza 2 works on two parallel similes. Examine the vowel sounds to show how these sounds help each simile convey its meaning. Find other examples of this technique.
4. What effect is achieved by the anapestic rhythm? Why is it so appropriate to the subject and theme of the poem?

from Childe Harold's Pilgrimage

The first two cantos of *Childe Harold's Pilgrimage,* published in 1812, recount Harold's travels through Spain, Portugal, and Greece. They are vivid in relating what the fictional traveler saw but offer little comment on the scenes. Canto III, published four years later, continues the journey and tells of Harold's travels in Belgium and Switzerland. However, now this melancholy and passionate traveler not only describes the scene but acts as commentator on the works of men.

Canto III

6

'Tis to create, and in creating live
A being more intense, that we endow
With form our fancy, gaining as we give
The life we image, even as I do now.
What am I? Nothing: but not so art thou,   5
Soul of my thought! [1] with whom I traverse earth,
Invisible but gazing, as I glow
Mix'd with thy spirit, blended with thy birth,
And feeling still with thee in my crush'd feelings' dearth.

7

Yet must I think less wildly:—I *have* thought   10
Too long and darkly, till my brain became,
In its own eddy boiling and o'erwrought,
A whirling gulf of phantasy and flame:
And thus, untaught in youth my heart to tame,
My springs of life were poison'd. 'Tis too late!   15
Yet am I changed; though still enough the same
In strength to bear what time can not abate,
And feed on bitter fruits without accusing Fate.

---

[1] **Soul of my thought:** Harold

8

Something too much of this:—but now 'tis past,
And the spell closes with its silent seal.
Long absent HAROLD re-appears at last;
He of the breast which fain no more would feel,
Wrung with the wounds which kill not, but ne'er heal,
Yet Time, who changes all, had alter'd him
In soul and aspect as in age: years steal
Fire from the mind as vigour from the limb,
And life's enchanted cup but sparkles near the brim.

9

His had been quaff'd too quickly, and he found
The dregs were wormwood; but he fill'd again,
And from a purer fount, on holier ground,
And deem'd its spring perpetual—but in vain!
Still round him clung invisibly a chain
Which gall'd for ever, fettering though unseen,
And heavy though it clank'd not; worn with pain,
Which pined although it spoke not, and grew keen,
Entering with every step he took through many a scene.

12

But soon he knew himself the most unfit
Of men to herd with Man; with whom he held
Little in common;—untaught to submit
His thoughts to others, though his soul was quell'd
In youth by his own thoughts; still uncompell'd,
He would not yield dominion of his mind
To spirits against whom his own rebell'd;
Proud though in desolation; which could find
A life within itself, to breathe without mankind.

13

Where rose the mountains, there to him were friends;
Where roll'd the ocean, thereon was his home;

Where a blue sky, and glowing clime, extends,
He had the passion and the power to roam;
The desert, forest, cavern, breaker's foam, 50
Were unto him companionship; they spake
A mutual language, clearer than the tome
Of his land's tongue, which he would oft forsake
For Nature's pages glass'd by sunbeams on the lake.

14

Like the Chaldean,[2] he could watch the stars, 55
Till he had peopled them with beings bright
As their own beams; and earth, and earthborn jars,
And human frailties, were forgotten quite:
Could he have kept his spirit to that flight
He had been happy; but this clay will sink 60
Its spark immortal, envying it the light
To which it mounts, as if to break the link
That keeps us from yon heaven which woos us to its brink.

15

But in Man's dwellings he became a thing
Restless and worn, and stern and wearisome, 65
Droop'd as a wild-born falcon with clipt wing,
To whom the boundless air alone were home:
Then came his fit again, which to o'er-come,
As eagerly the barr'd-up bird will beat
His breast and beak against his wiry dome 70
Till the blood tinge his plumage, so the heat
Of his impeded soul would through his bosom eat.

16

Self-exiled Harold wanders forth again,
With nought of hope left, but with less of gloom;
The very knowledge that he lived in vain, 75
That all was over on this side the tomb,
Had made Despair a smilingness assume,

[2] **Chaldean:** Babylonian experts in astronomy

Which, though 'twere wild,—as on the plunder'd wreck
When mariners would madly meet their doom
With draughts intemperate on the sinking deck,— 80
Did yet inspire a cheer, which he forbore to check.

17

Stop!—for thy tread is on an Empire's [3] dust!
An Earthquake's spoil is sepulchered below!
Is the spot mark'd with no colossal bust?
Nor column trophied for triumphal show? 85
None; but the moral's truth tells simpler so,
As the ground was before, thus let it be;—
How that red rain hath made the harvest grow!
And is this all the world has gain'd by thee,
Thou first and last of fields! king-making Victory? 90

18

And Harold stands upon this place of skulls,
The grave of France, the deadly Waterloo!
How in an hour the power which gave annuls
Its gifts, transferring fame as fleeting too!
In "pride of place" here last the eagle flew, 95
Then tore with bloody talon the rent plain,
Pierced by the shaft of banded nations through;
Ambition's life and labours all were vain;
He wears the shatter'd links of the world's broken chain.

19

Fit retribution! Gaul [4] may champ the bit 100
And foam in fetters;—but is Earth more free?
Did nations combat to make *One* submit;
Or league to teach all kings true sovereignty?
What! shall reviving Thraldom [5] again be
The patch'd-up idol of enlighten'd days? 105
Shall we, who struck the Lion down, shall we

---

[3] The defeat of Napoleon at Waterloo, June 18, 1815.
[4] **Gaul:** France
[5] **Thraldom:** serfdom, slavery

Pay the Wolf homage? proffering lowly gaze
And servile knees to thrones? No; *prove* before ye praise!

20

If not, o'er one fallen despot boast no more!
In vain fair cheeks were furrow'd with hot tears   110
For Europe's flowers long rooted up before
The trampler of her vineyards; in vain years
Of death, depopulation, bondage, fears,
Have all been borne, and broken by the accord
Of roused-up millions: all that most endears   115
Glory, is when the myrtle wreathes a sword
Such as Harmodius [6] drew on Athens' tyrant lord.

21

There was a sound of revelry by night,
And Belgium's capital had gathered then
Her beauty and her chivalry, and bright   120
The lamps shone o'er fair women and brave men;
A thousand hearts beat happily; and when
Music arose with its voluptuous swell,
Soft eyes looked love to eyes which spake again,
And all went merry as a marriage bell;   125
But hush! hark! a deep sound strikes like a rising knell!

22

Did ye not hear it?—No; 'twas but the wind,
Or the car rattling o'er the stony street;
On with the dance! let joy be unconfined;
No sleep till morn when youth and pleasure meet   130
To chase the glowing hours with flying feet—
But hark!—that heavy sound breaks in once more
As if the clouds its echo would repeat;
And nearer, clearer, deadlier than before!
Arm! Arm! it is—it is—the cannon's opening roar!   135

---

[6] **Harmodius:** a Greek patriot who slew the tyrannical ruler of Athens in 515 B.C.

23

Within a windowed niche of that high hall
Sate Brunswick's [7] fated chieftain; he did hear
That sound the first amidst the festival,
And caught its tone with death's prophetic ear;
And when they smiled because he deemed it near, 140
His heart more truly knew that peal too well
Which stretched his father on a bloody bier,[8]
And roused the vengeance blood alone could quell;
He rushed into the field, and, foremost fighting, fell.

24

Ah! then and there was hurrying to and fro, 145
And gathering tears, and tremblings of distress,
And cheeks all pale, which but an hour ago
Blushed at the praise of their own loveliness;
And there were sudden partings, such as press
The life from out young hearts, and choking sighs 150
Which ne'er might be repeated; who could guess
If ever more should meet those mutual eyes,
Since upon night so sweet such awful morn could rise!

25

And there was mounting in hot haste: the steed,
The mustering squadron, and the clattering car, 155
Went pouring forward with impetuous speed,
And swiftly forming in the ranks of war;
And the deep thunder peal on peal afar;
And near, the beat of the alarming drum
Roused up the soldier ere the morning star; 160
While thronged the citizens with terror dumb,
Or whispering, with white lips, "The foe! they come! they come!"

---

[7] The Duke of Brunswick who was later killed in the battle
[8] killed at the Battle of Auerstädt, 1806

26

And wild and high the "Cameron's gathering" [9] rose!
The war-note of Lochiel, which Albyn's hills
Have heard, and heard, too, have her Saxon foes: 165
How in the noon of night that pibroch thrills,
Savage and shrill! But with the breath which fills
Their mountain-pipe, so fill the mountaineers
With the fierce native daring which instils
The stirring memory of a thousand years, 170
And Evan's, Donald's, fame rings in each clansman's ears!

27

And Ardennes [10] waves above them her green leaves,
Dewy with nature's tear-drops as they pass,
Grieving, if aught inanimate e'er grieves,
Over the unreturning brave,—alas! 175
Ere evening to be trodden like the grass
Which now beneath them, but above shall grow
In its next verdure, when this fiery mass
Of living valor, rolling on the foe
And burning with high hope shall molder cold and low. 180

28

Last noon beheld them full of lusty life,
Last eve in beauty's circle proudly gay;
The midnight brought the signal-sound of strife,
The morn the marshaling in arms,—the day
Battle's magnificently-stern array! 185
The thunder-clouds close o'er it, which when rent
The earth is covered thick with other clay,
Which her own clay shall cover, heaped and pent,
Rider and horse—friend, foe—in one red burial blent!

---

[9] The Cameron clan under Lochiel went into battle to the sound of the pibroch, Scottish bagpipes.
[10] **Ardennes:** a wooded section in southern Belgium

In the remaining stanzas of Canto III, Byron in the guise of Harold visits Switzerland, commenting not only on the natural scene and on people like Rousseau, Gibbon, Voltaire, but also upon his own life and his attitude toward nature.

In Canto IV, Harold travels to Italy, which becomes the symbol of all human achievement in the arts, arms, and splendor. Having seen the decay of the works of man, Harold returns to the enduring world of nature.

178

There is a pleasure in the pathless woods,
There is a rapture on the lonely shore,
There is society, where none intrudes,
By the deep Sea, and music in its roar:
I love not Man the less, but Nature more, 5
From these our interviews, in which I steal
From all I may be, or have been before,
To mingle with the Universe, and feel
What I can ne'er express, yet cannot all conceal.

179

Roll on, thou deep and dark blue Ocean—roll! 10
Ten thousand fleets sweep over thee in vain;
Man marks the earth with ruin—his control
Stops with the shore; upon the watery plain
The wrecks are all thy deed, nor doth remain
A shadow of man's ravage, save his own, 15
When, for a moment, like a drop of rain,
He sinks into thy depths with bubbling groan,
Without a grave, unknell'd, uncoffin'd, and unknown.

180

His steps are not upon thy paths,—thy fields
Are not a spoil for him,—thou dost arise 20
And shake him from thee; the vile strength he wields
For earth's destruction thou dost all despise,
Spurning him from thy bosom to the skies,

And send'st him, shivering in thy playful spray
And howling, to his Gods where haply lies 25
His petty hope in some near port or bay,
And dashest him again to earth:—there let him lay.

181

The armaments which thunderstrike the walls
Of rock-built cities, bidding nations quake,
And monarchs tremble in their capitals, 30
The oak leviathans,[1] whose huge ribs make
Their clay creator the vain title take
Of lord of thee, and arbiter of war—
These are thy toys, and, as the snowy flake,
They melt into thy yeast of waves, which mar 35
Alike the Armada's [2] pride or spoils of Trafalgar.

182

Thy shores are empires, changed in all save thee—
Assyria, Greece, Rome, Carthage, what are they?
Thy waters wash'd them power while they were free,
And many a tyrant since; their shores obey 40
The stranger, slave, or savage; their decay
Has dried up realms to deserts:—not so thou;—
Unchangeable, save to thy wild waves' play,
Time writes no wrinkle on thine azure brow:
Such as creation's dawn beheld, thou rollest now. 45

183

Thou glorious mirror, where the Almighty's form
Glasses itself in tempests; in all time,—
Calm or convulsed, in breeze, or gale, or storm,
Icing the pole, or in the torrid clime
Dark-heaving—boundless, endless, and sublime, 50

---

[1] **oak leviathans:** large ships
[2] The Spanish Armada was defeated by the British fleet and by a storm in the English Channel in 1588.

The image of Eternity, the throne
Of the Invisible; even from out thy slime
The monsters of the deep are made; each zone
Obeys thee; thou goest forth, dread, fathomless, alone.

184

And I have loved thee, Ocean! and my joy 55
Of youthful sports was on thy breast to be
Borne, like thy bubbles, onward: from a boy
I wanton'd with thy breakers—they to me
Were a delight; and if the freshening sea
Made them a terror—'twas a pleasing fear, 60
For I was as it were a child of thee,
And trusted to thy billows far and near,
And laid my hand upon thy mane—as I do here.

185

My task is done, my song hath ceased, my theme
Has died into an echo; it is fit 65
The spell should break of this protracted dream.
The torch shall be extinguish'd which hath lit
My midnight lamp—and what is writ, is writ;
Would it were worthier! but I am not now
That which I have been—and my visions flit 70
Less palpably before me—and the glow
Which in my spirit dwelt is fluttering, faint, and low.

186

Farewell! a word that must be, and hath been—
A sound which makes us linger;—yet—farewell!
Ye! who have traced the Pilgrim to the scene 75
Which is his last, if in your memories dwell
A thought which once was his, if on ye swell
A single recollection, not in vain
He wore his sandal-shoon and scallop-shell;
Farewell! with *him* alone may rest the pain, 80
If such there were—with *you,* the moral of his strain!

For Discussion

1. What does the poet mean when he says " 'Tis to create, and in creating live/A being more intense"? In stanza 6, what fundamental question does the poet ask himself through his fictional character? As you read through the poem, explain the reason that the speaker was so concerned with that basic question.
2. What are the personal qualities of Harold given in stanzas 8 and 9? In what way is he the Byronic hero?
3. Beginning with stanza 12, Harold leaves the world of men and goes to nature. Is the nature he sought the same nature as contemplated by Wordsworth? How is nature like the hero himself? What dramatic contrast does this section form with stanza 15?
4. In stanza 17, Harold's journey takes him to Waterloo, the scene of Napoleon's defeat. What is Harold's attitude toward Napoleon's defeat? According to stanzas 19 and 20, why should Europe not boast about the fall of Napoleon? What does Harold say is the role and duty of the good ruler?
5. What dramatic contrast is achieved by reviewing the meaning of Waterloo in stanzas 17–20 and then describing the "revelry by night" before the battle? What further contrast is added in stanza 22 to the sounds of the dance?
6. How does Byron catch the mood of confusion and energy which permeated the preparation for battle? Point out examples of his ability to realize the force of the moment through concrete particulars. What is the relationship between stanza 28 and the stanzas which immediately precede it?
7. In the last section of Canto IV, quoted here, Byron returns to the theme of nature. Does he look upon nature as a teacher? What elements does he admire in nature?
8. Like many men, Byron is awed by the ocean. Stanza 179, the famous apostrophe to the ocean, details some of the wonderful terror and mystery and appeal of the water. What does Byron say of man's effect on the ocean? How

does the ocean remind man of his own insignificance? Why is the ocean the "image of Eternity"?
9. What is the nature of the images used by Byron in stanza 184 to describe his own delight in the ocean?
10. With what feelings does the poem end? How have the experiences in the poem affected the speaker? What overtones are present in the words "Pilgrim" and "sandal shoon"? What is the "moral of his strain"?
11. This poem is written in the difficult Spenserian stanza (see Glossary). Chart the rhythm and rhyme scheme of stanza 6, Canto III. What is the effect of the variation of the iambic patterns for the meaning of the stanza?

SONNET ON CHILLON [1]

Eternal spirit of the chainless mind!
   Brightest in dungeons, Liberty! thou art,
   For there thy habitation is the heart,
The heart which love of thee alone can bind;
And when thy sons to fetters are consigned,   5
   To fetters, and the damp vault's dayless gloom,
   Their country conquers with their martyrdom,
And freedom's fame finds wings on every wind.
Chillon! thy prison is a holy place,
   And thy sad floor an altar, for 'twas trod,   10
Until his very steps have left a trace
   Worn, as if thy cold pavement were a sod,
By Bonnivard! [2] May none those marks efface!
   For they appeal from tyranny to God.

[1] **Chillon:** a chateau on Lake Geneva
[2] **Bonnivard:** François Bonnivard, imprisoned in the dungeon of Chillon from 1530 to 1536

For Discussion

1. Examine carefully the syntax of the first two lines. What is the grammatical function of "Eternal spirit"? How is "Liberty" used grammatically?

2. In what way does Byron weave concrete and abstract terms in this sonnet? How does this weaving underscore the paradox stated in line 2?
3. This poem is concerned more with a political question than with a religious question. Why is the use of religious imagery appropriate in developing the ideas of the poem?
4. Plot the rhyme scheme of Byron's sonnet. Is it a Petrarchean or Shakespearean sonnet? How does the sestet relate to the octave?

STANZAS FOR MUSIC

There be none of Beauty's daughters
    With a magic like thee;
And like music on the waters
    Is thy sweet voice to me:
When, as if its sound were causing   5
The charmèd ocean's pausing,
The waves lie still and gleaming,
And the lulled winds seem dreaming.

And the midnight moon is weaving
    Her bright chain o'er the deep;   10
Whose breast is gently heaving,
    As an infant's asleep:
So the spirit bows before thee,
To listen and adore thee;
With a full but soft emotion,   15
Like the swell of summer's ocean.

For Discussion

1. The basic image of this poem is water—the ocean. How is this image developed in the first stanza? Is this an actual picture of the ocean?
2. What effect do the images of the second stanza have on the poem as a whole?
3. In lines 13–14, there is an implied religious connotation. Is such a connotation appropriate to a love poem? Discuss.

SO WE'LL GO NO MORE A-ROVING

So we'll go no more a-roving
 So late into the night,
Though the heart be still as loving,
 And the moon be still as bright.

For the sword outwears its sheath, 5
 And the soul wears out the breast,
And the heart must pause to breathe,
 And love itself have rest.

Though the night was made for loving,
 And the day returns too soon, 10
Yet we'll go no more a-roving
 By the light of the moon.

For Discussion

1. This poem is based on the refrain of an old Scottish song. Point out elements in the rhythm of the poem which account for its song-like quality.
2. What is the function of stanza 2? How does the rhythm change in the last lines of this stanza? What is the effect of this change?
3. How would you describe the tone of this poem: self-pitying; cavalier; rueful; resigned; wistful? Discuss.

For Composition

1. Write a theme of analysis in which you compare the concept of nature in Byron's poetry with the attitude toward nature in the poetry of Wordsworth. Select specific poems as examples to prove your statement.
2. In "Sonnet on Chillon" Byron makes concrete the abstract idea of Liberty by using the example of Bonnivard. Select an abstract word—love, honor, loyalty, patriotism, or one of your own choosing—and write a theme of definition by using an extended example.

John Keats

(1795-1821)

Although his career as a poet was cut short by his untimely death at the age of twenty-five, John Keats stands as one of the major English poets. In his poetry, much admired by modern critics, he communicated his ideal of Beauty in lines which fulfill his own poetic definition—that poetry "should strike the Reader as a wording of his own highest thoughts."

Keats is the poet of the particular detail. Shelley's world was too abstract for Keats, who preferred to render in concrete and sensuous images external objects and internal states. In poems like "The Eve of St. Agnes," he enables his readers to experience the sights, the sounds, the smell, the taste, the touch of the situation he explored. He was a lyricist of the highest rank.

ON FIRST LOOKING INTO CHAPMAN'S HOMER

Much have I travelled in the realms of gold,
    And many goodly states and kingdoms seen;
    Round many western islands have I been
Which bards in fealty to Apollo [1] hold.
Oft of one wide expanse had I been told   5
    That deep-browed Homer ruled as his demesne;
    Yet did I never breathe its pure serene
Till I heard Chapman speak out loud and bold:
Then felt I like some watcher of the skies
    When a new planet swims into his ken;   10

[1] **Apollo:** the Greek god of poetry

Or like stout Cortez [2] when with eagle eyes
   He stared at the Pacific—and all his men
Looked at each other with a wild surmise—
   Silent, upon a peak in Darien.[3]

[2] Historically, it was Balboa, not Cortez, who discovered the Pacific Ocean.
[3] **Darien:** district covering the eastern part of the isthmus that joins Central and South America

For Discussion

1. This sonnet tells of the delight which Keats felt on reading George Chapman's famous translation of Homer. How do the political metaphor and the reference to historical ages in the octave prepare for the emotion of the sestet?
2. How do the two similes used in the sestet help to communicate the emotion of the experience?
3. What happens to the entire poem if the last two lines are changed to:
    Smiled at each other with a glad surprise
    And laughed, upon a peak in Darien.
4. The sonnet is a very carefully controlled and limited form. Do you think this form is appropriate for a poem which expresses ideas of space and freedom? Discuss.

WHEN I HAVE FEARS

When I have fears that I may cease to be
   Before my pen has gleaned my teeming brain,
Before high-pilèd books, in charact'ry,
   Hold like rich garners the full-ripened grain;
When I behold, upon the night's starred face,   5
   Huge cloudy symbols of a high romance,
And think that I may never live to trace
   Their shadows, with the magic hand of chance;
And when I feel, fair creature of an hour!
   That I shall never look upon thee more,   10
Never have relish in the faery power
   Of unreflecting love!—then on the shore
Of the wide world I stand alone, and think
Till love and fame to nothingness do sink.

For Discussion

1. This sonnet is one sentence. How do the parts of this sentence relate to the form of the sonnet? What grammatical structure does Keats use to express his three fears?
2. Discuss the nature of the imagery used to point out each fear. In what way is the imagery appropriate to the fear? Consider carefully the diction used, and the connotations of the words and phrases.
3. The last two lines of this sonnet are particularly moving. How do these lines capture and complete the mood of the entire poem? How do vowel sounds used in these lines contribute to the meaning?

PROEM from ENDYMION

A thing of beauty is a joy for ever:
Its loveliness increases; it will never
Pass into nothingness; but still will keep
A bower quiet for us, and a sleep
Full of sweet dreams, and health, and quiet breathing.　5
Therefore, on every morrow, are we wreathing
A flowery band to bind us to the earth,
Spite of despondence, of the inhuman dearth
Of noble natures, of the gloomy days,
Of all the unhealthy and o'er-darkened ways　10
Made for our searching: yes, in spite of all,
Some shape of beauty moves away the pall
From our dark spirits. Such the sun, the moon,
Trees old, and young, sprouting a shady boon
For simple sheep; and such are daffodils　15
With the green world they live in; and clear rills
That for themselves a cooling covert make
'Gainst the hot season; the mid-forest brake,

126 • JOHN KEATS

    Rich with a sprinkling of fair musk-rose blooms:
And such too is the grandeur of the dooms   20
We have imagined for the mighty dead;
All lovely tales that we have heard or read:
An endless fountain of immortal drink,
Pouring unto us from the heaven's brink.

    Nor do we merely feel these essences   25
For one short hour; no, even as the trees
That whisper round a temple become soon
Dear as the temple's self, so does the moon,
The passion poesy, glories infinite,
Haunt us till they become a cheering light   30
Unto our souls, and bound to us so fast,
That, whether there be shine, or gloom o'ercast,
They always must be with us, or we die.

For Discussion

1. The opening lines of this introductory song are almost axiomatic in form; that is, they become a creed to be accepted, not to be discussed. What effect do the words "bower quiet," "sweet dreams," "quiet breathing" have on the authoritative statement?
2. What images of eternal beauty does Keats describe in lines 6–24? How are these images related to the first five lines of the poem? What does he mean by the "inhuman dearth/ Of noble natures" (lines 8–9)?
3. What is the meaning of "essences" (line 25)? What is the effect of the analogy in lines 26–28?
4. In a preface to this poem, Keats called it the work of a young man, a poem of "great inexperience, immaturity, and every error denoting a feverish attempt, rather than a deed accomplished." What evidence can you find in this selection to support the poet's criticism of his own work? Why do you think he allowed the poem to be published?

LA BELLE DAME SANS MERCI [1]

Oh, what can ail thee, knight-at-arms,
    Alone and palely loitering?
The sedge has withered from the lake,
    And no birds sing.

Oh, what can ail thee, knight-at-arms,   5
    So haggard and so woe-begone?
The squirrel's granary is full,
    And the harvest's done.

I see a lily on thy brow,
    With anguish moist and fever dew;   10
And on thy cheeks a fading rose
    Fast withereth too.

"I met a lady in the meads,[2]
    Full beautiful—a faery's child;
Her hair was long, her foot was light,   15
    And her eyes were wild.

"I made a garland for her head,
    And bracelets too, and fragrant zone;
She looked at me as she did love,
    And made sweet moan.   20

"I set her on my pacing steed,
    And nothing else saw all day long;
For sidelong would she bend and sing
    A faery's song.

"She found me roots of relish sweet,   25
    And honey wild, and manna-dew,

---

[1] "The Beautiful Lady without Pity"
[2] The knight's answer begins here.

And sure in language strange she said,
  'I love thee true.'

"She took me to her elfin grot,
  And there she wept, and sighed full sore,   30
And there I shut her wild, wild eyes,
  With kisses four.

"And there she lullèd me asleep,
  And there I dreamed—ah! woe betide!—
The latest dream I ever dreamed   35 *[could be last dream]*
  On the cold hill's side.

"I saw pale kings and princes too,
  Pale warriors, death-pale were they all,
They cried—'La belle Dame sans Merci
  Hath thee in thrall!'   40

"I saw their starved lips in the gloam,
  With horrid warning gapèd wide;
And I awoke, and found me here
  On the cold hill's side.

"And this is why I sojourn here   45
  Alone and palely loitering,
Though the sedge is withered from the lake,
  And no birds sing."

[Knight either died or his spirit died]

For Discussion

1. Like many old ballads, this poem is told in dialogue. What was the attitude of the first speaker toward the knight? What is the purpose of the references to the natural scene in stanzas 1–2? What effect does the reference to the lily and the rose in stanza 3 have on the poem?
2. The knight begins his story in stanza 4. Who is the lady?

What might this "faery's child" represent? Consider carefully the language used to describe her. Why does the lady weep and sigh "full sore"?
3. Consider carefully lines 25–28. What is the meaning of these lines? What are the connotations of the words used to describe the food?
4. What do the "pale kings and princes" tell the knight? Do you think this has a more general meaning? How does this message relate to the knight's finding himself on the "cold hill's side" and his explanation in the last stanza?
5. Notice the movement of scenes in the poem. Why might this movement be called circular? What effect is achieved by the similarity in the first and last stanzas? Plot the scenes in the poem and relate this scheme to its structure.

THE EVE OF ST. AGNES

1

St. Agnes' Eve [1]—Ah, bitter chill it was!
The owl, for all his feathers, was a-cold;
The hare limped trembling through the frozen grass,
And silent was the flock in woolly fold:
Numb were the beadsman's [2] fingers, while he told   5
His rosary, and while his frosted breath,
Like pious incense from a censer old,
Seemed taking flight for heaven, without a death,
Past the sweet Virgin's picture, while his prayer he saith.

2

His prayer he saith, this patient, holy man;   10
Then takes his lamp, and riseth from his knees,
And back returneth, meager, barefoot, wan.
Along the chapel aisle by slow degrees:
The sculptured dead, on each side, seem to freeze,

---

[1] **St. Agnes' Eve:** January 20th
[2] **beadsman:** a poor man paid to pray for a benefactor

Emprisoned in black, purgatorial rails: 15
Knights, ladies, praying in dumb orat'ries,[3]
He passeth by; and his weak spirit fails
To think how they may ache in icy hoods and mails.

3

Northward he turneth through a little door,
And scarce three steps, ere Music's golden tongue 20
Flattered to tears this aged man and poor;
But no—already had his deathbell rung;
The joys of all his life were said and sung:
His was harsh penance on St. Agnes' Eve:
Another way he went, and soon among 25
Rough ashes sat he for his soul's reprieve,
And all night kept awake, for sinners' sake to grieve.

4

That ancient beadsman heard the prelude soft;
And so it chanced, for many a door was wide,
From hurry to and fro. Soon, up aloft, 30
The silver, snarling trumpets 'gan to chide:
The level chambers, ready with their pride,
Were glowing to receive a thousand guests:
The carvéd angels, ever eager-eyed,
Stared, where upon their heads the cornice rests, 35
With hair blown back, and wings put crosswise on their breasts.

5

At length burst in the argent revelry,
With plume, tiara, and all rich array,
Numerous as shadows haunting faerily
The brain, new stuffed, in youth, with triumphs gay 40
Of old romance. These let us wish away,

---

[3] **dumb orat'ries:** "dumb" chapels because the knights and ladies are only sculptures

The Eve of St. Agnes • 131

And turn, sole-thoughted, to one lady there,
Whose heart had brooded, all that wintry day,
On love, and winked St. Agnes' saintly care,
As she had heard old dames full many times declare.   45

6

They told her how, upon St. Agnes' Eve,
Young virgins might have visions of delight,
And soft adorings from their loves receive
Upon the honeyed middle of the night,
If ceremonies due they did aright: 50
As, supperless to bed they must retire,
And couch supine their beauties, lily white;
Nor look behind, nor sideways, but require
Of Heaven with upward eyes for all that they desire.

7

Full of this whim was thoughtful Madeline: 55
The music, yearning like a god in pain,
She scarcely heard: her maiden eyes divine,
Fixed on the floor, saw many a sweeping train
Pass by—she heeded not at all: in vain
Came many a tiptoe, amorous cavalier,   60
And back retired; not cooled by high disdain,
But she saw not: her heart was otherwhere:
She sighed for Agnes' dreams, the sweetest of the year.

8

She danced along with vague, regardless eyes,
Anxious her lips, her breathing quick and short: 65
The hallowed hour was near at hand: she sighs
Amid the timbrels,[4] and the thronged resort
Of whisperers in anger, or in sport;
'Mid looks of love, defiance, hate, and scorn,
Hoodwinked with faery fancy; all amort,[5]   70

---

[4] **timbrels:** tambourines   [5] **amort:** as if dead

Save to St. Agnes and her lambs unshorn,
And all the bliss to be before to-morrow morn.

9

So, purposing each moment to retire,
She lingered still. Meantime, across the moors,
Had come young Porphyro, with heart on fire   75
For Madeline. Beside the portal doors,
Buttressed from moonlight, stands he, and implores
All saints to give him sight of Madeline.
But for one moment in the tedious hours,
That he might gaze and worship all unseen;   80
Perchance speak, kneel, touch, kiss—in sooth such things have been.

10

He ventures in: let no buzzed whisper tell:
All eyes be muffled, or a hundred swords
Will storm his heart, Love's fev'rous citadel:
For him, those chambers held barbarian hordes,   85
Hyena foemen, and hot-blooded lords,
Whose very dogs would execrations howl
Against his lineage: not one breast affords
Him any mercy, in that mansion foul,
Save one old beldame, weak in body and in soul.   90

11

Ah, happy chance! the agéd creature came,
Shuffling along with ivory-headed wand,
To where he stood, hid from the torch's flame,
Behind a broad hall-pillar, far beyond
The sound of merriment and chorus bland: 95
He startled her; but soon she knew his face,
And grasped his fingers in her palsied hand,
Saying, "Mercy, Porphyro! hide thee from this place;
They are all here to-night, the whole blood-thirsty race!

12

"Get hence! get hence! there's dwarfish Hildebrand;   100
He had a fever late, and in the fit
He curséd thee and thine, both house and land:
Then there's that old Lord Maurice, not a whit
More tame for his gray hairs—Alas me! flit!
Flit like a ghost away"—"Ah, Gossip [6] dear,   105
We're safe enough; here in this armchair sit,
And tell me how"—"Good saints! not here, not here;
Follow me, child, or else these stones will be thy bier."

13

He followed through a lowly archéd way,
Brushing the cobwebs with his lofty plume;   110
And as she muttered, "Well-a—well-a-day!"
He found him in a little moonlight room,
Pale, latticed, chill, and silent as a tomb.
"Now tell me where is Madeline," said he,
"Oh tell me, Angela, by the holy loom   115
Which none but secret sisterhood may see,
When they St. Agnes' wool are weaving piously." [7]

14

"St. Agnes! Ah! it is St. Agnes' Eve—
Yet men will murder upon holy days:
Thou must hold water in a witch's sieve,   120
And be liege-lord of all the elves and fays,
To venture so: it fills me with amaze
To see thee, Porphyro!—St. Agnes' Eve!
God's help! my lady fair the conjurer plays
This very night: good angels her deceive!   125
But let me laugh awhile, I've mickle time to grieve."

---

[6] **Gossip:** godmother
[7] Formerly on St. Agnes' Day, while the hymn *Agnus Dei* was sung, two lambs were sacrificed and their wool woven into cloth by nuns.

15

Feebly she laugheth in the languid moon,
While Porphyro upon her face doth look,
Like puzzled urchin on an agéd crone
Who keepeth closed a wond'rous riddlebook,   130
As spectacled she sits in chimney nook.
But soon his eyes grew brilliant, when she told
His lady's purpose; and he scarce could brook [8]
Tears, at the thought of those enchantments cold,
And Madeline asleep in lap of legends old.   135

16

Sudden a thought came like a full-blown rose,
Flushing his brow, and in his painéd heart
Made purple riot: then doth he propose
A stratagem, that makes the beldame start:
"A cruel man and impious thou art: 140
Sweet lady, let her pray, and sleep, and dream
Alone with her good angels, far apart
From wicked men like thee. Go, go!—I deem
Thou canst not surely be the same that thou didst seem."

17

"I will not harm her, by all saints I swear,"   145
Quoth Porphyro: "Oh may I ne'er find grace
When my weak voice shall whisper its last prayer,
If one of her soft ringlets I displace,
Or look with ruffian passion in her face:
Good Angela, believe me by these tears;   150
Or I will, even in a moment's space,
Awake, with horrid shout, my foemen's ears,
And beard them, though they be more fanged than wolves
     and bears."

---

[8] **brook:** keep back

18

"Ah! why wilt thou affright a feeble soul?
A poor, weak, palsy-stricken, churchyard thing,
Whose passing-bell may ere the midnight toll;
Whose prayers for thee, each morn and evening,
Were never missed."—Thus plaining, doth she bring
A gentler speech from burning Porphyro;
So woeful, and of such deep sorrowing,
That Angela gives promise she will do
Whatever he shall wish, betide her weal or woe.

19

Which was, to lead him, in close secrecy,
Even to Madeline's chamber, and there hide
Him in a closet, of such privacy
That he might see her beauty unespied,
And win perhaps that night a peerless bride,
While legioned faeries paced the coverlet,
And pale enchantment held her sleepy-eyed.
Never on such a night have lovers met,
Since Merlin paid his demon all the monstrous debt.[9]

20

"It shall be as thou wishest," said the dame:
"All cates [10] and dainties shall be storéd there
Quickly on this feast-night: by the tambour frame [11]
Her own lute thou wilt see: no time to spare,
For I am slow and feeble, and scarce dare
On such a catering trust my dizzy head.
Wait here, my child, with patience; kneel in prayer
The while: ah! thou must needs the lady wed,
Or may I never leave my grave among the dead."

---

[9] Merlin, the son of a demon, was imprisoned in a rock by Vivien, to whom he had taught magic.
[10] **cates:** delicacies
[11] **tambour frame:** embroidery frame shaped like a drum

21

So saying, she hobbled off with busy fear.
The lover's endless minutes slowly passed;
The dame returned, and whispered in his ear
To follow her; with agéd eyes aghast
From fright of dim espial. Safe at last,   185
Through many a dusky gallery, they gain
The maiden's chamber, silken, hushed, and chaste;
Where Porphyro took covert, pleased amain [12]
His poor guide hurried back with agues in her brain.

22

Her falt'ring hand upon the balustrade,   190
Old Angela was feeling for the stair,
When Madeline, St. Agnes' charméd maid,
Rose, like a missioned spirit, unaware:
With silver taper's light, and pious care,
She turned, and down the agéd gossip led   195
To a safe level matting. Now prepare,
Young Porphyro, for gazing on that bed;
She comes, she comes again, like ring-dove frayed [13] and fled.

23

Out went the taper as she hurried in;
Its little smoke, in pallid moonshine, died: 200
She closed the door, she panted, all akin
To spirits of the air, and visions wide:
No uttered syllable, or, woe betide!
But to her heart, her heart was voluble,
Paining with eloquence her balmy side;   205
As though a tongueless nightingale should swell
Her throat in vain, and die, heart-stifled, in her dell.

[12] **amain:** exceedingly
[13] **frayed:** frightened

24

A casement high and triple-arched there was,
All garlanded with carven imag'ries
Of fruits, and flowers, and bunches of knot-grass, 210
And diamonded with panes of quaint device,
Innumerable of stains and splendid dyes,
As are the tiger-moth's deep-damasked wings;
And in the midst, 'mong thousand heraldries,
And twilight saints, and dim emblazonings, 215
A shielded scutcheon blushed with blood of queens and kings.

25

Full on this casement shone the wintry moon,
And threw warm gules [14] on Madeline's fair breast,
As down she knelt for heaven's grace and boon;
Rose-bloom fell on her hands, together pressed, 220
And on her silver cross soft amethyst,
And on her hair a glory, like a saint:
She seemed a splendid angel, newly dressed,
Save wings, for heaven:—Porphyro grew faint:
She knelt, so pure a thing, so free from mortal taint. 225

26

Anon his heart revives: her vespers done,
Of all its wreathéd pearls her hair she frees;
Unclasps her warméd jewels one by one;
Loosens her fragrant bodice; by degrees
Her rich attire creeps rustling to her knees: 230
Half-hidden, like a mermaid in seaweed,
Pensive awhile she dreams awake, and sees,
In fancy, fair St. Agnes in her bed,
But dares not look behind, or all the charm is fled.

---

[14] **gules:** red

27

    Soon, trembling in her soft and chilly nest,
    In sort of wakeful swoon, perplexed she lay,
    Until the poppied warmth of sleep oppressed
    Her soothéd limbs, and soul fatigued away;
    Flown, like a thought, until the morrow-day;
    Blissfully havened both from joy and pain;
    Clasped like a missal where swart Paynims [15] pray;
    Blinded alike from sunshine and from rain,
As though a rose should shut, and be a bud again.

28

    Stol'n to this paradise, and so entranced,
    Porphyro gazed upon her empty dress,
    And listened to her breathing, if it chanced
    To wake into a slumberous tenderness;
    Which when he heard, that minute did he bless,
    And breathed himself: then from the closet crept,
    Noiseless as fear in a wide wilderness,
    And over the hushed carpet, silent, stepped,
And 'tween the curtains peeped, where, lo!—how fast she slept.

29

    Then by the bedside, where the faded moon
    Made a dim, silver twilight, soft he set
    A table, and, half anguished, threw thereon
    A cloth of woven crimson, gold, and jet:—
    Oh for some drowsy Morphean [16] amulet!
    The boisterous, midnight, festive clarion,
    The kettle-drum, and far-heard clarinet,
    Affray his ears, though but in dying tone:—
The hall door shuts again, and all the noise is gone.

---

[15] **swart Paynims:** dark-skinned pagans
[16] **Morphean:** sleep-inducing

30

And still she slept an azure-lidded sleep,
In blanchèd linen, smooth, and lavendered,
While he from forth the closet brought a heap
Of candied apple, quince, and plum, and gourd;   265
With jellies soother than the creamy curd,
And lucent syrups, tinct with cinnamon;
Manna and dates, in argosy transferred
From Fez; and spicèd dainties, every one,
From silken Samarcand to cedared Lebanon.   270

31

These delicates he heaped with glowing hand
On golden dishes and in baskets bright
Of wreathèd silver: sumptuous they stand
In the retirèd quiet of the night,
Filling the chilly room with perfume light.—   275
"And now, my love, my seraph fair, awake!
"Thou art my heaven, and I thine eremite: [17]
Open thine eyes, for meek St. Agnes' sake,
Or I shall drowse beside thee, so my soul doth ache."

32

Thus whispering, his warm, unnervèd arm   280
Sank in her pillow. Shaded was her dream
By the dusk curtains:—'twas a midnight charm
Impossible to melt as icèd stream:
The lustrous salvers in the moonlight gleam;
Broad golden fringe upon the carpet lies: 285
It seemed he never, never could redeem
From such a steadfast spell his lady's eyes;
So mused awhile, entoiled in woofèd phantasies.

[17] **eremite:** hermit; here it means "lover"

33

Awakening up, he took her hollow lute,—
Tumultuous,—and, in chords that tenderest be,   290
He played an ancient ditty, long since mute,
In Provence called, "La belle dame sans merci," [18]
Close to her ear touching the melody;—
Wherewith disturbed she uttered a soft moan:
He ceased—she panted quick—and suddenly   295
Her blue affrayéd eyes wide open shone:
Upon his knees he sank, pale as smooth-sculptured stone.

34

Her eyes were open, but she still beheld,
Now wide awake, the vision of her sleep:
There was a painful change, that nigh expelled   300
The blisses of her dream so pure and deep,
At which fair Madeline began to weep,
And moan forth witless words with many a sigh:
While still her gaze on Porphyro would keep;
Who knelt, with joinéd hands and piteous eye,   305
Fearing to move or speak, she looked so dreamingly.

35

"Ah, Porphyro!" said she, "but even now
Thy voice was at sweet tremble in mine ear,
Made tuneable with every sweetest vow;
And those sad eyes were spiritual and clear: 310
How changed thou art! how pallid, chill, and drear!
Give me that voice again, my Porphyro,
Those looks immortal, those complainings dear!
Oh leave me not in this eternal woe,
For if thou diest, my love, I know not where to go."   315

---

[18] See poem with same title on page 127.

36

Beyond a mortal man impassioned far
At these voluptuous accents, he arose,
Ethereal, flushed, and like a throbbing star
Seen 'mid the sapphire heaven's deep repose;
Into her dream he melted, as the rose   320
Blendeth its odor with the violet,—
Solution sweet: meantime the frost-wind blows
Like Love's alarum, pattering the sharp sleet
Against the window-panes; St. Agnes' moon hath set.

37

'Tis dark: quick pattereth the flaw-blown [19] sleet: 325
"This is no dream, my bride, my Madeline!"
'Tis dark: the icéd gusts still rave and beat:
"No dream, alas! alas! and woe is mine!
Porphyro will leave me here to fade and pine.—
Cruel! what traitor could thee hither bring?   330
I curse not, for my heart is lost in thine,
Though thou forsakest a deceivéd thing;—
A dove forlorn and lost with sick prunéd wing."

38

"My Madeline! sweet dreamer! lovely bride!
Say, may I be for aye thy vassal blest?   335
Thy beauty's shield, heart-shaped and vermeil dyed?
Ah, silver shrine, here will I take my rest
After so many hours of toil and quest,
A famished pilgrim,—saved by miracle.
Though I have found, I will not rob thy nest   340
Saving of thy sweet self; if thou think'st well
To trust, fair Madeline, to no rude infidel.

[19] **flaw-blown**: wind-blown

39

"Hark! 'tis an elfin-storm from faery land,
Of haggard seeming, but a boon indeed:
Arise—arise! the morning is at hand:— 345
The bloated wassailers will never heed:—
Let us away, my love, with happy speed;
There are no ears to hear or eyes to see,—
Drowned all in Rhenish [20] and the sleepy mead:
Awake! arise! my love, and fearless be, 350
For o'er the southern moors I have a home for thee."

40

She hurried at his words, beset with fears,
For there were sleeping dragons all around,
At glaring watch, perhaps, with ready spears—
Down the wide stairs a darkling way they found.— 355
In all the house was heard no human sound.
A chain-drooped lamp was flickering by each door;
The arras, rich with horseman, hawk, and hound,
Fluttered in the besieging wind's uproar;
And the long carpets rose along the gusty floor. 360

41

They glide, like phantoms, into the wide hall;
Like phantoms, to the iron porch they glide;
Where lay the porter, in uneasy sprawl,
With a huge empty flagon by his side:
The wakeful bloodhound rose, and shook his hide, 365
But his sagacious eye an inmate owns:
By one, and one, the bolts full easy slide:—
The chains lie silent on the footworn stones;—
The key turns, and the door upon its hinges groans.

[20] **Rhenish:** Rhine wine

42

And they are gone: ay, ages long ago 370
These lovers fled away into the storm.
That night the baron dreamt of many a woe,
And all his warrior-guests, with shade and form
Of witch, and demon, and large coffin-worm,
Were long be-nightmared. Angela the old 375
Died palsy-twitched, with meager face deform;
The beadsman, after thousand avés told,
For aye unsought for slept among his ashes cold.

For Discussion

1. The first stanza gives the setting carefully and clearly. Point out the images used to convey both mood and setting. What effect is achieved by the presence of the Beadsman in the first three stanzas? What dramatic contrast is afforded by stanzas 4–5?
2. Stanza 6 gives the legend of St. Agnes' Eve. What effect does the legend have on Madeline at the dance? How do stanzas 9–10 relate to Madeline's attitude? What romantic overtones are created by the fact of the feuding families?
3. What role does Angela play in the narrative? What is the effect of her laughter? What is the dramatic function of stanza 16? How does Porphyro persuade Angela to help him?
4. Stanzas 24–27 show Keats's ability to write rich, lush, sensuous verse, detailing sights, colors, and feelings. Point out examples of images you think are particularly appealing and effective.
5. What preparations does Porphyro make to complete the requirements of the legend of St. Agnes' Eve? Point out examples in stanzas 29–33 of Keats's ability to create a world rich and real through appeals to the senses.
6. What is Madeline's reaction when she wakes? Why is she fearful that her lover is in the castle?

7. After the lush imagery of the preceding stanzas, stanzas 40–42 seem harsh and barren. What dramatic function does this serve? How does the last stanza, which serves to tie together the threads of the narrative, add a dimension of reality to a story that sounds like a fairy tale?
8. Keats makes great use of contrast in this poem. Point out examples of the opposition of youth and old age, life and death, love and hate, cold and warmth. What clues to meaning do these contrasts give?

ODE ON A GRECIAN URN

Thou still unravished bride of quietness,
    Thou foster-child of silence and slow time,
Sylvan historian, who canst thus express
    A flowery tale more sweetly than our rime:
What leaf-fringed legend haunts about thy shape   5
    Of deities or mortals, or of both,
        In Tempe or the dales of Arcady?[1]
What men or gods are these? What maidens loath?
What mad pursuit? What struggle to escape?
    What pipes and timbrels? What wild ecstasy?   10

Heard melodies are sweet, but those unheard
    Are sweeter; therefore, ye soft pipes, play on;
Not to the sensual ear, but, more endeared,
    Pipe to the spirit ditties of no tone:
Fair youth, beneath the trees, thou canst not leave   15
    Thy song, nor ever can those trees be bare;
        Bold Lover, never, never canst thou kiss,
Though winning near the goal—yet, do not grieve;
    She cannot fade, though thou hast not thy bliss,
        Forever wilt thou love, and she be fair!   20

Ah, happy, happy, boughs! that cannot shed
    Your leaves, nor ever bid the spring adieu:

[1] **Tempe:** a valley in Greece; **Arcady:** a mountain in Greece

And, happy melodist, unwearied,
    Forever piping songs forever new;
More happy love! more happy, happy love!   25
    Forever warm and still to be enjoyed,
        Forever panting, and forever young;
All breathing human passion far above,
    That leaves a heart high-sorrowful and cloyed,
        A burning forehead, and a parching tongue.   30

Who are these coming to the sacrifice?
    To what green altar, O mysterious priest,
Lead'st thou that heifer lowing at the skies,
    And all her silken flanks with garlands dressed?
What little town by river or sea shore,   35
    Or mountain-built with peaceful citadel,
        Is emptied of this folk, this pious morn?
And, little town, thy streets for evermore
    Will silent be; and not a soul to tell
        Why thou art desolate, can e'er return.   40

O Attic [2] shape! Fair attitude! with brede [3]
    Of marble men and maidens overwrought,
With forest branches and the trodden weed;
    Thou, silent form, dost tease us out of thought
As doth eternity: cold pastoral! [4]   45
    When old age shall this generation waste,
        Thou shalt remain, in midst of other woe
Than ours, a friend to man, to whom thou say'st,
    "Beauty is truth, truth beauty,"—that is all
        Ye know on earth, and all ye need to know.   50

[2] **Attic:** refers to Attica in Greece
[3] **brede:** embroidery
[4] **cold pastoral:** poem in marble

For Discussion

    1. The ode begins with an apostrophe. The speaker addresses the urn, which is not a particular Greek urn but rather a

product of Keats's imagination. Why is the urn called a "sylvan historian"? What questions does the speaker ask the urn? In what way do these questions contrast with the first lines of the poem?
2. Stanzas 2–4 state what the urn depicts. Describe the scenes portrayed on the urn. Point out the concrete images which develop the description of each scene. How is the beauty and serenity of the moment captured in each scene?
3. What is the effect of the repetition of the word "happy" in stanza 3? Is the love depicted on the urn human love or is it an ideal conception?
4. What is the effect of introducing the sense of communal life in stanza 4? Does the speaker's sadness at the thought of the desolate town seem logical?
5. In the last stanza of the poem the speaker once again rivets our attention on the urn itself. How does he address the urn in this stanza? How can the urn "tease us out of thought/As doth eternity"? How does this final stanza sum up a basic attitude of Keats's thought, the sense of permanence in art as against a world of change? Do you think he is pointing to the superiority of art over human experience?

TO AUTUMN

Season of mists and mellow fruitfulness,
    Close bosom-friend of the maturing sun;
Conspiring with him how to load and bless
    With fruit the vines that round the thatch-eaves run;
To bend with apples the mossed cottage-trees,   5
    And fill all fruit with ripeness to the core;
        To swell the gourd, and plump the hazel shells
With a sweet kernel; to set budding more,
    And still more, later flowers for the bees,
    Until they think warm days will never cease,   10
        For Summer has o'er-brimmed their clammy cells.

Who hath not seen thee oft amid thy store?
    Sometimes whoever seeks abroad may find

Thee sitting careless on a granary floor,
    Thy hair soft-lifted by the winnowing wind;
Or on a half-reaped furrow sound asleep,
    Drowsed with the fume of poppies, while thy hook
        Spares the next swath and all its twinéd flowers:
And sometimes like a gleaner thou dost keep
    Steady thy laden head across a brook;
    Or by a cider-press, with patient look,
        Thou watchest the last oozings hours by hours.

Where are the songs of Spring? Ay, where are they?
    Think not of them, thou hast thy music too,—
While barréd clouds bloom the soft-dying day,
    And touch the stubble-plains with rosy hue;
Then in a wailful choir the small gnats mourn
    Among the river sallows, borne aloft
        Or sinking as the light wind lives or dies;
And full-grown lambs loud bleat from hilly bourn;
    Hedge-crickets sing; and now with treble soft
    The red-breast whistles from a garden-croft;
        And gathering swallows twitter in the skies.

For Discussion

1. Notice the series of infinitives used in stanza 1. What is the cumulative effect of these in developing the characteristics of autumn? This first stanza is not a sentence, merely a series of phrases. What effect is accomplished by this?
2. What image of autumn is seen in stanza 2? Is the mood of this stanza the same as that in stanza 1? Point out how the verbs and verb forms help to give the feeling of the stanza.
3. Stanza 3 picks up the sounds of autumn. Are these sounds consistent with the tranquility and serenity of the entire poem? Discuss. What is the effect of the monosyllables in this stanza? Is there a hint of deeper melancholy here?
4. Point out words and phrases in this formal ode which show Keats's use of sense impressions to convey mood and meaning.

ODE TO A NIGHTINGALE

My heart aches, and a drowsy numbness pains
   My sense, as though of hemlock I had drunk,
Or emptied some dull opiate to the drains
   One minute past, and Lethe-wards [1] had sunk:
'Tis not through envy of thy happy lot,   5
   But being too happy in thine happiness,—
      That thou, light-wingéd Dryad [2] of the trees,
         In some melodious plot
Of beechen green, and shadows numberless,
   Singest of summer in full-throated ease.   10

Oh, for a draught of vintage! that hath been
   Cooled a long age in the deep-delvéd earth,
Tasting of Flora [3] and the country green,
   Dance, and Provençal song,[4] and sunburnt mirth!
Oh, for a beaker full of the warm South,   15
   Full of the true, the blushful Hippocrene,[5]
      With beaded bubbles winking at the brim,
         And purple-stainéd mouth;
That I might drink, and leave the world unseen,
   And with thee fade away into the forest dim: 20

Fade far away, dissolve, and quite forget
   What thou among the leaves hast never known,
The weariness, the fever, and the fret
   Here, where men sit and hear each other groan;
Where palsy shakes a few, sad, last gray hairs,   25
   Where youth grows pale, and specter-thin, and dies;

---

[1] **Lethe-wards:** toward Lethe, the river of forgetfulness
[2] **Dryad:** nymph
[3] **Flora:** goddess of flowers
[4] **Provençal song:** music of troubadours in Provence in southern France
[5] **Hippocrene:** water from the fountain of the Muses that was supposed to give poetic inspiration

Ode to a Nightingale • 149

Where but to think is to be full of sorrow
And leaden-eyed despairs,
Where Beauty cannot keep her lustrous eyes,
Or new Love pine at them beyond tomorrow. 30

Away! away! for I will fly to thee,
Not charioted by Bacchus and his pards,[6]
But on the viewless wings of Poesy,
Though the dull brain perplexes and retards:
Already with thee! tender is the night, 35
And haply the Queen-Moon is on her throne,
Clustered around by all her starry Fays;[7]
But here there is no light,
Save what from heaven is with the breezes blown
Through verdurous glooms and winding mossy ways. 40

I cannot see what flowers are at my feet,
Nor what soft incense hangs upon the boughs,
But, in embalmèd darkness, guess each sweet
Wherewith the seasonable month endows
The grass, the thicket, and the fruit-tree wild; 45
White hawthorn, and the pastoral eglantine;
Fast fading violets covered up in leaves;
And mid-May's eldest child,
The coming musk-rose, full of dewey wine
The murmurous haunt of flies on summer eves. 50

Darkling I listen; and, for many a time
I have been half in love with easeful Death,
Called him soft names in many a musèd rime,
To take into the air my quiet breath;
Now more than ever seems it rich to die, 55
To cease upon the midnight with no pain,
While thou art pouring forth thy soul abroad
In such an ecstasy!

[6] **pards:** leopards which drew the car of Bacchus, the god of wine
[7] **Fays:** faery moon spirits in the court of the Queen

      Still wouldst thou sing, and I have ears in vain—
         To thy high requiem become a sod.   60

Thou wast not born for death, immortal bird!
    No hungry generations tread thee down;
The voice I hear this passing night was heard
    In ancient days by emperor and clown:
Perhaps the self-same song that found a path   65
      Through the sad heart of Ruth, when, sick for home,
         She stood in tears amid the alien corn; [8]
            The same that oft-times hath
Charmed magic casements, opening on the foam
    Of perilous seas, in faery lands forlorn.   70

Forlorn! the very word is like a bell
    To toll me back from thee to my sole self!
Adieu! the fancy cannot cheat so well
    As she is famed to do, deceiving elf.
Adieu! adieu! thy plaintive anthem fades   75
    Past the near meadows, over the still stream,
      Up the hill-side; and now 'tis buried deep
         In the next valley-glades:
Was it a vision, or a waking dream?
    Fled is that music:—Do I wake or sleep?   80

[8] Ruth, after the death of her husband, followed Naomi, her mother-in-law, to Bethlehem where she gleaned barley in the fields. See *Ruth* 2:3.

For Discussion

1. Keats wrote this poem in the garden of a house in Hampstead, a country suburb of London, where he had gone to recover his health. What is the setting of the poem—the time of day, the season of the year? How does the speaker portray his physical and spiritual feelings in stanza 1? What is his joy in "being too happy in thine happiness"? How does stanza 2 pick up the sense of joy? Discuss the contrasting images of youth and age in these stanzas.

2. What is the view of life in stanza 3? How does this relate to the speaker's wish to fade far away? What contrast is given between the world of reality and the world of fancy?
3. In stanza 4 the speaker reaches the bird through poetry; he is in control of the situation. How do his senses help him to gain this control? Point out examples which indicate the various senses used to gain this control. What image picks up an image used in stanza 2? What is the difference in meaning?
4. What is the meaning of "darkling" (line 51)? This stanza moves from the thoughts of the speaker about himself to the bird. What is the effect of this movement? What influence is the bird having on the speaker?
5. What does the bird become in stanza 7? What feeling is generated by the historical references?
6. What is the meaning and significance of the word "toll" (line 72)? In returning to his "sole self" is the speaker the same as he was in the opening stanza? What has the experience of listening and contemplating done for him? What is the meaning of the poem's final question?

For Composition

1. Keats's most famous line, "A thing of beauty is a joy for ever," is the statement of a man who loved deeply the beauty he saw in nature and art. Either by going to a museum or by studying a print, select a famous work of art—painting or sculpture—and write a theme expressing your reaction to the work. In the course of the paper, you might be describing the work itself, but your purpose should be to communicate to your reader the emotions you felt in coming in contact with artistic greatness.
2. As Keats talks of beauty we sometimes look at our surroundings and find them drab and uninspiring. Write a theme on the beautiful in the twentieth century. Consider whether we have lost the sense of the beautiful which Keats advocated or whether modern life has a beauty of its own in keeping with the tempo of the time. Select specific examples to prove your points.

Percy Bysshe Shelley

(1792–1822)

Percy Bysshe Shelley was a revolutionary and idealist, a dedicated seeker of an ideal world where love and the brotherhood of man would prevail. His poetry expresses his spirit of rebellion, his pervasive melancholy, his love of man and of freedom.

He used the objects of nature, which he worshiped, as images of his internal state. But, unlike the everyday world of nature that Wordsworth described, Shelley's was a world of clouds, light, motion, wind, and spaciousness. His skylark soars with a delicate and airy speed.

What makes Shelley a great poet is the sheer music and matchless spontaneity of his verse. Few poets have matched his clear-flowing melody and his lyric suggestion of a sublime world beyond the physical which man has never seen but which he knows must exist. His world stirs up sensations which bring each reader to the mystery of life, the attempt to find, as Shelley says, "a manifestation of something beyond the present and tangible."

OZYMANDIAS [1]

I met a traveller from an antique land
Who said: "Two vast and trunkless legs of stone
Stand in the desert. Near them on the sand,
Half sunk, a shattered visage lies, whose frown
And wrinkled lip and sneer of cold command   5
Tell that its sculptor well those passions read
Which yet survive, stamped on these lifeless things,
The hand that mocked them and the heart that fed;

[1] **Ozymandias:** Egyptian King whose real name was Raméses

And on the pedestal these words appear:
'My name is Ozymandias, king of kings: 10
Look on my works, ye Mighty, and despair!'
Nothing beside remains. Round the decay
Of that colossal wreck, boundless and bare
The lone and level sands stretch far away."

For Discussion

1. This poem, seemingly a direct statement repeating a conversation, moves beyond the literal statement to many deeper and more significant meanings. What precisely is the dramatic situation on the literal level? What hints are given by the language that the poet wants the reader to go beyond the literal level?
2. The poem's "traveller" presents two opposing pictures but he does not make a judgment. What irony is apparent in the juxtaposition of the description in the octave and the inscription given in the sestet?
3. Read carefully line 8. To whom do the words "hand" and "heart" refer? What figure of speech is being used?
4. Is the poet talking in this poem about the vanity of human desires or is he talking about the sense of permanence in art, or both? Discuss. Why might this poem be called a poetic parable?

SONG TO THE MEN OF ENGLAND

Men of England, wherefore plow
For the lords who lay ye low?
Wherefore weave with toil and care
The rich robes your tyrants wear?

Wherefore feed, and clothe, and save,   5
From the cradle to the grave,
Those ungrateful drones who would
Drain your sweat—nay, drink your blood?

Wherefore, Bees of England, forge
Many a weapon, chain, and scourge, 10
That these stingless drones may spoil
The forced produce of your toil?

Have ye leisure, comfort, calm,
Shelter, food, love's gentle balm?
Or what is it ye buy so dear 15
With your pain and with your fear?

The seed ye sow, another reaps;
The wealth ye find, another keeps;
The robes ye weave, another wears;
The arms ye forge, another bears. 20

Sow seed—but let no tyrant reap;
Find wealth—let no impostor heap;
Weave robes—let not the idle wear;
Forge arms—in your defense to bear.

Shrink to your cellars, holes, and cells; 25
In halls ye deck another dwells.
Why shake the chains ye wrought? Ye see
The steel ye tempered glance on ye.

With plow and spade, and hoe and loom,
Trace your grave, and build your tomb, 30
And weave your winding-sheet, till fair
England be your sepulcher.

For Discussion

1. This poem was occasioned by the labor troubles in England following the Napoleonic Wars. What was Shelley's attitude toward the ruling classes? From the details given in stanzas 1–4, describe the socio-economic condition of these men.

2. Note the metaphor given in line 7. How is this developed in the next stanza? How effective is this metaphor for the subject? What exactly do the workers "buy as dear"? What is this actually costing them?
3. How does Shelley's use of dramatic contrast and parallelism in stanzas 5 and 6 emphasize the action he is advocating? Do you think his imperative suggestions would be effective?
4. In the light of Shelley's indignant anger in the first six stanzas, why are the last two stanzas ironic? Why might the challenge given in these lines be even more persuasive than that given in stanzas 5 and 6? Discuss.
5. This poem has become a hymn of the British labor movement. What elements in the poem would contribute to its use for this purpose? Consider not only the theme but also the language and pace of the poem.

ODE TO THE WEST WIND

1

O wild West Wind, thou breath of Autumn's being,
Thou, from whose unseen presence the leaves dead
Are driven, like ghosts from an enchanter fleeing,

Yellow, and black, and pale, and hectic red,
Pestilence-stricken multitudes: O thou,   5
Who chariotest to their dark wintry bed

The wingéd seeds, where they lie cold and low,
Each like a corpse within its grave, until
Thine azure sister of the Spring shall blow

Her clarion o'er the dreaming earth, and fill   10
(Driving sweet buds like flocks to feed in air)
With living hues and odors plain and hill:

Wild Spirit, which art moving everywhere;
Destroyer and Preserver; hear, oh hear!

2

Thou on whose stream, 'mid the steep sky's commotion,   15
Loose clouds like earth's decaying leaves are shed,
Shook from the tangled boughs of heaven and ocean,

Angels of rain and lightning: there are spread
On the blue surface of thine airy surge,
Like the bright hair uplifted from the head   20

Of some fierce Maenad,[1] even from the dim verge
Of the horizon to the zenith's height
The locks of the approaching storm. Thou dirge

Of the dying year, to which this closing night
Will be the dome of a vast sepulcher,   25
Vaulted with all thy congregated might

Of vapors, from whose solid atmosphere
Black rain, and fire, and hail will burst: oh hear!

3

Thou who didst waken from his summer dreams
The blue Mediterranean, where he lay,   30
Lulled by the coil of his crystálline streams

Beside a pumice isle in Baiae's [2] bay,
And saw in sleep old palaces and towers
Quivering within the wave's intenser day,

All overgrown with azure moss and flowers   35
So sweet, the sense faints picturing them! Thou
For whose path the Atlantic's level powers

---

[1] **Maenad:** priestess of Bacchus, the god of wine
[2] **Baiae:** a seaside town at the western end of the Bay of Naples

Cleave themselves into chasms, while far below
The sea-blooms and the oozy woods which wear
The sapless foliage of the ocean, know 40

Thy voice, and suddenly grow gray with fear,
And tremble and despoil themselves: oh hear!

4

If I were a dead leaf thou mightest bear;
If I were a swift cloud to fly with thee;
A wave to pant beneath thy power, and share 45

The impulse of thy strength, only less free
Than Thou, O uncontrollable! If even
I were as in my boyhood, and could be

The comrade of thy wanderings over heaven,
As then, when to outstrip thy skyey speed 50
Scarce seemed a vision, I would ne'er have striven.

As thus with thee in prayer in my sore need.
Oh! lift me as a wave, a leaf, a cloud!
I fall upon the thorns of life! I bleed!

A heavy weight of hours has chained and bowed 55
One too like thee: tameless and swift and proud.

5

Make me thy lyre, even as the forest is:
What if my leaves are falling like its own!
The tumult of thy mighty harmonies

Will take from both a deep, autumnal tone, 60
Sweet though in sadness. Be thou, Spirit fierce,
My spirit! Be thou me, impetuous one!

Drive my dead thoughts over the universe
Like withered leaves to quicken a new birth!
And, by the incantation of this verse, 65

Scatter, as from an unextinguished hearth
Ashes and sparks, my words among mankind!
Be through my lips to unawakened earth

The trumpet of a prophecy! O Wind,
If Winter comes, can Spring be far behind? 70

For Discussion

1. In the first three sections of the poem, the speaker is viewing the activities of the wind, seeing its effects on natural objects. What details in Section 1 help the reader to see the wind as "Destroyer and Preserver"? How does this section introduce the idea of the cyclic process of the year?
2. How is the year image developed in Section 2? What aspect of the wind is described in this section? What is the meaning of "angels" (line 18) and of "dirge" (line 23)? Explain the image the poet is trying to develop in lines 15–20.
3. How does the imagery in Section 3 develop the dual role of the wind which the speaker assigned to it in Section 1?
4. In Section 4 the poem becomes more personal; we hear the "I" speaking. What likenesses does the speaker note between himself and the wind? Why does he pray to the wind in his "sore need"? How does this prayer relate to the pleas that end the first three sections?
5. The last section is the direct statement of the prayer. What exactly does the speaker wish from the wind? How does the music image help the section move from prayer to confidence? What role does the speaker see for the poets? Consider carefully the meaning of phrases like "dead thoughts" (line 63), "quicken a new birth" (line 64), "incantation of this verse" (line 65). What is the hope expressed at the end of the stanza?

6. In this poem Shelley makes use of an interlocking rhyme scheme followed by a couplet. Chart the rhyme scheme for the first section. What effect is achieved by the use of the interlocking rhyme to describe that which is "tameless, and swift, and proud"?

TO A SKYLARK

Hail to thee, blithe Spirit!
    Bird thou never wert,
That from Heaven, or near it,
    Pourest thy full heart
In profuse strains of unpremeditated art.   5

Higher still and higher
    From the earth thou springest
Like a cloud of fire;
    The blue deep thou wingest,
And singing still dost soar, and soaring ever singest.   10

In the golden lightning
    Of the sunken sun,
O'er which clouds are bright'ning,
    Thou dost float and run;
Like an unbodied joy whose race is just begun.   15

The pale purple even
    Melts around thy flight;
Like a star of Heaven
    In the broad daylight
Thou art unseen,—but yet I hear thy shrill delight,   20

Keen as are the arrows
    Of that silver sphere,
Whose intense lamp narrows
    In the white dawn clear,
Until we hardly see—we feel that it is there.   25

>   All the earth and air
>   With thy voice is loud,
>   As, when night is bare,
>   From one lonely cloud
> The moon rains out her beams, and Heaven is overflowed.   30

>   What thou art we know not;
>   What is most like thee?
>   From rainbow clouds there flow not
>   Drops so bright to see
> As from thy presence showers a rain of melody.   35

>   Like a Poet hidden
>   In the light of thought,
>   Singing hymns unbidden,
>   Till the world is wrought
> To sympathy with hopes and fears it heeded not: 40

>   Like a highborn maiden
>   In a palace tower,
>   Soothing her love-laden
>   Soul in secret hour
> With music sweet as love,—which overflows her bower: 45

>   Like a glowworm golden
>   In a dell of dew,
>   Scattering unbeholden
>   Its aërial hue
> Among the flowers and grass which screen it from the view: 50

>   Like a rose embowered
>   In its own green leaves,
>   By warm winds deflowered,
>   Till the scent it gives
> Makes faint with too much sweet these heavy-wingéd thieves.   55

    Sound of vernal showers
        On the twinkling grass,
    Rain-awakened flowers,
        All that ever was
Joyous and clear and fresh, thy music doth surpass.   60

    Teach us, Sprite or Bird,
        What sweet thoughts are thine;
    I have never heard
        Praise of love or wine
That panted forth a flood of rapture so divine.   65

    Chorus Hymeneal,[1]
        Or triumphal chaunt,
    Matched with thine would be all
        But an empty vaunt,
A thing wherein we feel there is some hidden want.   70

    What objects are the fountains
        Of thy happy strain?
    What fields, or waves, or mountains?
        What shapes of sky or plain?
What love of thine own kind? what ignorance of pain?   75

    With thy clear keen joyance
        Languor cannot be:
    Shadow of annoyance
        Never came near thee:
Thou lovest—but ne'er knew love's sad satiety.   80

    Waking or asleep,
        Thou of death must deem
    Things more true and deep
        Than we mortals dream—
Or how could thy notes flow in such a crystal stream?   85

[1] **Chorus Hymeneal:** marriage song

We look before and after,
    And pine for what is not:
Our sincerest laughter
    With some pain is fraught;
Our sweetest songs are those that tell of saddest thought.   90

Yet if we could scorn
    Hate and pride and fear;
If we were things born
    Not to shed a tear,
I know not how thy joy we ever should come near.   95

Better than all measures
    Of delightful sound,
Better than all treasures
    That in books are found,
Thy skill to poet were, thou scorner of the ground!   100

Teach me half the gladness
    That thy brain must know,
Such harmonious madness
    From my lips would flow,
The world should listen then—as I am listening now.   105

For Discussion

1. What does the speaker mean when he hails the skylark as "Bird thou never wert"? How is this greeting developed by the similes in stanzas 2–4? What, then, might the bird be?
2. The question asked in line 32 in a sense relates to the greeting given in lines 1–2. What use does the poet make of the four similes in stanzas 8–11? Discuss the ways in which each is like the bird.
3. In line 61 the speaker addresses the bird directly. What does he ask the bird to do? How does he compare the lot of man to the ideal of the bird? Is the description of life in lines 86–90 utterly pessimistic? Discuss.

4. The poet describes his poems as "harmonious madness." What does he mean by this? What does he hope the response to his poems will be?
5. Show how the meter and music of this poem fit the subject matter. What is the effect of the four short lines followed by the long fifth line?
6. Compare this poem to Keats's "Ode to a Nightingale" (see page 148). Do both poets identify with the bird? How do they differ in their final view of the bird? Are there any apparent differences in the imagery of the poems? Which poem has a better control of structure?

MUTABILITY

The flower that smiles today
    Tomorrow dies;
All that we wish to stay
    Tempts and then flies.
What is this world's delight?   5
Lightning that mocks the night,
    Brief even as bright.

Virtue, how frail it is!
    Friendship how rare!
Love, how it sells poor bliss   10
    For proud despair!
But we, though soon they fall,
Survive their joy, and all
    Which ours we call.

Whilst skies are blue and bright,   15
    Whilst flowers are gay,
Whilst eyes that change ere night
    Make glad the day;
Whilst yet the calm hours creep,
Dream thou—and from thy sleep   20
    Then wake to weep.

For Discussion

1. What essential human problem is this poem discussing? In what images does the poet present the problem? Are they abstract or concrete or both?
2. Is the last stanza essentially idealistic or realistic? Who might be the "thou" addressed in the last stanza? How does this provide a dimension of dramatic situation for the poem? Why do we as mortals "wake to weep"?
3. Discuss Shelley's use of diction in this poem, which bears the solemn title "Mutability." Take special care to note the heavy use of monosyllables. What effect is created?

STANZAS

Written in Dejection, near Naples

    The sun is warm, the sky is clear,
        The waves are dancing fast and bright,
    Blue isles and snowy mountains wear
        The purple noon's transparent might,
        The breath of the moist earth is light,   5
    Around its unexpanded buds;
        Like many a voice of one delight,
    The winds, the birds, the ocean floods,
The City's voice itself is soft like Solitude's.

    I see the Deep's untrampled floor   10
        With green and purple seaweeds strown;
    I see the waves upon the shore,
        Like light dissolved in star-showers, thrown:
        I sit upon the sands alone—
    The lightning of the noontide ocean   15
        Is flashing round me, and a tone
    Arises from its measured motion,
How sweet! did any heart now share in my emotion.

Alas! I have nor hope nor health,
    Nor peace within nor calm around,   20
Nor that content surpassing wealth
    The sage in meditation found,
And walked with inward glory crowned—
Nor fame, nor power, nor love, nor leisure.
    Others I see whom these surround—   25
Smiling they live, and call life pleasure;—
To me that cup has been dealt in another measure.

Yet now despair itself is mild,
    Even as the winds and waters are;
I could lie down like a tired child,   30
    And weep away the life of care
Which I have borne and yet must bear,
    Till death like sleep might steal on me,
And I might feel in the warm air
    My cheek grow cold, and hear the sea   35
Breathe o'er my dying brain its last monotony.

Some might lament that I were cold,
    As I, when this sweet day is gone,
Which my lost heart, too soon grown old,
    Insults with this untimely moan;   40
They might lament—for I am one
    Whom men love not—and yet regret,
Unlike this day, which, when the sun
    Shall on its stainless glory set,
Will linger, though enjoyed, like joy in memory yet.   45

For Discussion

1. When this poem was written Shelley was burdened by the death of his first wife, the death of his daughter, ill health, financial worries, and by the thought that he had failed as

a poet. What is the dramatic situation given in the first two stanzas? How do the elements the speaker sees in nature compare to his own state of mind? What very human—and therefore universal—wish does the speaker express?
2. Stanza 3 seems based on a principle of negatives. How does the use of negatives relate to the meaning of the stanza? Why can he not achieve the "content surpassing wealth" given to the meditative sage? What overtones are suggested by the word "cup" in line 27?
3. Note the transitional word "yet" beginning stanza 4. Is this used merely to indicate a change of thought or does it also indicate a change of tone and mood? What does the simile of the "tired child" mean? Is Shelley suggesting that in the face of the reverses which he cannot understand he is powerless to fight? Discuss.
4. How does the poet attempt to overcome what could have been maudlin self-pity? Consider, for example, the use of words and the comparison between the man and the day.
5. Trace the day image throughout the poem. What is the progression? What mood effect is achieved by this image? Is this merely a chronological way of achieving unity or does it have further symbolic meaning?

A LAMENT

1

O world! O life! O time!
On whose last steps I climb,
    Trembling at that where I had stood before;
When will return the glory of your prime?
        No more—oh, never more!   5

2

Out of the day and night
A joy has taken flight;
    Fresh spring, and summer, and winter hoar,
Move my faint heart with grief, but with delight
        No more—oh, never more!   10

For Discussion

1. The title itself would seem to indicate that this poem might be an example of Romantic self-pity. How does Shelley succeed in making the poem an expression of deep-felt emotion without becoming overly sentimental?
2. In an earlier version of the poem Shelley had the first line read "Oh time, oh night, oh day." What is the effect of the change he made? Is the final version better than the first attempt? Consider the movement and reference of the words.
3. How does the poet use sound in lines 5 and 6 to reinforce meaning?

from ADONAIS

An Elegy on the Death of John Keats, Author of Endymion, Hyperion, etc.

1

I weep for Adonais—he is dead!
Oh, weep for Adonais! though our tears
Thaw not the frost which binds so dear a head!
And thou, sad Hour, selected from all years
To mourn our loss, rouse thy obscure compeers,   5
And teach them thine own sorrow, say: "With me
Died Adonais; till the Future dares
Forget the Past, his fate and fame shall be
An echo and a light unto eternity!"

2

Where wert thou, mighty Mother, when he lay,   10
When thy Son lay, pierced by the shaft which flies
In darkness? where was lorn Urania [1]
When Adonais died? With veiléd eyes,

---
[1] **Urania:** the Muse of astronomy. Shelley uses it here to mean "heavenly love."

'Mid listening Echoes, in her Paradise
She sate, while one, with soft enamored breath, 15
Rekindled all the fading melodies,
With which, like flowers that mock the corse beneath,
He had adorned and hid the coming bulk of Death.

3

Oh, weep for Adonais—he is dead!
Wake, melancholy Mother, wake and weep! 20
Yet wherefore? Quench within their burning bed
Thy fiery tears, and let thy loud heart keep
Like his, a mute and uncomplaining sleep;
For he is gone where all things wise and fair
Descend:—oh, dream not that the amorous Deep 25
Will yet restore him to the vital air;
Death feeds on his mute voice, and laughs at our despair.

. . .

8

He will awake no more, oh, never more!—
Within the twilight chamber spreads apace, 65
The shadow of white Death, and at the door
Invisible Corruption waits to trace
His extreme way to her dim dwelling-place;
The eternal Hunger sits, but pity and awe
Soothe her pale rage, nor dares she to deface 70
So fair a prey, till darkness, and the law
Of change, shall o'er his sleep the mortal curtain draw.

9

Oh, weep for Adonais!—The quick Dreams,
The passion-wingéd Ministers of thought,
Who were his flocks, whom near the living streams 75
Of his young spirit he fed, and whom he taught
The love which was its music, wander not,—

Wander no more, from kindling brain to brain,
But droop there, whence they sprung; and mourn their lot
   Round the cold heart, where, after their sweet pain,   80
They ne'er will gather strength, or find a home again.

10

And one with trembling hands clasps his cold head,
And fans him with her moonlight wings, and cries:
"Our love, our hope, our sorrow is not dead;
See, on the silken fringe of his faint eyes,   85
Like dew upon a sleeping flower, there lies
A tear some Dream has loosened from his brain."
Lost Angel of a ruined Paradise!
She knew not 'twas her own; as with no stain
She faded, like a cloud which had outwept its rain.   90

In the stanzas omitted the poet calls on nature, beauty, mythological personages, and other poets to mourn the dead Adonais. Such a train of mourners is a convention of the elegy.

36

Our Adonais has drunk poison—oh!
What deaf and viperous murderer could crown
Life's early cup with such a draught of woe?
The nameless worm would now itself disown:
It felt, yet could escape the magic tone   320
Whose prelude held all envy, hate, and wrong,
But what was howling in one breast alone,
Silent with expectation of the song,
Whose master's hand is cold, whose silver lyre unstrung.

37

Live thou,[19] whose infamy is not thy fame!   325
Live! fear no heavier chastisement from me,
Thou noteless blot on a remembered name!

[19] **thou:** the reviewer who criticized Keats's poetry

But be thyself, and know thyself to be!
And ever at thy season be thou free
To spill the venom when thy fangs o'erflow: 330
Remorse and Self-contempt shall cling to thee;
Hot Shame shall burn upon thy secret brow,
And like a beaten hound tremble thou shalt—as now.

38

Nor let us weep that our delight is fled
Far from these carrion kites that scream below; 335
He wakes or sleeps with the enduring dead;
Thou canst not soar where he is sitting now.—
Dust to the dust! but the pure spirit shall flow
Back to the burning fountain whence it came,
A portion of the Eternal, which must glow 340
Through time and change, unquenchably the same,
Whilst thy cold embers choke the sordid hearth of shame.

39

Peace, peace! he is not dead; he doth not sleep—
He hath awakened from the dream of life—
'Tis we who, lost in stormy visions, keep 345
With phantoms an unprofitable strife,
And in mad trance strike with our spirit's knife
Invulnerable nothings.—*We* decay
Like corpses in a charnel; fear and grief
Convulse us and consume us day by day, 350
And cold hopes swarm like worms within our living clay.

40

He has outsoared the shadow of our night;
Envy and calumny and hate and pain,
And that unrest which men miscall delight,
Can touch him not and torture not again; 355
From the contagion of the world's slow stain

He is secure, and now can never mourn
A heart grown cold, a head grown gray in vain;
Nor, when the spirit's self has ceased to burn,
With sparkless ashes load an unlamented urn.   360

41

He lives, he wakes—'tis Death is dead, not he;
Mourn not for Adonais.—Thou young Dawn,
Turn all thy dew to splendor, for from thee
The spirit thou lamentest is not gone;
Ye caverns and ye forests, cease to moan!   365
Cease, ye faint flowers and fountains, and thou Air,
Which like a mourning veil thy scarf hadst thrown
O'er the abandoned Earth, now leave it bare
Even to the joyous stars which smile on its despair!

42

He is made one with Nature: there is heard   370
His voice in all her music, from the moan
Of thunder, to the song of night's sweet bird;
He is a presence to be felt and known
In darkness and in light, from herb and stone,
Spreading itself where'er that Power may move   375
Which has withdrawn his being to its own;
Which wields the world with never-wearied love,
Sustains it from beneath, and kindles it above.

43

He is a portion of the loveliness
Which once he made more lovely: he doth bear   380
His part, while the one Spirit's plastic stress
Sweeps through the dull dense world, compelling there
All new successions to the forms they wear;
Torturing the unwilling dross that checks its flight
To its own likeness, as each mass may bear;   385

And bursting in its beauty and its might
From trees and beasts and men into the Heaven's light.

44

The splendors of the firmament of time
May be eclipsed, but are extinguished not;
Like stars to their appointed height they climb, 390
And death is a low mist which cannot blot
The brightness it may veil. When lofty thought
Lifts a young heart above its mortal lair,
And love and life contend in it, for what
Shall be its earthly doom, the dead live there 395
And move like winds of light on dark and stormy air.

. . .

52

The One remains, the many change and pass; 460
Heaven's light forever shines, Earth's shadows fly;
Life, like a dome of many-colored glass,
Stains the white radiance of Eternity,
Until Death tramples it to fragments,—Die,
If thou wouldst be with that which thou dost seek! 465
Follow where all is fled!—Rome's azure sky,
Flowers, ruins, statues, music, words, are weak
The glory they transfuse with fitting truth to speak.

53

Why linger, why turn back, why shrink, my Heart?
Thy hopes are gone before: from all things here 470
They have departed; thou shouldst now depart!
A light is past from the revolving year,
And man, and woman; and what still is dear
Attracts to crush, repels to make thee wither.
The soft sky smiles,—the low wind whispers near; 475
'Tis Adonais calls! oh, hasten thither,
No more let Life divide what Death can join together.

54

That Light whose smile kindles the Universe,
That Beauty in which all things work and move,
That Benediction which the eclipsing Curse 480
Of birth can quench not, that sustaining Love
Which, through the web of being blindly wove
By man and beast and earth and air and sea,
Burns bright or dim, as each are mirrors of
The fire for which all thirst, now beams on me, 485
Consuming the last clouds of cold mortality.

55

The breath whose might I have invoked in song
Descends on me; my spirit's bark is driven
Far from the shore, far from the trembling throng
Whose sails were never to the tempest given; 490
The massy earth and spheréd skies are riven!
I am borne darkly, fearfully, afar;
Whilst, burning through the inmost veil of Heaven,
The soul of Adonais, like a star,
Beacons from the abode where the Eternal are. 495

For Discussion

1. The dignified mood of the elegy is created partly through the use of conventions honored in classical literature; for example, early in the poem there is an invocation to a muse. Whom does Shelley select as the muse? Why is his choice an apt one? What is the basic statement of the first three stanzas? How would you describe the tone of these stanzas?
2. Adonais is pictured in a pastoral setting. How is this image developed in stanza 9? How do the images in this stanza afford dramatic opposition to the personification to be found in stanza 8?

3. In stanzas 36–38 Shelley makes a direct attack against the reviewer who condemned Keats's poems and, according to Shelley, hastened the poet's death. In what terms does the poet describe the reviewer? What fate does Shelley foresee for the reviewer? In your opinion, is the denunciation overstated?
4. The mood of the poem changes in stanza 39 from dignified mourning to elation. What is responsible for this change in mood? How has Keats "outsoared the shadow of our night"? Notice that the poem is becoming more personal, reflecting many of Shelley's own thoughts about the fate of the Romantic poets. What is his attitude toward life as expressed in these stanzas? What is his attitude toward death?
5. Where does Shelley place Keats in stanzas 42–44? Why are his references especially appropriate for a poet like Keats? Explain the meaning of lines 392–396.
6. Like many other poets Shelley uses the elegy to portray his own feelings and emotions. Explain the ideal world which Shelley establishes in stanzas 52–55. What is its relationship to the reality of human life?
7. The traditional ending of an elegy is the canonization of the dead person. How does Shelley deal with this convention? What is the influence of the dead Keats on the poet?

For Composition

1. Write a critical paper in which you discuss Shelley's use of natural objects to express his personal feelings. Choose two images from specific poems and examine them carefully, pointing out specific lines which prove your points.
2. Shelley, like all men, is concerned with the concept of change, the lack of permanence in the world. What effect does change have on the life of a human being, be it a change of day to night, of seasons, of place, of ideas? Write a theme using an incident or happening within your own experience that brought you to a greater understanding of the way change affects the individual.

ROMANTIC PROSE WRITERS

The eighteenth century was a period of great prose—written with outstanding clarity and directness of expression. The most popular prose form was the essay, and writers such as Addison and Steele, Defoe and Swift used it with great skill to make their perceptive observations of people, places, and events. The essay was used as a platform from which the writers sought to cultivate taste, to hold up to ridicule the excesses of boorishness and foppery, and to provide conversational matter for the popular coffeehouses. Although the form declined in popularity toward the end of the eighteenth century and although poetry seemed the more proper vehicle for presenting the thoughts and feelings of the Romantics, the Romantic Movement and its interest in imagination and the commonplace were not confined to poets alone. In a period of outstanding poetry, writers like Charles Lamb, William Hazlitt, and Thomas De Quincey responded to Romantic impulses and kept alive the tradition of English prose.

Publications such as *Blackwood's Magazine* and the *London Magazine* provided a market for the essays of Lamb, Hazlitt, and De Quincey. Freed from the space restrictions of the newspaper essay that prevailed in the eighteenth century, these writers made the essay longer, more personal, and more varied in theme and subject. The light and easy view of these essays, their conversational tone, and the emergence of the writer's personality in their pages established the personal essay in the form which it has kept to the present.

Charles Lamb was one of the best liked of the essayists of the Romantic period, and he remains the favorite of many people. He wrote the *Essays of Elia*, for which he is most famous, in his forties; and before this he had written some poetry, plays, and a prose narrative. His bright and witty letters, filled with informal criticisms of literature, with comments about his work, his boredom, his circle of friends, his life in the city of London are excellent examples of his writing and contain many of the elements he expanded in his essays.

The *Essays of Elia* display much of the man himself. Under the mask of Elia, Lamb indulged in the most characteristic of Romantic tendencies—personal memoirs, reminiscences of past life. Time and again in the essays Lamb returns to the world of childhood, weaving autobiographical details and fanciful imaginings into a reality of its own. His style is not the plain style which had as its end clarity and directness. He was more concerned with creating a mood and with evoking a response. To do this he used the rambling, ornate style more typical of the seventeenth century than of his own age. His is a style not often imitated well; in the hands of lesser writers it becomes little more than mawkish sentimentality. However, his wry observations of London and his cherished recollections of past days are models for the personal essay.

William Hazlitt, like Lamb, was a friend and confidant of the Romantic poets and, like Lamb, came to the personal essay late in life. Hazlitt's first fame came as a literary critic. His two major works of criticism, *Lectures on the English Poets* and *The English Comic Writers* stand today as highpoints in the history of literary criticism. He had a passionate interest in literature but was not above allowing his radical political convictions and personal bias to color his criticism. What he enjoyed, he wrote about with enthusiasm and directness; what he disliked, he condemned.

In his personal essays, particularly those in *The Round Table* and *Table Talk*, he presented pictures of his time, its literature, and its manners. He himself states that the essays are an attempt "to recollect all I have ever observed or thought upon a subject and to express it as nearly as I can." Unlike Lamb, who was concerned with creating a character for his essays, Hazlitt covered a wide range of human affairs from the trivial to the great and fundamental issues of life. Less didactic than his eighteenth-century counterparts, he yet shared with them clarity and directness of style.

Thomas De Quincey's early fame rested on *Confessions of an English Opium Eater*, a powerful and imaginative book which was the first major step in his proposed literary career, a career he had determined on early in his boyhood. Most of his work appeared originally in magazines and was collected only shortly before his death. His subjects are taken from personal experience, politics, history, and literature.

De Quincey's criticism has both the virtues and faults of the Romanticism of which he was a part. Placing heavy emphasis on feeling, he viewed literature with his own jaundiced eye. Although he was widely read, he dealt only with the major figures of English literature in his criticism. Of his contemporaries, he praised highly Wordsworth and Coleridge, calling *Lyrical Ballads* a great work of art and a book which had had great personal influence on him. He dismissed Byron, Shelley, and Keats as canting poets and attacked Hazlitt vehemently. Perhaps the only virtue he found in Shelley was the poet's classical learning.

De Quincey advocated "impassioned prose," elaborate and musical. Attempting to penetrate beneath the surface of things, he advocated a style which would extend the range of prose into the realm of poetry. The display of great learning, the sprinkling of classical allusions, the seemingly illogical digressions can, at times, make his writing ponderous and weighty. At its best, however, his prose conveys the mind of a critic of penetrating ability, if biased opinions.

Charles Lamb

(1775–1834)

In his essays, Lamb expressed his opinions on whatever attracted his attention. He loved London and saw romance in its streets and people. He saw the strange and extraordinary in the trivial and matter-of-fact incidents of life; and he recounted his impressions in an informal, graceful, and witty style that revealed as much about himself as it did about the subjects of his essays.

It is this personal quality which accounts for Lamb's prominent role in the development of the familiar essay. He gives his own acute and wry observations in graceful, flowing sentences which meander with the charm of fine conversation, the result of a subtle craftsmanship characterized by urbanity and good taste.

Lamb could be delicately nostalgic and wistful, as in "Dream Children"; or he could be lively and humorous, as in "A Dissertation Upon Roast Pig." Whatever the subject, Lamb showed himself to be a gentle person, sympathetic to mankind, but amused by the contradiction and follies of people, including himself. These essays are, in Lamb's words, "a talk with the reader; and they do nothing else."

DREAM CHILDREN: A REVERIE

Children love to listen to stories about their elders, when *they* were children; to stretch their imagination to the conception of a traditionary great-uncle, or grandame, whom they never saw. It was in this spirit that my little ones crept about me the other evening to hear about their great-grandmother Field, who lived in a great house in Norfolk (a hundred times bigger than that in which they and papa lived) which had been the scene—so at least it was generally believed in that part of the country—of the tragic incidents which they had lately become familiar with from the ballad of the Children in the Wood. Certain it is that the whole story of the children and their cruel uncle was to be seen fairly carved out in wood upon the chimney-piece of the great hall, the whole story down to the Robin Redbreasts, till a foolish rich person pulled it down to set up a marble one of modern invention in its stead, with no story upon it. Here Alice put out one of her dear mother's looks, too tender to be called upbraiding. Then I went on to say how religious and how good their great-grandmother Field was, how beloved and respected by everybody, though she was not indeed the mistress of this great house, but had only the charge of it (and yet in some respects she might be said to be the mistress of it too) committed to her by the owner, who preferred living in a newer and more fashionable mansion which he had purchased somewhere in the adjoining county; but still she lived in it in a manner as if it had been her own, and kept up the dignity of the great house in a sort while she lived, which afterwards came to decay, and was nearly pulled down, and all its old ornaments stripped and carried away to the owner's other house, where they were set up, and looked as awkward as if someone were to carry away the old tombs they had seen lately at the Abbey, and stick them up in Lady C.'s tawdry gilt drawing-room. Here John smiled, as much as to say, "that would be foolish, indeed." And then I told how, when she came to die, her funeral was attended by a concourse of all the poor, and some of the gentry too, of the neighborhood for many miles round, to show their respect for her memory, because she had been such a good and religious woman; so good indeed that she knew all the Psaltery by heart, ay, and a great part of the Testament besides. Here little Alice spread her hands. Then I told what a tall, upright, graceful person their great-grandmother Field once was; and how in her youth she was esteemed the best dancer—here Alice's little right foot played an involuntary movement, till upon my looking grave, it desisted—the best dancer, I was saying, in the county, till a cruel disease, called a cancer, came, and bowed her down with pain; but it could never bend her good spirits, or make them stoop, but they were still upright, because she was so good and religious. Then I told how she was used to sleep by herself in a lone chamber of the great lone house; and how she believed that an apparition of two infants was to be seen at midnight gliding up and down the great staircase near where she slept, but she said "those innocents would do her no harm"; and how frightened I used to be, though in those days I had my maid sleep with me, because I was never half so good or religious as she—and yet I never saw the infants. Here John expanded all his eyebrows and tried to look courageous. Then I told how good she was to all her grandchildren, having us to the great house in the holidays, where I in particular used to spend many hours by myself, in gazing upon the old busts of the twelve Caesars, that had been emperors of Rome, till the old marble heads would seem to live again, or I to be turned into marble with them; how I never could be tired with roaming about that huge mansion, with its vast empty rooms, with their worn-out hangings, fluttering tapestry, and carved oaken panels, with the gilding almost rubbed out—sometimes in the spacious old-fashioned gardens, which I had almost to myself, unless when now and then a solitary gardening man would cross me—and how the nectarines and peaches hung upon the walls without my ever offering to pluck them, because they were forbidden fruit, unless now and then—and because I had more pleasure in strolling about among the old melancholy-looking yew-trees, or the firs, and picking up the red berries, and the fir apples, which were good for nothing but to look at—or in lying about upon the fresh grass, with all the fine garden smells around me—or basking in the orangery, till I could almost fancy myself ripening too along with the oranges and the limes in that grateful warmth—or in watching the dace [1] that darted to and fro in the fishpond, at the bottom of the garden, with here and there a great sulky pike hanging midway down the water in silent state, as if it mocked at their impertinent friskings—I had more pleasure in these busy-idle diversions than in all the sweet flavors of peaches, nectarines, oranges, and such-like common baits of children. Here John slyly deposited back upon the plate a bunch of grapes which, not unobserved by Alice, he had meditated dividing with her, and both seemed willing to relinquish them for the present as irrelevant. Then in somewhat a more heightened tone, I told how, though their great-grandmother Field loved all her grandchildren, yet in an especial manner she might be said to love their uncle, John L——, because he was so handsome and spirited a youth, and a king to the rest of us; and, instead of moping about in solitary corners, like some of us, he would mount the most mettlesome horse he could get, when but an imp no bigger than themselves, and make it carry him half over the county in a morning, and join the hunters when there were any out—and yet he loved the old great house and gardens too, but had too much spirit to be always pent up within their boundaries—and how their uncle grew up to man's estate as brave as he was handsome, to the admiration of everybody, but of their great-grandmother Field most especially; and how he used to carry me upon his back when I was a lame-footed boy—for he was a good bit older than me—many a mile when I could not walk for pain;—and how in after-life he became lame-footed too, and I did not always (I fear) make allowances enough for him when he was impatient, and in pain, nor remember sufficiently how considerate he had been to me when I was lame-footed; and how when he died, though he had not been dead an hour, it seemed as if he had died a great while ago, such a distance there is betwixt life and death; and how I bore his death as I thought pretty well at first, but afterwards it haunted and haunted me; and though

[1] **dace:** a kind of small fish

I did not cry or take it to heart as some do, and as I think he would have done if I had died, yet I missed him all day long, and knew not till then how much I had loved him. I missed his kindness, and I missed his crossness, and wished him to be alive again, to be quarreling with him (for we quarreled sometimes), rather than not have him again, and was as uneasy without him, as he, their poor uncle, must have been when the doctor took off his limb. Here the children fell a-crying, and asked if their little mourning which they had on was not for Uncle John, and they looked up, and prayed me not to go on about their uncle, but to tell them some stories about their pretty dead mother. Then I told how for seven long years, in hope sometimes, sometimes in despair, yet persisting ever, I courted the fair Alice W——n; and, as much as children could understand, I explained to them what coyness, and difficulty, and denial meant in maidens—when suddenly, turning to Alice, the soul of the first Alice looked out at her eyes with such a reality of representment, that I became in doubt which of them stood there before me, or whose that bright hair was; and while I stood gazing, both the children gradually grew fainter to my view, receding, and still receding till nothing at last but two mournful features were seen in the uttermost distance, which without speech, strangely impressed upon me the effects of speech: "We are not of Alice, nor of thee, nor are we children at all. The children of Alice call Bartrum father. We are nothing; less than nothing, and dreams. We are only what might have been, and must wait upon the tedious shores of Lethe millions of ages before we have existence and a name"—and immediately awaking, I found myself quietly seated in my bachelor armchair, where I had fallen asleep, with the faithful Bridget [2] unchanged by my side—but John L. (or James Elia) was gone forever.

[2] **Bridget:** Lamb's sister Mary

For Discussion

1. In this essay Lamb blends reality and fantasy. The great-grandmother is actually Lamb's own grandmother; Uncle John is Lamb's brother John. What function do these details have in the essay? What do they show about the personal feelings of Lamb?
2. At pivotal points during the essay we see the reactions of Alice and John to the story being told. Chart these reactions. Do the children seem interested in the story? What is their attitude toward the storyteller? What actions make them appear lifelike?
3. In the course of the evening, stories are told about several people. For whose benefit is the story of Uncle John told? What is the effect on the children?
4. Examine the sentences in this essay and note the varied structure. What tone is suggested by the long sentences and by the "and then" transitions?
5. What is the mood of this essay? Do the final sentences change the mood or do they add a further dimension to the reverie? Discuss. What is the relationship between the real world and the world of the dream children?
6. What characteristics of the personal essay are demonstrated in "Dream Children"? Consider not only the subject and mood but also the construction and the phrasing.
7. Compare the prose style of Lamb with that of Jonathan Swift. How do they differ? Which one seems more modern? Discuss.

A DISSERTATION UPON ROAST PIG

Mankind, says a Chinese manuscript, which my friend M. was obliging enough to read and explain to me, for the first seventy thousand ages ate their meat raw, clawing or biting it from the living animal, just as they do in Abyssinia to this day. This period is not obscurely hinted at by their great Confucius in the second chapter of his *Mundane Mutations,* where he designates a kind of golden age by the term *Cho-fang,* literally the Cook's Holiday. The manuscript goes on to say, that the art of roasting, or rather broiling (which I take to be the elder brother) was accidentally discovered in the manner following. The swine-herd, Ho-ti, having gone out into the woods one morning, as his manner was, to collect mast for his hogs, left his cottage in the care of his eldest son Bo-bo, a great lubberly boy, who being fond of playing with fire, as younkers of his age commonly are, let some sparks escape into a bundle of straw, which kindling quickly, spread the conflagration over every part of their poor mansion, till it was reduced to ashes. Together with the cottage (a sorry antediluvian makeshift of a building, you may think it), what was of much more importance, a fine litter of new farrowed pigs, no less than nine in number, perished. China pigs have been esteemed a luxury all over the East from the remotest periods that we read of. Bo-bo was in the utmost consternation, as you may think, not so much for the sake of the tenement, which his father and he could easily build up again with a few dry branches, and the labor of an hour or two, at any time, as for the loss of the pigs. While he was thinking what he should say to his father, and wringing his hands over the smoking remnants of one of those untimely sufferers, an odor assailed his nostrils, unlike any scent which he had before experienced. What could it proceed from?—not from the burnt cottage—he had smelt that smell before—indeed this was by no means the first accident of the kind which had occurred through the negligence of this unlucky young firebrand. Much less did it resemble that of any known herb, weed, or flower. A premonitory moistening at the same time overflowed his nether lip. He knew not what to think. He next stooped down to feel the pig, if there were any signs of life in it. He burnt his fingers, and to cool them he applied them in his booby fashion to his mouth. Some of the crumbs of the scorched skin had come away with his fingers, and for the first time in his life (in the world's life indeed, for before him no man had known it) he tasted—*crackling!* Again he felt and fumbled at the pig. It did not burn him so much now, still he licked his fingers from a sort of habit. The truth at length broke into his slow understanding, that it was the pig that smelt so, and the pig that tasted so delicious; and surrendering himself up to the newborn pleasure, he fell to tearing up whole handfuls of the scorched skin with the flesh next it, and was cramming it down his throat in his beastly fashion, when his sire entered amid the smoking rafters, armed with retributory cudgel, and finding how affairs stood, began to rain blows upon the young rogue's shoulders, as thick as hailstones, which Bo-bo heeded not any more than if they had been flies. The tickling pleasure, which he experienced in his lower regions, had rendered him quite callous to any inconveniences he might feel in those remote quarters. His father might lay on, but he could not beat him from his pig, till he had fairly made an end of it, when, becoming a little more sensible of his situation, something like the following dialogue ensued.

"You graceless whelp, what have you got there devouring? Is it not enough that you have burnt me down three houses with your dog's tricks, and be hanged to you, but you must be eating fire, and I know not what—what have you got there, I say?"

"Oh, father, the pig, the pig, do come and taste how nice the burnt pig eats."

The ears of Ho-ti tingled with horror. He cursed his son, and he cursed himself that ever he should beget a son that should eat burnt pig.

Bo-bo, whose scent was wonderfully sharpened since morning, soon raked out another pig, and fairly rending it asunder, thrust the lesser half by main force into the fists of Ho-ti, still shouting out, "Eat, eat, eat the burnt pig, father, only taste— O Lord"—with such-like barbarous ejaculations, cramming all the while as if he would choke.

Ho-ti trembled in every joint while he grasped the abominable thing, wavering whether he should not put his son to death for an unnatural young monster, when the crackling scorching his fingers, as it had done his son's, and applying the same remedy to them, he in his turn tasted some of its flavor, which, make what sour mouths he would for a pretence, proved not altogether displeasing to him. In conclusion (for the manuscript here is a little tedious) both father and son fairly sat down to the mess, and never left off till they had despatched all that remained of the litter.

Bo-bo was strictly enjoined not to let the secret escape, for the neighbors would certainly have stoned them for a couple of abominable wretches, who could think of improving upon the good meat which God had sent them. Nevertheless, strange stories got about. It was observed that Ho-ti's cottage was burnt down now more frequently than ever. Nothing but fires from this time forward. Some would break out in broad day, others in the night-time. As often as the sow farrowed, so sure was the house of Ho-ti to be in a blaze; and Ho-ti himself, which was the more remarkable, instead of chastising his son, seemed to grow more indulgent to him than ever. At length they were watched, the terrible mystery discovered, and father and son summoned to take their trial at Pekin, then an inconsiderable assize town. Evidence was given, the obnoxious food itself produced in court, and verdict about to be pronounced, when the foreman of the jury begged that some of the burnt pig, of which the culprits stood accused, might be handed into the box. He handled it, and they all handled it, and burning their fingers, as Bo-bo and his father had done before them, and nature prompting to each of them the same remedy, against the face of all the facts, and the clearest charge which judge had ever given—to the surpise of the whole court, townsfolk, strangers, reporters, and all present—without leaving the box, or any manner of consultation whatever, they brought in a simultaneous verdict of Not Guilty.

The judge, who was a shrewd fellow, winked at the manifest iniquity of the decision; and, when the court was dismissed, went privily, and bought up all the pigs that could be had for love or money. In a few days his lordship's town house was observed to be on fire. The thing took wing, and now there was nothing to be seen but fires in every direction. Fuel and pigs grew enormously dear all over the district. The insurance offices one and all shut up shop. People built slighter and slighter every day, until it was feared that the very science of architecture would in no long time be lost to the world. Thus this custom of firing houses continued, till in process of time, says my manuscript, a sage arose, like our Locke, who made a discovery, that the flesh of swine, or indeed of any other animal, might be cooked (*burnt,* as they called it) without the necessity of consuming a whole house to dress it. Then first began the rude form of a gridiron. Roasting by the string, or spit, came in a century or two later, I forget in whose dynasty. By such slow degrees, concludes the manuscript, do the most useful, and seemingly the most obvious arts, make their way among mankind.——

Without placing too implicit faith in the account above given, it must be agreed that if a worthy pretext for so dangerous an experiment as setting houses on fire (especially in these days) could be assigned in favor of any culinary object, that pretext and excuse might be found in ROAST PIG.

Of all the delicacies in the whole *mundus edibilis*,[1] I will maintain it to be the most delicate—*princeps obsoniorum*.[2]

I speak not of your grown porkers—things between pig and pork—those hobble-dehoys—but a young and tender suckling—under a moon old—guiltless as yet of the sty—with no original speck of the *amor immunditiae*,[3] the hereditary failing of the first parent, yet manifest—his voice as yet not broken, but something between a childish treble, and a grumble—the mild forerunner, or *praeludium,* of a grunt.

He must be roasted. I am not ignorant that our ancestors ate them seethed, or boiled—but what a sacrifice of the exterior tegument!

---

[1] **mundus edibilis:** world of edibles [2] **princeps obsoniorum:** prince of delicacies [3] **amor immunditiae:** love of the unclean

There is no flavor comparable, I will contend, to that of the crisp, tawny, well-watched, not over-roasted, *crackling*, as it is well called—the very teeth are invited to their share of the pleasure at this banquet in overcoming the coy, brittle resistance—with the adhesive oleaginous—O call it not fat—but an indefinable sweetness growing up to it—the tender blossoming of fat—fat cropped in the bud—taken in the shoot—in the first innocence—the cream and quintessence of the child-pig's yet pure food—the lean, no lean, but a kind of animal manna—or, rather, fat and lean (if it must be so) so blended and running into each other, that both together make but one ambrosian result, or common substance.

Behold him, while he is doing—it seemeth rather a refreshing warmth, than a scorching heat, that he is so passive to. How equably he twirleth round the string!—Now he is just done. To see the extreme sensibility of that tender age, he hath wept out his pretty eyes—radiant jellies—shooting stars.—

See him in the dish, his second cradle, how meek he lieth!—wouldst thou have had this innocent grow up to the grossness and indocility which too often accompany maturer swinehood? Ten to one he would have proved a glutton, a sloven, an obstinate, disagreeable animal—wallowing in all manner of filthy conversation—from these sins he is happily snatched away—

> Ere sin could blight, or sorrow fade,
> Death came with timely care—[4]

his memory is odoriferous—no clown curseth, while his stomach half rejecteth, the rank bacon—no coal-heaver bolteth him in reeking sausages—he hath a fair sepulchre in the grateful stomach of the judicious epicure—and for such a tomb might be content to die.

[4] A quotation from Coleridge's "Epitaph on an Infant"

He is the best of sapors. Pineapple is great. She is indeed almost too transcendent—a delight, if not sinful, yet so like to sinning, that really a tender-conscienced person would do well to pause—too ravishing for mortal taste, she woundeth and excoriateth the lips that approach her—like lovers' kisses, she biteth—she is a pleasure bordering on pain from the fierceness and insanity of her relish—but she stoppeth at the palate—she meddleth not with the appetite—and the coarsest hunger might barter her consistently for a mutton chop.

Pig—let me speak his praise—is no less provocative of the appetite, than he is satisfactory to the criticalness of the censorious palate. The strong man may batten on him, and weakling refuseth not his mild juices.

Unlike to mankind's mixed characters, a bundle of virtues and vices, inexplicably intertwisted, and not to be unravelled without hazard, he is—good throughout. No part of him is better or worse than another. He helpeth, as far as his little means extend, all around. He is the least envious of banquets. He is all neighbors' fare.

I am one of those, who freely and ungrudgingly impart a share of the good things of this life which fall to their lot (few as mine are in this kind) to a friend. I protest I take as great an interest in my friend's pleasures, his relishes, and proper satisfactions, as in mine own. "Presents," I often say, "endear Absents." Hares, pheasants, partridges, snipes, barn-door chickens (those "tame villatic fowl"), capons, plovers, brawn, barrels of oysters, I dispense as freely as I receive them. I love to taste them, as it were, upon the tongue of my friend. But a stop must be put somewhere. One would not, like Lear, "give everything." I make my stand upon pig. Methinks it is an ingratitude to the Giver of all good flavors, to extra-domiciliate or send out of the house, slightingly (under pretext of friendship, or I know not what), a blessing so particularly adapted, predestined, I may say, to my individual palate.—It argues an insensibility.

I remember a touch of conscience in this kind at school. My good old aunt, who never parted from me at the end of a holiday without stuffing a sweetmeat, or some nice thing, into my pocket, had dismissed me one evening with a smoking plum-cake, fresh from the oven. On my way to school (it was over London Bridge) a grey-headed old beggar saluted me (I have no doubt at this time of day that he was a counterfeit). I had no pence to console him with, and in the vanity of self-denial, and the very coxcombry of charity, schoolboy-like, I made him a present of—the whole cake! I walked on a little, buoyed up, as one is on such occasions, with a sweet soothing of self-satisfaction; but before I had got to the end of the bridge, my better feelings returned, and I burst into tears, thinking how ungrateful I had been to my good aunt, to go and give her good gift away to a stranger, that I had never seen before, and who might be a bad man for aught I knew; and then I thought of the pleasure my aunt would be taking in thinking that I—I myself, and not another—would eat her nice cake—and what should I say to her the next time I saw her—how naughty I was to part with her pretty present!—and the odor of that spicy cake came back upon my recollection, and the pleasure, and the curiosity I had taken in seeing her make it, and her joy when she sent it to the oven, and how disappointed she would feel that I had never had a bit of it in my mouth at last—and I blamed my impertinent spirit of alms-giving, and out-of-place hypocrisy of goodness, and above all I wished never to see the face again of that insidious, good-for-nothing, old grey impostor.

Our ancestors were nice in their method of sacrificing these tender victims. We read of pigs whipped to death with something of a shock, as we hear of any other obsolete custom. The age of discipline is gone by, or it would be curious to inquire (in a philosophical light merely) what effect this process might have towards intenerating and dulcifying [5] a substance, naturally so mild and dulcet as the flesh of young pigs. It looks

[5] **intenerating and dulcifying:** making tender and sweet

like refining a violet. Yet we should be cautious, while we condemn the inhumanity, how we censure the wisdom of the practice. It might impart a gusto.—

I remember an hypothesis, argued upon by the young students, when I was at St. Omer's [6] and maintained with much learning and pleasantry on both sides, "Whether, supposing that the flavor of a pig who obtained his death by whipping (*per flagellationem extremam*) superadded a pleasure upon the palate of a man more intense than any possible suffering we can conceive in the animal, is man justified in using that method of putting the animal to death?" I forget the decision.

His sauce should be considered. Decidedly, a few bread crumbs, done up with his liver and brains, and a dash of mild sage. But, banish, dear Mrs. Cook, I beseech you, the whole onion tribe. Barbecue your whole hogs to your palate, steep them in shalots, stuff them out with plantations of the rank and guilty garlic; you cannot poison them, or make them stronger than they are—but consider, he is a weakling—a flower.

[6] **St. Omer's:** a college conducted by the Jesuits in France for English boys

For Discussion

1. The opening of this essay has elements of an academic dissertation: the Chinese manuscript, the reference to Confucius's *Mundane Mutations,* the term *Cho-fang.* What is the purpose of these references? How do they prepare the reader for the story of Ho-ti and Bo-bo?
2. The story of the discovery of crackling is told with whimsical good humor. How does Lamb use language to create humorous incongruity? Point out examples of deliberate exaggeration which are humorous.
3. Why did Ho-ti wish to keep the discovery of roast pig a secret? When people discovered the secret, what did they think it necessary to do to have roast pig? Find examples in the essay of elements from Lamb's own time applied to the ancient situation. What effect is intended?

4. The second section of the essay is in tone a rapturous hymn in praise of roast pig. Does Lamb use the elevated style and the mixture of learned and common words with the same effect in this section of the essay as he did in the first section? Why is this praise so humorous?
5. From the incident about the plum-cake, do you think Lamb was really selfish? Why or why not? Does his observation about charity have any truth to it? Discuss.

For Composition

1. Using the informal essay style, write a short essay on one of the following topics: (a) a memory of someone I knew as a child; (b) in praise of my favorite food; (c) how my vanity got the better of me.
2. Write a critical paper on Lamb's use of language to create humor. Try to analyze his use of words, the construction of his sentences, and his use of foreign phrases as elements of this humor.

William Hazlitt

(1778–1830)

William Hazlitt was a vigorous and perceptive person with an enormous interest in what was going on in the world and in the arts. Few writers have had a greater passion for freedom of thought and action. In his critical capacity, he was able to appreciate not only the best literature of his own age but that of other periods. His style in his essays is forceful and direct, befitting a desire to praise what is good and to condemn what is bad.

Hazlitt's personal essays are models of the familiar prose style. His principle is "to write as any one would speak in common conversation who had a thorough command and choice of words, or who could discourse with ease, force, and perspicuity." His sentences are leaner than the ornate sentences of Lamb, and they come directly to the heart of the matter. It is through the tightness of sentence structure, through the heavy use of quotations, through the references to people and places, and through the precision of diction, that we come to know the man Hazlitt.

ON GOING A JOURNEY

One of the pleasantest things in the world is going a journey; but I like to go by myself. I can enjoy society in a room; but out of doors, nature is company enough for me. I am then never less alone than when alone.

"The fields his study, nature was his book."

I cannot see the wit of walking and talking at the same time. When I am in the country I wish to vegetate like the country. I am not for criticizing hedge-rows and black cattle. I go out of town in order to forget the town and all that is in it. There are those who for this purpose go to watering-places, and carry the metropolis with them. I like more elbow-room and fewer incumbrances. I like solitude, when I give myself up to it, for the sake of solitude; nor do I ask for

> "a friend in my retreat,
> Whom I may whisper solitude is sweet."

The soul of a journey is liberty, perfect liberty, to think, feel, do, just as one pleases. We go a journey chiefly to be free of all impediments and of all inconveniences; to leave ourselves behind, much more to get rid of others. It is because I want a little breathing-space to muse on indifferent matters, where Contemplation

> "May plume her feathers and let grow her wings,
> That in the various bustle of resort
> Were all too ruffled, and sometimes impair'd,"

that I absent myself from the town for a while, without feeling at a loss the moment I am left by myself. Instead of a friend in a post-chaise or in a Tilbury,[1] to exchange good things with, and vary the same stale topics over again, for once let me have a truce with impertinence. Give me the clear blue sky over my head, and the green turf beneath my feet, a winding road before me, and three hours' march to dinner—and then to thinking! It is hard if I cannot start some game on these lone heaths. I laugh, I run, I leap, I sing for joy. From the point of yonder rolling cloud I plunge into my past being, and revel there, as the sun-burnt Indian plunges headlong into the wave that wafts him to his native shore. Then long-forgotten things, like "sunken wrack and sumless treasuries," burst upon my eager sight, and I begin to feel, think, and be

[1] **Tilbury:** a two wheeled carriage without a top

myself again. Instead of an awkward silence, broken by attempts at wit or dull common-places mine is that undisturbed silence of the heart which alone is perfect eloquence. No one likes puns, alliterations, antitheses, argument, and analysis better than I do; but I sometimes had rather be without them. "Leave, oh, leave me to my repose!" I have just now other business in hand, which would seem idle to you, but is with me "very stuff of the conscience." Is not this wild rose sweet without a comment? Does not this daisy leap to my heart set in its coat of emerald? Yet if I were to explain to you the circumstance that has so endeared it to me, you would only smile. Had I not better then keep it to myself, and let it serve me to brood over, from here to yonder craggy point, and from thence onward to the far-distant horizon? I should be but bad company all that way, and therefore prefer being alone. I have heard it said that you may, when the moody fit comes on, walk or ride on by yourself, and indulge your reveries. But this looks like a breach of manners, a neglect of others, and you are thinking all the time that you ought to rejoin your party. "Out upon such half-faced fellowship," say I. I like to be either entirely to myself, or entirely at the disposal of others; to talk or be silent, to walk or sit still, to be sociable or solitary. I was pleased with an observation of Mr. Cobbett's, that "he thought it a bad French custom to drink our wine with our meals, and that an Englishman ought to do only one thing at a time." So I cannot talk and think, or indulge in melancholy musing and lively conversation by fits and starts. "Let me have a companion of my way," says Sterne,[2] "were it but to remark how the shadows lengthen as the sun declines." It is beautifully said; but, in my opinion, this continual comparing of notes interferes with the involuntary impression of things upon the mind, and hurts the sentiment. If you only hint what you feel in a kind of dumb show, it is insipid: if you have to explain it, it is making a toil of a pleasure. You cannot read the book of nature without being perpetually put

[2] **Sterne:** Laurence Sterne (1713–1768), English novelist

to the trouble of translating it for the benefit of others. I am for this synthetical method on a journey in preference to the analytical. I am content to lay in a stock of ideas then, and to examine and anatomise them afterwards. I want to see my vague notions float like the down of the thistle before the breeze, and not to have them entangled in the briars and thorns of controversy. For once, I like to have it all my own way; and this is impossible unless you are alone, or in such company as I do not covet. I have no objection to argue a point with any one for twenty miles of measured road, but not for pleasure. If you remark the scent of a bean-field crossing the road, perhaps your fellow-traveller has no smell. If you point to a distant object, perhaps he is short-sighted, and has to take out his glass to look at it. There is a feeling in the air, a tone in the colour of a cloud, which hits your fancy, but the effect of which you are unable to account for. There is then no sympathy, but an uneasy craving after it, and a dissatisfaction which pursues you on the way, and in the end probably produces ill-humour. Now I never quarrel with myself, and take all my own conclusions for granted till I find it necessary to defend them against objections. It is not merely that you may not be of accord on the objects and circumstances that present themselves before you—these may recall a number of objects, and lead to associations too delicate and refined to be possibly communicated to others. Yet these I love to cherish, and sometimes still fondly clutch them, when I can escape from the throng to do so. To give way to our feelings before company seems extravagance or affectation; and, on the other hand, to have to unravel this mystery of our being at every turn, and to make others take an equal interest in it (otherwise the end is not answered), is a task to which few are competent. We must "give it an understanding, but no tongue." My old friend Coleridge, however, could do both. He could go on in the most delightful explanatory way over hill and dale a summer's day, and convert a landscape into a didactic poem or a Pindaric ode. . . .

In general, a good thing spoils out-of-door prospects: it should be reserved for Table-talk. Lamb is for this reason, I take it, the worst company in the world out of doors; because he is the best within. I grant, there is one subject on which it is pleasant to talk on a journey; and that is, what one shall have for supper when we get to our inn at night. The open air improves this sort of conversation or friendly altercation, by setting a keener edge on appetite. Every mile of the road heightens the flavour of the viands we expect at the end of it. How fine it is to enter some old town, walled and turreted, just at approach of night-fall, or to come to some straggling village, with the lights streaming through the surrounding gloom; and then, after inquiring for the best entertainment that the place affords, to "take one's ease at one's inn"! These eventful moments in our lives' history are too precious, too full of solid, heart-felt happiness to be frittered and dribbled away in imperfect sympathy. I would have them all to myself, and drain them to the last drop: they will do to talk of or to write about afterwards. What a delicate speculation it is, after drinking whole goblets of tea—

"The cups that cheer, but not inebriate,"

and letting the fumes ascend into the brain, to sit considering what we shall have for supper—eggs and a rasher, a rabbit smothered in onions, or an excellent veal-cutlet! Sancho in such a situation once fixed upon cow-heel; and his choice, though he could not help it, is not to be disparaged. Then, in the intervals of pictured scenery and Shandean[3] contemplation, to catch the preparation and the stir in the kitchen (getting ready for the gentleman in the parlour). . . . These hours are sacred to silence and to musing, to be treasured up in the memory, and to feed the source of smiling thoughts hereafter. I would not waste them in idle talk; or if I must have the integrity of fancy broken in upon, I would rather it were by a stranger than a friend. A stranger takes his hue

[3] **Shandean:** careless, good-humored (from Sterne's *Tristram Shandy*)

and character from the time and place; he is a part of the furniture and costume of an inn. If he is a Quaker, or from the West Riding of Yorkshire, so much the better. I do not even try to sympathise with him, and he breaks no squares. (How I love to see the camps of the gypsies, and to sigh my soul into that sort of life. If I express this feeling to another, he may qualify and spoil it with some objection.) I associate nothing with my travelling companion but present objects and passing events. In his ignorance of me and my affairs, I in a manner forget myself. But a friend reminds one of other things, rips up old grievances, and destroys the abstraction of the scene. He comes in ungraciously between us and our imaginary character. Something is dropped in the course of conversation that gives a hint of your profession and pursuits; or from having some one with you, that knows the less sublime portions of your history, it seems that other people do. You are no longer a citizen of the world; but your "unhoused free condition is put into circumscription and confine." The *incognito* of an inn is one of its striking privileges—"lord of one's self, uncumber'd with a name." Oh! it is great to shake off the trammels of the world and of public opinion—to lose our importunate, tormenting, everlasting personal identity in the elements of nature, and become the creature of the moment, clear of all ties—to hold to the universe only by a dish of sweet-breads, and to owe nothing but the score of the evening —and no longer seeking for applause and meeting with contempt, to be known by no other title than *the Gentleman in the parlour*! One may take one's choice of all characters in this romantic state of uncertainty as to one's real pretensions, and become indefinitely respectable and negatively right-worshipful. We baffle prejudice and disappoint conjecture; and from being so to others, begin to be objects of curiosity and wonder even to ourselves. We are no more those hackneyed common-places that we appear in the world; an inn restores us to the level of nature, and quits scores with society! . . . It was on the tenth of April, 1798, that I sat down to a volume of the *New Eloise*,[4] at the inn at Llangollen, over a bottle of sherry and a cold chicken. The letter I chose was that in which St. Preux describes his feelings as he first caught a glimpse from the heights of the Jura of the Pays de Vaud, which I had brought with me as a *bon bouche* [5] to crown the evening with. It was my birthday, and I had for the first time come from a place in the neighbourhood to visit this delightful spot. The road to Llangollen turns off between Chirk and Wrexham; and on passing a certain point you come all at once upon the valley, which opens like an amphitheatre, broad, barren hills rising in majestic state on either side, with "green upland swells that echo to the bleat of flocks" below, and the river Dee babbling over its stony bed in the midst of them. The valley at this time "glittered green with sunny showers," and a budding ash-tree dipped its tender branches in the chiding stream. How proud, how glad I was to walk along the high road that overlooks the delicious prospect, repeating the lines which I have just quoted from Mr. Coleridge's poems! But besides the prospect which opened beneath my feet, another also opened to my inward sight, a heavenly vision, on which were written, in letters large as Hope could make them, these four words, LIBERTY, GENIUS, LOVE, VIRTUE; which have since faded into the light of common day, or mock my idle gaze.

"The beautiful is vanished, and returns not."

Still I would return some time or other to this enchanted spot; but I would return to it alone. What other self could I find to share that influx of thoughts, of regret, and delight, the fragments of which I could hardly conjure up to myself, so much have they been broken and defaced. I could stand on some tall rock, and overlook the precipice of years that separates me from what I then was. I was at that time going shortly to visit the poet whom I have above named. Where is he now? Not only I myself have changed; the world which

[4] **New Eloise:** sentimental novel by Jean Jacques Rousseau
[5] **bon bouche:** choice morsel

was then new to me, has become old and incorrigible. Yet will I turn to thee in thought, O sylvan Dee, in joy, in youth and gladness as thou then wert; and thou shalt always be to me the river of Paradise, where I will drink of the waters of life freely!

There is hardly anything that shows the short-sightedness or capriciousness of the imagination more than travelling does. With change of place we change our ideas; nay, our opinions and feelings. We can by an effort indeed transport ourselves to old and long-forgotten scenes, and then the picture of the mind revives again; but we forget those that we have just left. It seems that we can think but of one place at a time. The canvas of the fancy is but of a certain extent, and if we paint one set of objects upon it, they immediately efface every other. We cannot enlarge our conceptions, we only shift our point of view. The landscape bares its bosom to the enraptured eye, we take our fill of it, and seem as if we could form no other image of beauty or grandeur. We pass on, and think no more of it: the horizon that shuts it from our sight, also blots it from our memory like a dream. In travelling through a wild barren country I can form no idea of a woody and cultivated one. It appears to me that all the world must be barren, like what I see of it. In the country we forget the town, and in town we despise the country. "Beyond Hyde Park," says Sir Fopling Flutter, "all is a desert." All that part of the map that we do not see before us is a blank. The world in our conceit of it is not much bigger than a nutshell. It is not one prospect expanded into another, county joined to county, kingdom to kingdom, lands to seas, making an image voluminous and vast;—the mind can form no larger idea of space than the eye can take in at a single glance. The rest is a name written in a map, a calculation of arithmetic. For instance, what is the true signification of that immense mass of territory and population known by the name of China to us? An inch of pasteboard on a wooden globe, of no more account than a China orange! Things near us are seen of the size of life; things at a distance are diminished to the size of the understanding. We measure the universe by ourselves, and even comprehend the texture of our being only piece-meal. In this way, however, we remember an infinity of things and places. The mind is like a mechanical instrument that plays a great variety of tunes, but it must play them in succession. One idea recalls another, but it at the same time excludes all others. In trying to renew old recollections, we cannot as it were unfold the whole web of our existence; we must pick out the single threads. So in coming to a place where we have formerly lived, and with which we have intimate associations, every one must have found that the feeling grows more vivid the nearer we approach the spot, from the mere anticipation of the actual impression: we remember circumstances, feelings, persons, faces, names that we had not thought of for years; but for the time all the rest of the world is forgotten!—To return to the question I have quitted above:

I have no objection to go to see ruins, aqueducts, pictures, in company with a friend or a party, but rather the contrary, for the former reason reversed. They are intelligible matters, and will bear talking about. The sentiment here is not tacit, but communicable and overt. Salisbury Plain is barren of criticism, but Stonehenge [6] will bear a discussion antiquarian, picturesque, and philosophical. In setting out on a party of pleasure, the first consideration always is where we shall go to: in taking a solitary ramble, the question is what we shall meet with by the way. "The mind is its own place"; nor are we anxious to arrive at the end of our journey. I can myself do the honours indifferently well to works of art and curiosity. I once took a party to Oxford with no mean *éclat*—shewed them that seat of the Muses at a distance,

"With glistering spires and pinnacles adorn'd—"

descanted on the learned air that breathes from the grassy quadrangles and stone walls of halls and colleges—was at home

[6] **Stonehenge:** a large group of prehistoric stone pillars on Salisbury Plain

in the Bodleian;[7] and at Blenheim[8] quite superseded the powdered Cicerone[9] that attended us, and that pointed in vain with his wand to commonplace beauties in matchless pictures. As another exception to the above reasoning, I should not feel confident in venturing on a journey in a foreign country without a companion. I should want at intervals to hear the sound of my own language. There is an involuntary antipathy in the mind of an Englishman to foreign manners and notions that requires the assistance of social sympathy to carry it off. As the distance from home increases, this relief, which was at first a luxury, becomes a passion and an appetite. A person would almost feel stifled to find himself in the deserts of Arabia without friends and countrymen: there must be allowed to be something in the view of Athens or old Rome that claims the utterance of speech; and I own that the Pyramids are too mighty for any single contemplation. In such situations, so opposite to all one's ordinary train of ideas, one seems a species by one's-self, a limb torn off from society, unless one can meet with instant fellowship and support.—Yet I did not feel this want or craving very pressing once, when I first set my foot on the laughing shores of France. Calais was peopled with novelty and delight. The confused, busy murmur of the place was like oil and wine poured into my ears; nor did the mariners' hymn, which was sung from the top of an old crazy vessel in the harbour, as the sun went down, send an alien sound into my soul. I only breathed the air of general humanity. I walked over "the vine-covered hills and gay regions of France," erect and satisfied; for the image of man was not cast down and chained to the foot of arbitrary thrones: I was at no loss for language, for that of all the great schools of painting was open to me. The whole is vanished like a shade. Pictures, heroes, glory, freedom, all are fled: nothing remains but the Bourbons and the French people!—There is

[7] **Bodleian:** University Library
[8] **Blenheim:** palace belonging to the Duke of Marlborough
[9] **Cicerone:** guide

undoubtedly a sensation in travelling into foreign parts that is to be had nowhere else; but it is more pleasing at the time than lasting. It is too remote from our habitual associations to be a common topic of discourse or reference, and, like a dream or another state of existence, does not piece into our daily modes of life. It is an animated but a momentary hallucination. It demands an effort to exchange our actual for our ideal identity; and to feel the pulse of our old transports revive very keenly, we must "jump" all our present comforts and connexions. Our romantic and itinerant character is not to be domesticated. Dr. Johnson remarked how little foreign travel added to the facilities of conversation in those who had been abroad. In fact, the time we have spent there is both delightful, and in one sense instructive; but it appears to be cut out of our substantial, downright existence, and never to join kindly on to it. We are not the same, but another, and perhaps more enviable individual, all the time we are out of our own country. We are lost to ourselves, as well as our friends. So the poet somewhat quaintly sings,

"Out of my country and myself I go."

Those who wish to forget painful thoughts, do well to absent themselves for a while from the ties and objects that recall them; but we can be said only to fulfill our destiny in the place that gave us birth. I should on this account like well enough to spend the whole of my life in travelling abroad, if I could anywhere borrow another life to spend afterwards at home!

For Discussion

1. What reason does Hazlitt give for going a journey alone? How do the references to solitude and freedom develop this idea? What does he mean by "that undisturbed silence of the heart which alone is perfect eloquence"?

2. Why does Hazlitt object to Laurence Sterne's statement? Is Hazlitt saying that the contemplation of nature is an end in itself and not a means to human communication? Discuss. How would you relate these statements to Wordsworth's concept of poetry?
3. What human difficulties does Hazlitt point out which would interfere with his pleasure? How valid is his point that there are "associations too delicate and too refined to be possibly communicated to others"? Why does he approve of Coleridge on a journey and disapprove of Lamb?.
4. What topic does Hazlitt consider to be suitable conversation for a journey? Why does Hazlitt prefer to talk to a stranger? What exactly delights him about the "incognito of an inn"? Is his assuming of a role done only for amusement or does it have a necessary human function?
5. His account of his stay at the inn in Llangollen is poetical in its lyric quality. What makes it so? Why is Hazlitt emphatic in his wish to return to this spot alone? What has the view of the River Dee meant to him?
6. Do you agree with his statement "we measure the universe by ourselves, and even comprehend the texture of our being only piece-meal"? Discuss.
7. What situations, for Hazlitt, require a companion? How does he distinguish these from the times necessary for solitary freedom?
8. What effect is produced by the quotations, the parallel structure, and the foreign phrases? How would you describe the tone of the essay? Does it seem dated?
9. What Romantic qualities are apparent in this essay in its subject matter, treatment, and revelation of personality?

For Composition

1. In imitation of Hazlitt's style, write a personal essay on one of the following topics or on one of your own choosing: (a) seeing a friend; (b) buying a car; (c) hearing a song.
2. Hazlitt notes four words—liberty, genius, love, virtue—which were a special guide to him. Discuss in a theme the relevance of one of these words to you as a student.

Thomas De Quincey

(1785–1859)

Thomas De Quincey's reputation rests on his imaginative and impassioned prose, which often takes on some of the best qualities of poetry in its diction, rhythm, and music. In the 150 essays which have been identified as his, he covers a wide field of human experience—personal, political, social, historical, philosophical, and literary.

As a literary critic, De Quincey was among the first to recognize the influence of psychology on literature. He insisted that the truth of literature would be substantiated by human experience. The theory is most admirably demonstrated in the justly famous "On the Knocking at the Gate in Macbeth," where he uses an actual crime to prove his feelings about the play.

The prose of De Quincey is heavily ornate, with long involved sentences, language heavy with classical learning, and seemingly irrelevant digressions. At its best, his essays demonstrate the critic who has a subtlety of mind and a sensitive feeling for the power of literature and the literature of power.

ON THE KNOCKING AT THE GATE IN MACBETH [1]

From my boyish days I had always felt a great perplexity on one point in *Macbeth*. It was this: the knocking at the gate which succeeds to the murder of Duncan produced to my feel-

---

[1] Before reading this selection, read the murder scene in *Macbeth*, Act II, Scenes 2–3.

ings an effect for which I never could account. The effect was that it reflected back upon the murderer a peculiar awfulness and a depth of solemnity; yet, however obstinately I endeavored with my understanding to comprehend this, for many years I never could see *why* it should produce such an effect.

Here I pause for one moment to exhort the reader never to pay any attention to his understanding when it stands in opposition to any other faculty of his mind. The mere understanding, however useful and indispensable, is the meanest faculty in the human mind and the most to be distrusted; and yet the great majority of people trust to nothing else—which may do for ordinary life, but not for philosophical purposes. Of this, out of ten thousand instances that I might produce, I will cite one. Ask of any person whatsoever who is not previously prepared for the demand by a knowledge of perspective, to draw in the rudest way the commonest appearance which depends upon the laws of that science—as, for instance, to represent the effect of two walls standing at right angles to each other, or the appearance of the houses on each side of a street, as seen by a person looking down the street from one extremity. Now, in all cases, unless the person has happened to observe in pictures how it is that artists produce these effects, he will be utterly unable to make the smallest approximation to it. Yet why? For he has actually seen the effect every day of his life. The reason is that he allows his understanding to overrule his eyes. His understanding, which includes no intuitive knowledge of the laws of vision, can furnish him with no reason why a line which is known and can be proved to be a horizontal line should not *appear* a horizontal line; a line that made any angle with the perpendicular less than a right angle would seem to him to indicate that his houses were all tumbling down together. Accordingly he makes the line of his houses a horizontal line, and fails of course to produce the effect demanded. Here then is one instance out of many, in which not only the understanding is allowed to overrule the eyes, but where the understanding is positively allowed to obliterate the eyes, as it were; for not only does the man believe the evidence of his understanding in opposition to that of his eyes, but (what is monstrous) the idiot is not aware that his eyes ever gave such evidence. He does not know that he has seen (and therefore *quoad* [1] his consciousness has *not* seen) that which he *has* seen every day of his life.

But to return from this digression. My understanding could furnish no reason why the knocking at the gate in *Macbeth* should produce any effect, direct or reflected. In fact, my understanding said positively that it could *not* produce any effect. But I knew better; I felt that it did; and I waited and clung to the problem until further knowledge should enable me to solve it. At length, in 1812, Mr. Williams made his *début* on the stage of Ratcliffe Highway, and executed those unparalleled murders which have procured for him such a brilliant and undying reputation.[2] On which murders, by the way, I must observe, that in one respect they have had an ill effect, by making the connoisseur in murder very fastidious in his taste and dissatisfied with anything that has been since done in that line. All other murders look pale by the deep crimson of his; and, as an amateur once said to me in a querulous tone, "There has been absolutely nothing *doing* since his time, or nothing that's worth speaking of." But this is wrong, for it is unreasonable to expect all men to be great artists, and born with the genius of Mr. Williams. Now it will be remembered that in the first of these murders (that of the Marrs) the same incident (of a knocking at the door soon after the work of extermination was complete)[3] did actually occur which the genius of Shakespeare has invented; and all good judges, and the most eminent dilettanti, acknowledged the felicity of Shakespeare's suggestion as soon as it was actually realized. Here, then, was a fresh proof that I had been

---

[1] **quoad:** as far as his consciousness is concerned
[2] In December, 1811, John Williams murdered two families—the Marrs and the Williamsons in Ratcliffe Highway, in a disreputable part of London.
[3] A servant of the Marrs, who had been sent out to buy some oysters, knocked at the door of the house just after the murders had occurred.

right in relying on my own feeling in opposition to my understanding; and again I set myself to study the problem. At length I solved it to my own satisfaction; and my solution is this—Murder, in ordinary cases, where the sympathy is wholly directed to the case of the murdered person, is an incident of coarse and vulgar horror; and for this reason—that it flings the interest exclusively upon the natural but ignoble instinct by which we cleave to life: an instinct which, as being indispensable to the primal law of self-preservation, is the same in kind (though different in degree) amongst all living creatures. This instinct, therefore, because it annihilates all distinctions, and degrades the greatest of men to the level of "the poor beetle that we tread on," exhibits human nature in its most abject and humiliating attitude. Such an attitude would little suit the purposes of the poet. What then must he do? He must throw the interest on the murderer. Our sympathy must be with *him* (of course I mean a sympathy of comprehension, a sympathy by which we enter into his feelings, and are made to understand them—not a sympathy of pity or approbation). In the murdered person all strife of thought, all flux and reflux of passion and of purpose, are crushed by one overwhelming panic; the fear of instant death smites him "with its petrific mace."[4] But in the murderer, such a murderer as a poet will condescend to, there must be raging some great storm of passion—jealousy, ambition, vengeance, hatred—which will create a hell within him; and into this hell we are to look.

In *Macbeth,* for the sake of gratifying his now enormous and teeming faculty of creation, Shakespeare has introduced two murderers; and, as usual in his hands, they are remarkably discriminated: but—though in Macbeth the strife of mind is greater than in his wife, the tiger spirit not so awake, and his feelings caught chiefly by contagion from her—yet, as both were finally involved in the guilt of murder, the murderous mind of necessity is finally to be presumed in both.

[4] **petrific:** petrifying. From Milton's *Paradise Lost,* X, 293.

This was to be expressed; and on its own account, as well as to make it a more proportionable antagonist to the unoffending nature of their victim, "the gracious Duncan," and adequately to expound "the deep damnation of his taking off," this was to be expressed with peculiar energy. We were to be made to feel that the human nature—i.e., the divine nature of love and mercy, spread through the hearts of all creatures, and seldom utterly withdrawn from man—was gone, vanished, extinct, and that the fiendish nature had taken its place. And, as this effect is marvelously accomplished in the *dialogues* and *soliloquies* themselves, so it is finally consummated by the expedient under consideration; and it is to this that I now solicit the reader's attention. If the reader has ever witnessed a wife, daughter, or sister, in a fainting fit, he may chance to have observed that the most affecting moment in such a spectacle is *that* in which a sign and a stirring announce the recommencement of suspended life. Or, if the reader has ever been present in a vast metropolis on the day when some great national idol was carried in funeral pomp to his grave, and, chancing to walk near the course through which it passed, has felt powerfully, in the silence and desertion of the streets and in the stagnation of ordinary business, the deep interest which at that moment was possessing the heart of man—if all at once he should hear the death-like stillness broken up by the sound of wheels rattling away from the scene, and making known that the transitory vision was dissolved, he will be aware that at no moment was his sense of the complete suspension and pause in ordinary human concerns so full and affecting as at that moment when the suspension ceases, and the goings-on of human life are suddenly resumed. All action in any direction is best expounded, measured, and made apprehensible, by reaction. Now apply this to the case in *Macbeth*. Here, as I have said, the retiring of the human heart and the entrance of the fiendish heart was to be expressed and made sensible. Another world has stepped in; and the murderers are taken out of the region of human things, human purposes, human desires. They are transfigured: Lady Macbeth is "unsexed"; Macbeth has forgot that he was born of woman; both are conformed to the image of devils; and the world of devils is suddenly revealed. But how shall this be conveyed and made palpable? In order that a new world may step in, this world must for a time disappear. The murderers, and the murder, must be insulated—cut off by an immeasurable gulf from the ordinary tide and succession of human affairs—locked up and sequestered in some deep recess; we must be made sensible that the world of ordinary life is suddenly arrested—laid asleep—tranced—racked into a dread armistice; time must be annihilated; relation to things without abolished; and all must pass self-withdrawn into a deep syncope and suspension of earthly passion. Hence it is that, when the deed is done, when the work of darkness is perfect, then the world of darkness passes away like a pageantry in the clouds: the knocking at the gate is heard, and it makes known audibly that the reaction has commenced; the human has made its reflux upon the fiendish: the pulses of life are beginning to beat again; and the reestablishment of the goings-on of the world in which we live first makes us profoundly sensible of the awful parenthesis that had suspended them.

O mighty poet! Thy works are not as those of other men, simply and merely great works of art, but are also like the phenomena of nature, like the sun and the sea, the stars and the flowers, like frost and snow, rain and dew, hail-storm and thunder, which are to be studied with entire submission of our own faculties, and in the perfect faith that in them there can be no too much or too little, nothing useless or inert, but that, the farther we press in our discoveries, the more we shall see proofs of design and self-supporting arrangement where the careless eye had seen nothing but accident!

For Discussion

1. This essay is one of the most famous of the Romantic criticisms on Shakespeare. What effect was produced in De Quincey by the knocking on the gate? What is the relationship between the meaning of the second paragraph and that of the first paragraph? What distinction does De Quincey make between understanding and feeling?
2. The murder committed by J. Williams helps to prove that the knocking by the porter "reflected back upon the murderer a peculiar awfulness and a depth of solemnity." What does De Quincey mean by "sympathy"? Why, according to De Quincey, must the poet "throw the interest on the murderer"?
3. What does De Quincey mean by "all action in any direction is best expounded, measured, and made apprehensible by reaction"? Why is this statement pivotal to his theory on the murder?
4. How exactly does the knocking at the gate indicate that "the human has made its reflux upon the fiendish"? Do you think—and feel—that this explanation is valid? Discuss.
5. Is the final paragraph of this essay a considered critical judgment or do you think that it overly stresses feeling? Discuss the relationship which De Quincey establishes between the truth of nature and the truth of art. Is this a typical Romantic characteristic?
6. De Quincey tends to digress in his work. Point out examples of digression in this essay. Do they detract from the meaning and effectiveness of the essay or add to it? Discuss.

For Composition

1. Write a theme in which you discuss the dramatic relationship between suspense and humor in a play, motion picture, or television program you have recently seen.
2. Write a theme in which you explore how the truth of a particular work of literature has been substantiated by actual experience.

VICTORIAN PROSE WRITERS

England during the Victorian Period was at the height of her power as a world leader both politically and economically. This was the time when the sun never set on the British Empire. This was the period of great nationalistic pride, of staggering material progress, of great advances in science and industry. However, it was also a period which called into question some of the fundamental principles and values upon which English life was built, a period of social unrest, of crass self-interest, of exploitation of the poor and the working classes. Such conflict, of course, is almost inevitable in an age which compressed the accomplishments of centuries into a span of less than seventy years.

Popularly used, the word "Victorian" connotes for many people a smug, prudish society which inflicted upon the world ornately gaudy architecture, sentimentalized painting, overstuffed furniture, and sternly Puritanical attitudes toward life and sex. Certainly, it was a sober age. The country as a whole followed the example of the court where Victoria and her husband, Prince Albert, gave an image of utter respectability, close family ties, and strict morality.

To overemphasize this side of Victorian life is to miss the great variety of the life of the times and to ignore the great issues which went deep into the lives of the Victorian people. One of the major causes of unrest was the Industrial Revolution that had been at work for a long time, transforming the lives of millions of the people. While the industrialization of England brought material progress, it also brought misery. The hundred thousand looms that rapidly replaced handcraftsmen put hundreds of thousands of men out of work, sending them wandering through the country. Industrialization had the evil effects of creating the "dark Satanic mills" and the dark slums which caused further misery, hardship, and degradation. Work went on sixteen hours a day, seven days a week. For the poor there was no English Sunday.

While the poor suffered under these conditions, the capitalists and merchants grew wealthy and surrounded themselves with material comforts. They were justified in the selfishness of their pursuits not only by the concept of laissez-faire or free trade, but also by the doctrines of Utilitarianism. This was the name given to a theory first set forth by Jeremy Bentham, which taught that all law ought to be directed toward happiness and that the best law gives the greatest happiness to the greatest number. The bourgeois employers applied this theory very much to themselves, and thus were encouraged in their self-interest.

Some reform had of course been made. The Reform Bill of 1832 had succeeded in giving the vote to the lower middle class and in abolishing unequal representation in Parliament. Labor unions were slowly coming into existence; attempts were made to raise the educational level of the poor and to extend to them the franchise. There was undeniable, if localized, prosperity and definite progress based on technological advances and scientific discoveries. The prosperity and the political and social reforms that had been accomplished lulled the less perceptive Victorians into a smug and self-satisfied complacency that progress was assured and that problems were well on the way to solution. Yet underneath the surface were deep issues that caused great unrest and occupied to a great degree the writers and thinkers of the period.

The great scientific achievements of the age, celebrated in the Crystal Palace Exhibition in London in 1851, created serious intellectual and religious problems. Lyell's work in geology and Darwin's *Origin of Species* and *Descent of Man*, which put forth the theory of the evolution of man and questioned the validity of the Biblical story of creation, rocked the religious stability of the country.

Utilitarianism and Deism further deepened the raging religious controversies. The worldliness among the clergy of the Established Church weakened religious observance. Around the middle of the century, the Oxford Movement, launched by a group of zealous High Church Anglicans, attempted to revitalize the religious fervor of the English people. Although many of the leaders of the movement, including John Henry Newman, became Roman Catholics as a result of their investigations, the movement itself helped to make clear to Anglican Churchmen that they must concern themselves with the problems of a changing world.

The Victorian writers wrote for the middle class fireside public, the group which held the political power under the constitutional monarchy. They attempted to refine the tastes of the merchant class which believed that ostentatious display of wealth was good for art and architecture. The problem of education was continually debated in the press, particularly as it concerned the relationship between science and the classics. Fiction in all forms, from the "penny dreadfuls" to the novels of the great masters of the form, was available in inexpensive editions for a ready market. Sensing the pressing moral problems of the age, the Victorian writers turned to a didactic prose as the means to educate the masses and to combat the spread of materialistic values. Although some fine poetry was produced, the Victorian Age was an age of great prose writers. Outstanding among them are Macaulay, Carlyle, Arnold, Newman, and Stevenson.

Thomas Babington Macaulay was as much a literary man as he was a historian. He conceived of history as "philosophy teaching by examples" and said, in his essay "History," that the "perfect historian must possess an imagination sufficiently powerful to make his narrative affecting and picturesque." Certainly, as a historian Macaulay had a good general comprehension of the forces which mold history; as a writer of vivid and compelling prose, he stands as a man who helped popularize the art of history.

His major work, *History of England,* shows Macaulay at his best—and his worst. A firm believer in the natural progress of society and in the political institutions of Great Britain in their historical continuity, he presented an eloquent and nationalistic narrative. Proud of his time, Macaulay had gathered facts to prove that the increase in wealth, population, power, and the spread of knowledge meant, of necessity, that life must be better than it had been in the past. Professional historians have attacked Macaulay for this tendency, for although the glorification of the present appealed to the self-interest of the rising middle class, it gave little in the way of an objective evaluation of the time. However, as the epitome of the spirit of Imperial England—the man of honor assured of the rightness of progress—Macaulay is the man "in whose work the character and spirit of an age is exhibited in miniature."

Thomas Carlyle was perhaps the most significant of the literary men of his age, an independent and turbulent man who exerted a strong moral force on the Victorians. His was a warring battle against the complacency and hypocrisy of the time; *quackery* and *cant* were the words he used to describe the cliché thinking and pretentious orations of the Victorians satisfied with themselves and with the state of the nation. With all the vehemence of a Biblical prophet, Carlyle enunciated a doctrine of work and duty under the leadership of his "hero," the true aristocrat.

His fame was firmly established by the *History of the French Revolution,* an exciting and dramatic work which presented history as a series of great scenes. His purpose was both social and political. He showed how the revolutionary leaders failed to carry out their social duties, and how the aristocracy was supplanted by unscrupulous merchants, bankers, and industrialists who ignored the needs of the people. Carlyle, an aristocratic radical, had little sympathy for democratic ideals, maintaining that the only right the ordinary man has is the right to be well governed.

In *Past and Present,* a topical book written during the period of agricultural and labor unrest, he maintained that rule should be in the hands of an exceptional man or hero. In his own age, he looked for a new aristocracy of industrial leaders to replace the decadent and ineffectual landed gentry.

In all his prose writings, Matthew Arnold, a staunch opponent of the materialism of the "populace, Philistines, and barbarians," advocated an approach to life based upon culture and education.

His major literary criticism is to be found in *On Translating Homer, The Study of Celtic Literature,* and the volumes of *Essays in Criticism.* He looked upon literature, "the best that has been thought and said," as the means of overcoming the narrow provincialism of the complacent Victorians, whom he called Philistines. He placed a high moral value on literature, stressing its "high seriousness" and its function as a "criticism of life."

His social criticism was based on much the same persuasive order as was his literary criticism, and was an outgrowth of it. In *Culture and Anarchy,* he forcefully recommended the spread of culture through education to prevent anarchy. Culture, in his usage, was the desire for perfection and the wish to see reason and the will of God prevail for all; it was not the province of the few. The ideal of "sweetness and light" was not a means for doing as one liked but a way to rid the country of the pettiness of class distinctions, a way to bring a system of values to a time too concerned with materialism.

John Henry Newman was a leading figure in the Oxford Movement which shook the foundations of the Anglican Church. Later, as a Roman Catholic priest and cardinal, he was to be a leading figure in what was termed the Catholic

Literary Revival. His was an eloquent and persuasive voice advocating traditional values to combat the spread of materialism.

Although his writings include poetry, historical novels, essays, and sermons, Newman is best known today for two works: *Apologia pro Vita Sua* and *The Idea of a University*. The former is a defense of his religious conversion written in direct and straightforward language. It is one man's account of his own confrontation of the problem of belief and has rightly been termed one of the greatest spiritual autobiographies in the world.

The Idea of a University was originally a series of lectures given in Dublin when the bishops of Ireland were attempting to found a Catholic university. Although the university never succeeded, the lectures Newman delivered stand as a classic statement in defense of a liberal education.

The prose works of Robert Louis Stevenson seem almost alien to the world of the polemical prose writers, but they were a vital part of the world of the Victorian reading public. As a poet, an essayist, a short story writer, and a novelist, Stevenson reminded his readers of the spirit of romance and adventure which has intrigued man in all periods of history. Moreover, the popularity of his fiction attested to a reading public anxious for good fiction.

Stevenson helped to popularize the short story form in England. Influenced by the writings of Edgar Allan Poe, he wrote stories filled with mystery and terror. These same traits are essential ingredients in the great juvenile adventure novels, *Treasure Island* and *Kidnapped*. In works like *The Strange Case of Dr. Jekyll and Mr. Hyde* and *The Master of Ballantrae* he exhibits the tendency for analysis and character probing which is the dominant interest in modern fiction.

Thomas Babington Macaulay

(1800–1859)

Although he is today most remembered as one of the great amateur historians, Thomas Babington Macaulay also wrote essays, biographies, literary criticism, and book reviews. He saw history as a colorful and exciting pageant. His major historical work, the five-volume *History of England,* is as swift-moving as a novel; its characters and details are as alive as those in a play.

One of the great prose stylists in English literature, Macaulay achieved his effects through sharply dramatic contrasts and paradoxes expressed in elaborate parallelisms. This is done with an energy and graphic quality that is reminiscent of the style of the orator. His work stands as a prime example of his own principle that the art of history is "the art of interesting the affections and presenting pictures of the imagination."

LONDON COFFEEHOUSES

The coffeehouse must not be dismissed with a cursory mention. It might indeed at that time have been not improperly called a most important political institution. No Parliament had sat for years. The municipal council of the city had ceased to speak the sense of the citizens. Public meetings, harangues, resolutions, and the rest of the modern machinery of agitation had not yet come into fashion. Nothing resembling the modern newspaper existed. In such circumstances the coffeehouses were the chief organs through which the public opinion of the metropolis vented itself.

The first of these establishments had been set up, in the time of the Commonwealth, by a Turkey merchant, who had acquired among the Mohammedans a taste for their favorite beverage. The convenience of being able to make appointments in any part of the town, and of being able to pass evenings socially at a very small charge, was so great that the fashion spread fast. Every man of the upper or middle class went daily to his coffeehouse to learn the news and to discuss it. Every coffeehouse had one or more orators to whose eloquence the crowd listened with admiration, and who soon became what the journalists of our own time have been called, a fourth Estate of the realm. The court had long seen with uneasiness the growth of this new power in the state. An attempt had been made, during Danby's administration,[1] to close the coffeehouses. But men of all parties missed their usual places of resort so much that there was an universal outcry. The government did not venture, in opposition to a feeling so strong and general, to enforce a regulation of which the legality might well be questioned. Since that time ten years had elapsed, and during those years the number and influence of the coffeehouses had been constantly increasing. Foreigners remarked that the coffeehouse was that which especially distinguished London from all other cities; that the coffeehouse was the Londoner's home, and that those who wished to find a gentleman commonly asked, not whether he lived in Fleet Street or Chancery Lane, but whether he frequented the Grecian or the Rainbow. Nobody was excluded from these places who laid down his penny at the bar. Yet every rank and profession, and every shade of religious and political opinion, had its own headquarters. There were houses near Saint James' Park where fops congregated, their heads and shoulders covered with black or flaxen wigs, not less ample than those which are now worn by the Chancellor and by the Speaker of the House of Commons. The wig came from Paris; and so did the rest of the fine gentleman's orna-

[1] **Danby's administration:** during the reign of Charles II

ments, his embroidered coat, his fringed gloves, and the tassel which upheld his pantaloons. The conversation was in that dialect which, long after it had ceased to be spoken in fashionable circles, continued, in the mouth of Lord Foppington,[2] to excite the mirth of theaters. The atmosphere was like that of a perfumer's shop. Tobacco in any other form than that of richly scented snuff was held in abomination. If any clown, ignorant of the usages of the house, called for a pipe, the sneers of the whole assembly and the short answers of the waiters soon convinced him that he had better go somewhere else. Nor, indeed, would he have had far to go. For, in general, the coffeerooms reeked with tobacco like a guardroom; and strangers sometimes expressed their surprise that so many people should leave their own firesides to sit in the midst of eternal fog and stench.

Nowhere was the smoking more constant that at Will's. That celebrated house, situated between Covent Garden and Bow Street, was sacred to polite letters. There the talk was about poetical justice and the unities of place and time. There was a faction for Perrault and the moderns, a faction for Boileau [3] and the ancients. One group debated whether *Paradise Lost* ought not to have been in rhyme. To another an envious poetaster demonstrated that *Venice Preserved* [4] ought to have been hooted from the stage. Under no roof was a greater variety of figures to be seen. There were earls in stars and garters, clergymen in cassocks and bands, pert Templars,[5] sheepish lads from the universities, translators and index makers in ragged coats of frieze.[6] The great press was to get near the chair where John Dryden sat. In winter that chair was always in the warmest nook by the fire; in summer it stood in the balcony. To bow to the Laureate, and to hear his

[2] **Lord Foppington:** one of the characters in Vanbrugh's play, *The Relapse*
[3] **Boileau:** French writer. During the 17th century the writers quarreled as to whether the ancient or the modern writers were superior.
[4] **Venice Preserved:** play by Thomas Otway
[5] **Templars:** name given to lawyers and students who lived in the Temple, a section of London owned in medieval times by Knights Templar
[6] **frieze:** coarse woolen fabric

opinion of Racine's [7] last tragedy or of Bossu's [8] treatise on epic poetry, was thought a privilege. A pinch from his snuffbox was an honor sufficient to turn the head of a young enthusiast. There were coffeehouses where the first medical men might be consulted. Doctor John Radcliffe, who, in the year 1685, rose to the largest practice in London, came daily, at the hour when the Exchange was full, from his house in Bow Street, then a fashionable part of the capital, to Garaway's, and was to be found, surrounded by surgeons and apothecaries, at a particular table. There were Puritan coffeehouses where no oath was heard, and where lank-haired men discussed election and reprobation through their noses; Jew coffeehouses where dark-eyed money-changers from Venice and from Amsterdam greeted each other; and Popish coffeehouses where, as good Protestants believed, Jesuits planned, over their cups, another great fire, and cast silver bullets to shoot the King.

These gregarious habits had no small share in forming the character of the Londoner of that age. He was, indeed, a different being from the rustic Englishman. There was not then the intercourse which now exists between the two classes. Only very great men were in the habit of dividing the year between town and country. Few esquires came to the capital thrice in their lives. Nor was it yet the practice of all citizens in easy circumstances to breathe the fresh air of the fields and woods during some weeks of every summer. A cockney, in a rural village, was stared at as much as if he had intruded into a kraal [9] of Hottentots. On the other hand, when the Lord of a Lincolnshire or Shropshire manor appeared in Fleet Street, he was as easily distinguished from the resident population as a Turk or a lascar.[10] His dress, his gait, his accent, the manner in which he stared at the shops, stumbled into the gutters, ran against the porters, and stood under the

[7] **Racine:** one of the leading French playwrights of the 17th century
[8] **Bossu:** French critic
[9] **kraal:** village of huts built within a stockade
[10] **lascar:** a sailor of East India

waterspouts, marked him out as an excellent subject for the operations of swindlers and banterers. Bullies jostled him into the kennel. Hackney coachmen splashed him from head to foot. Thieves explored with perfect security the huge pockets of his horseman's coat, while he stood entranced by the splendor of the Lord Mayor's show. Money droppers, sore from the cart's tail,[11] introduced themselves to him, and appeared to him the most honest, friendly gentlemen that he had ever seen. Painted women, the refuse of Lewkner Lane and Whetstone Park, passed themselves on him for countesses and maids of honor. If he asked his way to Saint James', his informants sent him to Mile End.[12] If he went into a shop, he was instantly discerned to be a fit purchaser of everything that nobody else would buy, of secondhand embroidery, copper rings, and watches that would not go. If he rambled into any fashionable coffeehouse, he became a mark for the insolent derision of fops and the grave waggery of Templars. Enraged and mortified, he soon returned to his mansion, and there, in the homage of his tenants, and the conversation of his boon companions, found consolation for the vexations and humiliations which he had undergone. There he was once more a great man, and saw nothing above himself except when at the assizes[13] he took his seat on the bench, near the Judge, or when at the muster of the militia he saluted the Lord Lieutenant.

[11] **cart's tail:** thieves were dragged through the streets, tied to a cart
[12] **Mile End:** a poor district in London
[13] **assizes:** sessions of judges of the superior courts in every county of England

For Discussion

1. What, according to Macaulay, was the prime function of the coffeehouse in the seventeenth century? What was the attitude of the court toward the coffeehouses? Why?
2. How does Macaulay capture the spirit of the different coffeehouses and the people who frequented them? What topics were discussed in the various houses?
3. What was the attitude of the Londoners toward the "rustic

Englishman"? What does this reveal about the Londoners? How do the details help to evoke the feeling of the city?
4. As an example of Macaulay's style, look back at the paragraph beginning "Nowhere was the smoking . . ." on page 220. How does he use the technique of balanced sentences and antithesis to develop the idea of this paragraph?

LONDON STREETS

The position of London, relatively to the other towns of the empire, was, in the time of Charles II, far higher than at present. For at present the population of London is little more than six times the population of Manchester[1] or of Liverpool.[2] In the days of Charles II the population of London was more than seventeen times the population of Bristol or of Norwich. It may be doubted whether any other instance can be mentioned of a great kingdom in which the first city was more than seventeen times as large as the second. There is reason to believe that in 1685 London had been, during about half a century, the most populous capital in Europe. The inhabitants, who are now at least nineteen hundred thousand, were then probably little more than half a million. . . .

We should greatly err if we were to suppose that any of the streets and squares then bore the same aspect as at present. The great majority of the houses, indeed, have, since that time, been wholly, or in great part, rebuilt. If the most fashionable parts of the capital could be placed before us, such as they then were, we should be disgusted by their squalid appearance, and poisoned by their noisome atmosphere. In Covent Garden[3] a filthy and noisy market was held close to the dwellings of the great. Fruit women screamed, carters fought, cabbage stalks and rotten apples accumulated in heaps at the thresholds of the Countess of Berkshire and of the Bishop of Durham.

---
[1] **Manchester:** cotton manufacturing center in western England
[2] **Liverpool:** shipping port on the west coast of England
[3] **Covent Garden:** London's largest fruit and flower market

The center of Lincoln's Inn Fields [4] was an open space where the rabble congregated every evening, within a few yards of Cardigan House and Winchester House, to hear mountebanks harangue, to see bears dance, and to set dogs at oxen. Rubbish was shot in every part of the area. Horses were exercised there. The beggars were as noisy and importunate as in the worst-governed cities of the Continent. A Lincoln's Inn mumper [5] was a proverb. The whole fraternity knew the arms and liveries of every charitably disposed grandee in the neighborhood, and, as soon as his lordship's coach and six appeared, came hopping and crawling in crowds to persecute him. These disorders lasted, in spite of many accidents, and of some legal proceedings, till, in the reign of George II, Sir Joseph Jekyll, Master of the Rolls, was knocked down and nearly killed in the middle of the square. Then at length palisades were set up, and a pleasant garden laid out.

Saint James' Square was a receptacle for all the offal and cinders, for all the dead cats and dead dogs of Westminster. At one time a cudgel player kept the ring there. At another time an impudent squatter settled himself there, and built a shed for rubbish under the windows of the gilded saloons in which the first magnates of the realm, Norfolk, Ormond, Kent, and Pembroke, gave banquets and balls. It was not till these nuisances had lasted through a whole generation, and till much had been written about them, that the inhabitants applied to Parliament for permission to put up rails, and to plant trees.

When such was the state of the region inhabited by the most luxurious portion of society, we may easily believe that the great body of the population suffered what would now be considered as insupportable grievances. The pavement was detestable; all foreigners cried shame upon it. The drainage was so bad that in rainy weather the gutters soon became torrents. Several facetious poets have commemorated the

[4] **Lincoln's Inn Fields:** a square in London around which are located lawyers' offices
[5] **mumper:** beggar

fury with which these black rivulets roared down Snow Hill and Ludgate Hill, bearing to Fleet Ditch a vast tribute of animal and vegetable filth from the stalls of butchers and greengrocers. This flood was profusely thrown to right and left by coaches and carts. To keep as far from the carriage road as possible was therefore the wish of every pedestrian. The mild and timid gave the wall. The bold and athletic took it. If two roisterers met, they cocked their hats in each other's faces and pushed each other about till the weaker was shoved toward the kennel.[6] If he was a mere bully he sneaked off, muttering that he should find a time. If he was pugnacious, the encounter probably ended in a duel behind Montague House.

The houses were not numbered. There would indeed have been little advantage in numbering them; for of the coachmen, chairmen,[7] porters, and errand boys of London, a very small proportion could read. It was necessary to use marks which the most ignorant could understand. The shops were therefore distinguished by painted or sculptured signs, which gave a gay and grotesque aspect to the streets. The walk from Charing Cross to Whitechapel lay through an endless succession of Saracens' Heads, Royal Oaks, Blue Bears, and Golden Lambs, which disappeared when they were no longer required for the direction of the common people.

When the evening closed in, the difficulty and danger of walking about London became serious indeed. The garret windows were opened, and pails were emptied, with little regard to those who were passing below. Falls, bruises, and broken bones were of constant occurrence. For, till the last year of the reign of Charles II, most of the streets were left in profound darkness. Thieves and robbers plied their trade with impunity; yet they were hardly so terrible to peaceable citizens as another class of ruffians. It was a favorite amusement of dissolute young gentlemen to swagger by night about

[6] **kennel:** street gutter
[7] **chairmen:** men employed to carry a person in a sedan chair, a wheelless vehicle much used in the 17th and 18th centuries

the town, breaking windows, upsetting sedans, beating quiet men, and offering rude caresses to pretty women. Several dynasties of these tyrants had, since the Restoration, domineered over the streets. The Muns and Tityre Tus had given place to the Hectors, and the Hectors had been recently succeeded by the Scourers. At a later period rose the Nicker, the Hawcubite, and the yet more dreaded name of Mohawk. The machinery for keeping the peace was utterly contemptible. There was an act of Common Council which provided that more than a thousand watchmen should be constantly on the alert in the city, from sunset to sunrise, and that every inhabitant should take his turn of duty. But this act was negligently executed. Few of those who were summoned left their homes; and those few generally found it more agreeable to tipple in alehouses than to pace the streets. . . .

For Discussion

1. In this essay Macaulay uses the description of the streets of London to indicate the values held by some of the people of the seventeenth century. What is the condition of Covent Garden, Lincoln's Inn Fields, and Saint James' Square? Is Macaulay justified in the inference he draws from this? Discuss.
2. Why were the houses not numbered? What difficulties faced the city dweller at night? What was the state of the "machinery for keeping the peace"?
3. What does this short selection tell us about the attitude of the seventeenth-century Londoner toward the physical welfare of the citizens and the beauty of the city?

For Composition

1. Based on what you have learned about London from the two selections, write a description of the city from the point of view of a rustic squire seeing it for the first time.
2. Using some of the parallelism that characterizes Macaulay's style, write a short description of a typical street in your city or town.

Thomas Carlyle

(1795–1881)

Thomas Carlyle stands as one of the great men of letters, a historian and essayist who attacked the selfish individualism of the Victorian period and the placing of personal pleasure over social duty. He viewed history as the record of great men; "all things that we see standing accomplished in the world are properly the outer material result, the practical realization and embodiment of Thoughts that dwelt in the Great Men sent into the world; the soul of the whole world's history, it may be justly considered, were the history of these." The concept of the hero was Carlyle's hope for the progress of the world; he sought an aristocracy of talent which would lead all men to their proper duty. This emphasis on the worth of the individual was further developed in *Heroes and Hero-Worship,* in much of his literary criticism, and in his philosophy of history. The "hero" becomes a creative personality molding and shaping his age and serving as the guide for the masses.

Although Carlyle as historian is not always reliable, he is a master of the art of history by "lightning flashes." Bewildering at first by its noisy and emphatic language, by its explosive exclamations, by its tangled syntax, and by the multiplicity of Biblical and literary allusions, the writing succeeds in capturing the mood and spirit of the historical moment. Read aloud, as Carlyle probably would have wanted it to be read, it has the energy and vitality of the reformer indignantly declaiming against materialism, greed, stupidity, and pettiness.

STORMING THE BASTILLE

The Bastille [1] is besieged!

On, then, all Frenchmen, that have hearts in your bodies! Roar with all your throats, of cartilage and metal, ye sons of liberty; stir spasmodically whatsoever of utmost faculty is in you, soul, body, or spirit; for it is the hour! Smite, thou Louis Tournay, cartwright of the Marais, old soldier of the Regiment Dauphiné; [2] smite at the Outer Drawbridge chain, though the fiery hail whistles round thee! Never, over nave or felloe [3] did thy axe strike such a stroke. Down with it, man; down with it to Orcus [4]: let the whole accursed edifice sink thither, and tyranny be swallowed up forever! Mounted, some say, on the roof of the guard-room, some "on bayonets stuck into joints of the wall," Louis Tournay smites, brave Aubin Bonnemère (also an old soldier) seconding him: the chain yields, breaks; the huge drawbridge slams down, thundering (*avec fracas*). Glorious: and yet, alas, it is still but the outworks. The Eight grim Towers, with their Invalide [5] musketry, their paving stones and cannon-mouths, still soar aloft intact;—Ditch yawning impassable, stone-faced; the inner Drawbridge with its *back* towards us: the Bastille is still to take!

To describe this Siege of the Bastille (thought to be one of the most important in History) perhaps transcends the talents of mortals. Could one but, after infinite reading, get to understand so much as the plan of the building! But there is open Esplanade, at the end of the Rue Saint-Antoine; there are such Forecourts, *Cour Avancé, Cour de l'Orme,* arched Gateway (where Louis Tournay now fights); then new drawbridges,

---

[1] **Bastille:** French state prison, stormed by mobs in Paris on July 14, 1789
[2] **Regiment Dauphiné:** Regiment of the Dauphin or King's son
[3] **felloe:** exterior rim or segment of the rim of a wheel
[4] **Orcus:** the Underworld in Roman mythology
[5] **Invalide:** veteran

dormant-bridges, rampart-bastions, and the grim Eight Towers; a labyrinthic Mass, high-frowning there, of all ages from twenty years to four hundred and twenty;—beleaguered, in this its last hour, as we said, by mere Chaos come again! Ordnance of all calibers; throats of all capacities; men of all plans, every man his own engineer: seldom since the war of Pygmies and Cranes was there seen so anomalous a thing. Half-pay Elie is home for a suit of regimentals; no one would heed him in colored clothes: half-pay Hulin is haranguing Gardes Françaises in the Palace de Grève. Frantic Patriots pick up the grapeshots; bear them, still hot (or seemingly so), to the Hôtel-de-Ville:—Paris, you perceive, is to be burnt! Flesselles is "pale to the very lips"; for the roar of the multitude grows deep. Paris wholly has got to the acme of its frenzy; whirled, all ways, by panic madness. At every street-barricade, there were whirls simmering a minor whirlpool,—strengthening the barricade, since God knows what is coming; and all minor whirlpools play distractedly into that grand Fire-Mahlstrom which is lashing round the Bastile.

And so it lashes and it roars. Cholat the wine-merchant has become an impromptu cannoneer. See Georget, of the Marine Service, fresh from Brest [6] ply the King of Siam's cannon. Singular (if we were not used to the like): Georget lay, last night, taking his ease at his inn; the King of Siam's cannon also lay, knowing nothing of *him*, for a hundred years. Yet now, at the right instant, they have got together, and discourse eloquent music. For, hearing what was toward, Georget sprang from the Brest Diligence, and ran. Gardes Françaises [7] also will be here, with real artillery: were not the walls so thick!—Upwards from the Esplanade, horizontally from all neighboring roofs and windows, flashes one irregular deluge of musketry, without effect. The Invalides lie flat, firing comparatively at their ease from behind stone; hardly through portholes, show the tip of a nose. We fall, shot; and make no impression!

[6] **Brest:** French seaport   [7] **Gardes Françaises:** French guards

Let conflagration rage; of whatsoever is combustible! Guardrooms are burnt, Invalides messrooms. A distracted "Peruke-maker with two fiery torches" is for burning "the saltpeters of the arsenal";—had not a woman run screaming; had not a Patriot, with some tincture of Natural Philosophy, instantly struck the wind out of him (butt of musket on pit of stomach), overturned barrels, and stayed the devouring element. A young beautiful lady, seized escaping in these Outer Courts, and thought falsely to be De Launay's [8] daughter, shall be burnt in De Launay's sight; she lies swooned on a paillasse [9]: but again a Patriot, it is brave Aubin Bonnemère the old soldier, dashes in, and rescues her. Straw is burnt; three cartloads of it, hauled thither, go up in white smoke: almost to the choking of Patriotism itself; so that Elie had, with singed brows, to drag back one cart; and Réole the "gigantic haberdasher" another. Smoke as of Tophet; [10] confusion as of Babel; noise as of the Crack of Doom!

Blood flows; the aliment of new madness. The wounded are carried into houses of the Rue Cerisaie; the dying leave their last mandate not to yield till the accursed Stronghold fall. And yet, alas, how fall? The walls are so thick! Deputations, three in number, arrive from the Hôtel-de-Ville; Abbé Fauchet (who was of one) can say, with what almost superhuman courage of benevolence. These wave their Town-flag in the arched Gateway; and stand, rolling their drum; but to no purpose. In such Crack of Doom, De Launay cannot hear them, dare not believe them: they return, with justified rage, the whew of lead still singing in their ears. What to do? The Firemen are here, squirting with their fire pumps on the Invalides cannon, to wet the touchholes; they unfortunately cannot squirt so high; but produce only clouds of spray. Individuals of classical knowledge propose *catapults*. Santerre,[11] the sonorous Brewer of the Suburb Saint-Antoine, advises

---

[8] **De Launay:** governor of the Bastille who was killed after its capture
[9] **paillasse:** straw bed
[10] **Tophet:** places outside Jerusalem where refuse is burned, therefore, "Hell"
[11] **Santerre:** leader of Parisian revolutionary mob

rather that the place be fired by a "mixture of phosphorus and oil-of-turpentine spouted up through forcing pumps": O Spinola-Santerre,[12] hast thou the mixture *ready*? Every man his own engineer! And still the fire-deluge abates not: even women are firing, and Turks; at least one woman (with her sweetheart), and one Turk. Gardes Françaises have come: real cannon, real cannoneers. Usher Maillard is busy; half-pay Elie, half-pay Hulin rage in the midst of thousands.

How the great Bastille Clock ticks (inaudible) in its Inner Court there, at its ease, hour after hour; as if nothing special, for it or the world, were passing! It tolled One when the firing began; and is now pointing towards Five, and still the firing slakes not.—Far down, in their vaults, the seven Prisoners hear muffled din as of earthquakes; their Turnkeys answer vaguely.

Woe to thee, De Launay, with thy poor hundred Invalides! Broglie is distant, and his ears heavy: Besenval hears, but can send no help. One poor troop of Hussars has crept, reconnoitering, cautiously along the Quais, as far as Pont Neuf. "We are come to join you," said the Captain, for the crowd seems shoreless. A large-headed dwarfish individual, of smoke-bleared aspect, shambles forward, opening his blue lips, for there is sense in him; and croaks: "Alight then, and give up your arms!" The Hussar-Captain is too happy to be escorted to the Barriers, and dismissed on parole. Who the squat individual was? Men answer, It is M. Marat, author of the excellent pacific *Avis au Peuple!* Great truly, O thou remarkable Dogleech, is this thy day of emergence and new-birth: and yet this same day come four years—!—But let the curtains of the Future hang.

What shall De Launay do? One thing only De Launay could have done: what he said he would do. Fancy him sitting, from the first, with lighted taper, within arm's length of the Powder-Magazine; motionless, like old Roman Senator, or

---

[12] **Spinola-Santerre:** Santerre is compared with an Italian general Spinola who captured a fortress in Holland in 1625.

Bronze Lamp-holder; coldly apprising Thuriot, and all men, by a slight motion of his eye, what his resolution was:—Harmless, he sat there, while unharmed; but the King's Fortress, meanwhile, could, might, would, or should, in nowise be surrendered, save to the King's Messenger: one old man's life is worthless, so it be lost with honor; but think, ye brawling *canaille*,[13] how will it be when a whole Bastille springs skyward!—In such statuesque, taper-holding attitude, one fancies De Launay might have left Thuriot, the Red Clerks of the Basoche, Curé of Saint-Stephen and all the tagrag-and-bobtail of the world, to work their will.

And yet, withal, he could not do it. Hast thou considered how each man's heart is so tremulously responsive to the hearts of all men; hast thou noted how omnipotent is the very sound of many men? How their shriek of indignation palsies the strong soul; their howl of contumely withers with unfelt pangs? The Ritter Gluck confessed that the ground-tone of the noblest passage, in one of his noblest Operas, was the voice of the Populace he had heard at Vienna, crying to their Kaiser: Bread! Bread! Great is the combined voice of men; the utterance of their *instincts,* which are truer than their thoughts: it is the greatest a man encounters, among the sounds and shadows which make up this World of Time. He who can resist that, has his footing somewhere *beyond* Time. De Launay could not do it. Distracted, he hovers between two; hopes in the middle of despair; surrenders not his Fortress; declares that he will blow it up, seizes torches to blow it up, and does not blow it. Unhappy old De Launay, it is the death-agony of thy Bastille and thee! Jail, Jailoring, and Jailor, all three, such as they may have been, must finish.

For four hours now has the World-Bedlam roared: call it the World-Chimera,[14] blowing fire! The poor Invalides have sunk under their battlements, or rise only with reversed muskets: they have made a white flag of napkins; go beating

[13] **canaille:** mob
[14] **chimera:** a mythological fire-breathing monster

the *chamade*,[15] or seeming to beat, for one can hear nothing. The very Swiss [16] at the Portcullis look weary of firing; disheartened in the fire-deluge: a porthole at the drawbridge is opened, as by one that would speak. See Hussier Maillard, the shifty man! On his plank, swinging over the abyss of that stone Ditch; plank resting on parapet, balanced by weight of Patriots,—he hovers perilous: such a Dove towards such an Ark! Deftly, thou shifty Usher: one man already fell; and lies smashed, far down there, against the masonry; Usher Maillard falls not; deftly, unerring he walks, with outspread palm. The Swiss holds a paper through his porthole; the shifty Usher snatches it, and returns. Terms of surrender: Pardon, immunity to all! Are they accepted?—*"Foi d'officier,* On the word of an officer," answers half-pay Hulin,—or half-pay Elie,—for men do not agree on it, "they are!" Sinks the drawbridge,— Usher Maillard bolting it when down; rushes-in the living deluge: the Bastille is fallen! *Victoire! La Bastille est prise!* [17]

[15] **chamade:** a drum signal for a conference between enemies
[16] **Swiss:** Swiss mercenary soldiers hired by the French
[17] **Victoire! La Bastille est prise!:** Victory! The Bastille is taken!

For Discussion

1. What is the effect of Carlyle's using a narrator to describe the taking of the Bastille? What devices of syntax does he use to convey the drama of the action?
2. To allow the reader to become immersed in the whole of this dramatic moment, Carlyle shows both sides, those attacking the Bastille and those defending it. What is the situation outside? How does this differ from the situation inside the Bastille? What is the effect of Carlyle's using the names of the people? How are their emotions conveyed?
3. What plans are devised for taking the Bastille? Why does De Launay not blow up the Bastille? What does Carlyle say about the voice of a mob?
4. Discuss the imagery which Carlyle uses to describe the spectacle, particularly the images of fire and blood.

CAPTAINS OF INDUSTRY [1]

If I believed that Mammonism with its adjuncts was to continue henceforth the one serious principle of our existence, I should reckon it idle to solicit remedial measures from any Government, the disease being insusceptible of remedy. Government can do much, but it can in no wise do all. Government, as the most conspicuous object in Society, is called upon to give signal of what shall be done; and, in many ways, to preside over, further, and command the doing of it. But the Government cannot do, by all its signalling and commanding, what the Society is radically indisposed to do. In the long-run every Government is the exact symbol of its People, with their wisdom and unwisdom; we have to say, Like People like Government.—The main substance of this immense Problem of Organising Labour and first of all of Managing the Working Classes, will, it is very clear, have to be solved by those who stand practically in the middle of it; by those who themselves work and preside over work. Of all that can be enacted by any Parliament in regard to it, the germs must already lie potentially extant in those two Classes, who are to obey such enactment. A Human Chaos *in* which there is no light, you vainly attempt to irradiate by light shed *on* it: order never can arise there.

But it is my firm conviction that the 'Hell of England' will *cease* to be that of 'not making money;' that we shall get a nobler Hell and a nobler Heaven! I anticipate light *in* the Human Chaos, glimmering, shining more and more; under manifold true signals from without That light shall shine. Our deity no longer being Mammon,—O Heavens, each man will then say to himself: "Why such deadly haste to make money? I shall not go to Hell, even if I do not make money! There is another Hell, I am told!" Competition, at railway-speed, in all branches of commerce and work will then abate: —good felt-hats for the head, in every sense, instead of seven-

[1] from *Past and Present*

feet lath-and-plaster hats on wheels, will then be discoverable! Bubble-periods,[2] with their panics and commercial crises, will again become infrequent; steady modest industry will take the place of gambling speculation. To be a noble Master, among noble Workers, will again be the first ambition with some few; to be a rich Master only the second. How the Inventive Genius of England, with the whirr of its bobbins and billy-rollers shoved somewhat into the backgrounds of the brain, will contrive and devise, not cheaper produce exclusively, but fairer distribution of the produce at its present cheapness! By degrees, we shall again have a Society with something of Heroism in it, something of Heaven's Blessing on it; we shall again have, as my German friend asserts, 'instead of Mammon-Feudalism with unsold cotton-shirts and Preservation of the Game, noble just Industrialism and Government by the Wisest!' . . .

The Leaders of Industry, if Industry is ever to be led, are virtually the Captains of the World; if there be no nobleness in them, there will never be an Aristocracy more. But let the Captains of Industry consider: once again, are they born of other clay than the old Captains of Slaughter; doomed forever to be no Chivalry, but a mere gold-plated *Doggery,*—what the French well name *Canaille,* 'Doggery' with more or less gold carrion at its disposal? Captains of Industry are the true Fighters, henceforth recognisable as the only true ones: Fighters against Chaos, Necessity and the Devils and Jötuns,[3] and lead on Mankind in that great, and alone true, and universal warfare; the stars in their courses fighting for them,[4] and all Heaven and all Earth saying audibly, Well-done! Let the Captains of Industry retire into their own hearts, and ask solemnly, If there is nothing but vulturous hunger, for fine wines, valet reputation and gilt carriages, discoverable there?

[2] A reference to the "South Sea bubble" of 1720
[3] **Jötuns:** Giants in Norse mythology
[4] Judges 5:20

Of hearts made by the Almighty God I will not believe such a thing. Deep-hidden under wretchedest godforgetting Cants, Epicurisms, Dead-Sea Apisms; forgotten as under foulest fat Lethe mud and weeds, there is yet, in all hearts born into this God's-World, a spark of the Godlike slumbering. Awake, O nightmare sleepers; awake, arise, or be forever fallen! This is not playhouse poetry; it is sober fact. Our England, our world cannot live as it is. It will connect itself with a God again, or go down with nameless throes and fire-consummation to the Devils. Thou who feelest aught of such a Godlike stirring in thee, any faintest intimation of it as through heavy-laden dreams, follow *it,* I conjure thee. Arise, save thyself, be one of those that save thy country. . . .

Love of men cannot be bought by cash-payment; and without love, men cannot endure to be together. You cannot lead a Fighting World without having it regimented, chivalried: the thing, in a day, becomes impossible; all men in it, the highest at first, the very lowest at last, discern consciously, or by a noble instinct, this necessity. And can you any more continue to lead a Working World unregimented, anarchic? I answer, and the Heavens and Earth are now answering, No! The thing becomes not 'in a day' impossible; but in some two generations it does. . . .

And there is a virtual Industrial Aristocracy as yet only half-alive, spellbound amid money-bags and ledgers; and an actual Idle Aristocracy seemingly near dead in somnolent delusions, in trespasses and double-barrels; 'sliding,' as on inclined-planes, which every new year they *soap* with new Hansard's-jargon under God's sky, and so are 'sliding' ever faster, towards a 'scale' and balance-scale whereon is written *Thou art found Wanting:* [5]—in such days, after a generation or two, I say, it does become, even to the low and simple, very palpably impossible! No Working World, any more than a Fighting World, can be led on without a noble Chivalry of Work, and laws and fixed rules which follow out of that,—far

[5] Daniel 5:27

nobler than any Chivalry of Fighting was. As an anarchic multitude on mere Supply-and-demand, it is becoming inevitable that we dwindle in horrid suicidal convulsions, and self-abrasion, frightful to the imagination, into *Chactaw* Workers. With wigwam and scalps,—with palaces and thousand-pound bills; with savagery, depopulation, chaotic desolation! Good Heavens, will not one French Revolution and Reign of Terror suffice us, but must there be two? There will be two if needed; there will be twenty if needed; there will be precisely as many as are needed. The Laws of Nature will have themselves fulfilled. That is a thing certain to me.

Your gallant battle-hosts and work-hosts, as the others did, will need to be made loyally yours; they must and will be regulated, methodically secured in their just share of conquest under you;—joined with you in veritable brotherhood, sonhood, by quite other and deeper ties than those of temporary day's wages! How would mere redcoated regiments, to say nothing of chivalries, fight for you, if you could discharge them on the evening of the battle, on payment of the stipulated shillings,—and they discharge you on the morning of it! Chelsea Hospitals,[6] pensions, promotions, rigorous lasting covenant on the one side and on the other, are indispensable even for a hired fighter. The Feudal Baron, much more,—how could he subsist with mere temporary mercenaries round him, at sixpence a day; ready to go over to the other side, if sevenpence were offered? He could not have subsisted;—and his noble instinct saved him from the necessity of even trying! The Feudal Baron had a Man's Soul in him; to which anarchy, mutiny, and the other fruits of temporary mercenaries, were intolerable: he had never been a Baron otherwise, but had continued a Chactaw and Bucanier. He felt it precious, and at last it became habitual, and his fruitful enlarged existence included it as a necessity, to have men round him who in heart loved him; whose life he watched over with rigour yet with love; who were prepared to give their life for him, if need

[6] **Chelsea Hospital:** a home for aged or disabled soldiers

came. It was beautiful; it was human! Man lives not otherwise, nor can live contented, anywhere or anywhen. Isolation is the sum-total of wretchedness to man. To be cut off, to be left solitary: to have a world alien, not your world; all a hostile camp for you; not a home at all, of hearts and faces who are yours, whose you are! It is the frightfulest enchantment; too truly a work of the Evil One. To have neither superior, nor inferior, nor equal, united manlike to you. Without father, without child, without brother. Man knows no sadder destiny. . . .

Awake, ye noble Workers, warriors in the one true war: all this must be remedied. It is you who are already half-alive, whom I will welcome into life; whom I will conjure in God's name to shake off your enchanted sleep, and live wholly! Cease to count scalps, gold-purses; not in these lies your or our salvation. Even these, if you count only these, will not long be left. Let bucaniering be put far from you; alter, speedily abrogate all laws of the bucaniers, if you would gain any victory that shall endure. Let God's justice, let pity, nobleness and manly valour, with more gold-purses or with fewer, testify themselves in this your brief Life-transit to all the Eternities, the Gods and Silences. It is to you I call; for ye are not dead, ye are already half-alive: there is in you a sleepless dauntless energy, the prime-matter of all nobleness in man. Honour to you in your kind. It is to you I call: ye know at least this, That the mandate of God to His creature man is: Work! The future Epic of the World rests not with those that are near dead, but with those that are alive, and those that are coming into life.

Look around you. Your world-hosts are all in mutiny, in confusion, destitution; on the eve of fiery wreck and madness! They will not march farther for you, on the sixpence a day and supply-and-demand principle: they will not; nor ought they, nor can they. Ye shall reduce them to order, begin reducing them. To order, to just subordination; noble loyalty in return for noble guidance. Their souls are driven nigh mad;

let yours be sane and ever saner. Not as a bewildered bewildering mob; but as a firm regimented mass, with real captains over them, will these men march any more. All human interests, combined human endeavours, and social growths in this world, have, at a certain stage of their development, required organising: and Work, the grandest of human interests, does now require it.

God knows, the task will be hard: but no noble task was ever easy. This task will wear away your lives, and the lives of your sons and grandsons: but for what purpose, if not for tasks like this, were lives given to men? Ye shall cease to count your thousand-pound scalps, the noble of you shall cease? . . .

Difficult? Yes, it will be difficult. The short-fibre cotton; that too was difficult. The waste cotton-shrub, long useless, disobedient, as the thistle by the wayside,—have ye not conquered it; made it into beautiful bandana webs; white woven shirts for men; bright-tinted air-garments wherein flit goddesses? Ye have shivered mountains asunder, made the hard iron pliant to you as soft putty: the Forest-giants, Marsh-jötuns bear sheaves of golden grain; Ægir the Sea-demon [7] himself stretches his back for a sleek highway to you, and on Fire-horses and Windhorses ye career.[8] Ye are most strong. Thor red-bearded, with his blue sun-eyes, with his cheery heart and strong thunder-hammer, he and you have prevailed. Ye are most strong, ye Sons of the icy North, of the far East,—far marching from your rugged Eastern Wildernesses, hitherward from the grey Dawn of Time! Ye are Sons of the *Jötun*-land; the land of Difficulties Conquered. Difficult? You must try this thing. Once try it with the understanding that it will and shall have to be done. Try it as ye try the paltrier thing, making of money! I will bet on you once more, against all Jötuns, Tailor-gods, Double-barrelled Law-wards, and Denizens of Chaos whatsoever!

---

[7] **Ægir:** a giant in Norse mythology
[8] 2 Kings 2:11

For Discussion

1. This essay is from *Past and Present,* a work written to supply a remedy for the economic and labor troubles in England during the 1830's and 1840's. As the title suggests, Carlyle compares the present situation with some of the great ages in the past to find a cure for the present ills. What is the situation in England as Carlyle sees it in the opening section of the essay? What does he mean by "Mammonism"? What is the relationship between government and the deeper issue involved?
2. What distinction is Carlyle making with the references to "light on" and "light in"? What does the statement "To be a noble Master, among noble Workers, will again be the first ambition with some few" reveal about Carlyle?
3. Carlyle's address to the "Leaders of Industry" was particularly meaningful for his own day. What role does he assign them? What does he say is their frequent motivation? What prediction of chaos does he make? Why?
4. What is the situation among the working classes as Carlyle pictures it in the fifth paragraph? What is Carlyle's attitude toward the landed gentry and aristocracy? Would he use the term aristocracy to describe these people?
5. Define Carlyle's concept of "Chivalry of Work." How effective is the reference to the Feudal Baron? How does his contrast of the isolated man and the men who surround the Feudal Baron develop the ideal of "Chivalry of Work"?
6. The last few paragraphs of this selection are an impassioned plea to the Captains of Industry, the "noble Workers, warriors in the one true sense." What exactly does Carlyle wish them to do? Do you think his arguments are particularly apt and effective for this audience? What are the implications of his idea of "just subordination"? Discuss the effectiveness of Carlyle's style in presenting this argument? Is it too emotional? Is it logically presented? In what way does his handling of the elements of sentence structure, diction, and allusion make his argument more persuasive? Discuss.
7. Study the last four paragraphs of this essay. What is the

effect of the imperative? What methods does Carlyle use to involve his readers? Considering his audience, the Captains of Industry, do you think they are particularly effective? Discuss.
8. Read the last four paragraphs aloud. Does the style of writing seem more like that of an orator than that of a writer? Discuss.

For Composition

1. Using Carlyle's method in "Storming the Bastille," write a description recreating a colorful event you have recently witnessed.
2. Write a theme in which you discuss Carlyle's concept of "just subordination." Could such a concept work in a democratic society? What are its dangers and limitations?

Matthew Arnold

(1822–1888)

Matthew Arnold was one of the most influential figures of Victorian literature and life. Strongly opposed to the materialism of the times, he effectively criticized the social, religious, and educational institutions of Victorian England. In an age of great scientific achievements, Arnold was the spokesman for the humanities against what was for him the inadequacy of science alone to bring man to a proper understanding of himself, his world, and the values of life.

Arnold's hope to combat the materialism and scientific utilitarianism of his day was education. A classicist in training and in temperament, Arnold saw in literature, "the best that has been thought and said in the world," the means whereby man could "see life steadily and see it whole." He rejected the idea that literature was merely a decorative study; the deep study of the ideals and values of the past was the way to "relate the results of modern science to our need for conduct, our need for beauty."

Though often somber and intensely serious, his writings are always vigorous and challenging; his ideas are sharply presented in language which is classical in structure and diction. His power as a writer and a thinker is based on his own fair-minded humaneness and his ability to be a stimulating and provocative commentator on his times.

SWEETNESS AND LIGHT [1]

The disparagers of culture make its motive curiosity; sometimes, indeed, they make its motive mere exclusiveness and vanity. The culture which is supposed to plume itself on a smattering of Greek and Latin is a culture which is begotten by nothing so intellectual as curiosity; it is valued either out of sheer vanity and ignorance or else as an engine of social and class distinction, separating its holder, like a badge or title, from other people who have not got it. No serious man would call this *culture,* or attach any value to it, as culture, at all. To find the real ground for the very differing estimate which serious people will set upon culture, we must find some motive for culture in the terms of which may lie a real ambiguity; and such a motive the word *curiosity* gives us.

I have before now pointed out [2] that we English do not, like the foreigners, use this word in a good sense as well as in a bad sense. With us the word is always used in a somewhat disapproving sense. A liberal and intelligent eagerness about the things of the mind may be meant by a foreigner when he speaks of curiosity, but with us the word always conveys a certain notion of frivolous and unedifying activity. In the *Quarterly Review,* some little time ago, was an estimate of the celebrated French critic, M. Sainte-Beuve,[3] and a very inadequate estimate it in my judgment was. And its inadequacy consisted chiefly in this: that in our English way it left out of sight the double sense really involved in the word *curiosity,* thinking enough was said to stamp M. Sainte-Beuve with blame if it was said that he was impelled in his operations as a critic by curiosity, and omitting either to perceive that M. Sainte-Beuve himself, and many other people with him, would consider that this was praiseworthy and not blameworthy, or to

[1] From *Culture and Anarchy*
[2] In "The Function of Criticism at the Present Time"
[3] **M. Sainte-Beuve:** Charles Augustin Sainte-Beuve, a leading French literary critic of the 19th century

point out why it ought really to be accounted worthy of blame and not of praise. For as there is a curiosity about intellectual matters which is futile, and merely a disease, so there is certainly a curiosity,—a desire after the things of the mind simply for their own sakes and for the pleasure of seeing them as they are,—which is, in an intelligent being, natural and laudable. Nay, and the very desire to see things as they are, implies a balance and regulation of mind which is not often attained without fruitful effort, and which is the very opposite of the blind and diseased impulse of mind which is what we mean to blame when we blame curiosity. Montesquieu [4] says: "The first motive which ought to impel us to study is the desire to augment the excellence of our nature, and to render an intelligent being yet more intelligent." This is the true ground to assign for the genuine scientific passion, however manifested, and for culture, viewed simply as a fruit of this passion; and it is a worthy ground, even though we let the term *curiosity* stand to describe it.

But there is of culture another view, in which not solely the scientific passion, the sheer desire to see things as they are, natural and proper in an intelligent being, appears as the ground of it. There is a view in which all the love of our neighbour, the impulses towards action, help, and beneficence, the desire for removing human error, clearing human confusion, and diminishing human misery, the noble aspiration to leave the world better and happier than we found it,— motives eminently such as are called social,—come in as part of the grounds of culture, and the main and preëminent part. Culture is then properly described not as having its origin in curiosity, but as having its origin in the love of perfection; it is *a study of perfection*. It moves by the force, not merely or primarily of the scientific passion for pure knowledge, but also of the moral and social passion for doing good. As, in the first view of it, we took for its worthy motto Montesquieu's words: "To render an intelligent being yet more intelligent!"

[4] **Charles de Montesquieu:** French jurist and philosopher (1689–1755)

so, in the second view of it, there is no better motto which it can have than these words of Bishop Wilson:[5] "To make reason and the will of God prevail!"

Only, whereas the passion for doing good is apt to be overhasty in determining what reason and the will of God say, because its turn is for acting rather than thinking and it wants to be beginning to act; and whereas it is apt to take its own conceptions, which proceed from its own state of development and share in all the imperfections and immaturities of this, for a basis of action; what distinguishes culture is, that it is possessed by the scientific passion as well as by the passion of doing good; that it demands worthy notions of reason and the will of God, and does not readily suffer its own crude conceptions to substitute themselves for them. And knowing that no action or institution can be salutary and stable which is not based on reason and the will of God, it is not so bent on acting and instituting, even with the great aim of diminishing human error and misery ever before its thoughts, but that it can remember that acting and instituting are of little use, unless we know how and what we ought to act and to institute.

This culture is more interesting and more far-reaching than that other, which is founded solely on the scientific passion for knowing. But it needs times of faith and ardor, times when the intellectual horizon is opening and widening all round us, to flourish in. And is not the close and bounded intellectual horizon within which we have long lived and moved now lifting up, and are not new lights finding free passage to shine in upon us? For a long time there was no passage for them to make their way in upon us, and then it was of no use to think of adapting the world's action to them. Where was the hope of making reason and the will of God prevail among people who had a routine which they had christened reason and the will of God, in which they were inextricably bound, and beyond which they had no power of looking? But now the iron force of adhesion to the old routine,—social, political,

[5] **Bishop Wilson:** Thomas Wilson (1663–1755)

religious,—has wonderfully yielded; the iron force of exclusion of all which is new has wonderfully yielded. The danger now is, not that people should obstinately refuse to allow anything but their old routine to pass for reason and the will of God, but either that they should allow some novelty or other to pass for these too easily, or else that they should underrate the importance of them altogether, and think it enough to follow action for its own sake, without troubling themselves to make reason and the will of God prevail therein. Now, then, is the moment for culture to be of service, culture which believes in making reason and the will of God prevail, believes in perfection, is the study and pursuit of perfection, and is no longer debarred, by a rigid invincible exclusion of whatever is new, from getting acceptance for its ideas, simply because they are new.

The moment this view of culture is seized, the moment it is regarded not solely as the endeavor to see things as they are, to draw towards a knowledge of the universal order which seems to be intended and aimed at in the world, and which it is a man's happiness to go along with or his misery to go counter to,—to learn, in short, the will of God,—the moment, I say, culture is considered not merely as the endeavor to *see* and *learn* this, but as the endeavor, also, to make it *prevail,* the moral, social, and beneficent character of culture becomes manifest. The mere endeavor to see and learn the truth for our own personal satisfaction is indeed a commencement for making it prevail, a preparing the way for this, which always serves this, and is wrongly, therefore, stamped with blame absolutely in itself and not only in its caricature and degeneration. But perhaps it has got stamped with blame, and disparaged with the dubious title of curiosity, because in comparison with this wider endeavor of such great and plain utility it looks selfish, petty, and unprofitable.

And religion, the greatest and most important of the efforts by which the human race has manifested its impulse to perfect itself,—religion, that voice of the deepest human experience,—does not only enjoin and sanction the aim which is the great aim of culture, the aim of setting ourselves to ascertain what perfection is and to make it prevail; but also, in determining generally in what human perfection consists, religion comes to a conclusion identical with that which culture,—culture seeking the determination of this question through *all* the voices of human experience which have been heard upon it, of art, science, poetry, philosophy, history, as well as of religion, in order to give a greater fulness and certainty to its solution,—likewise reaches. Religion says: *The kingdom of God is within you;* and culture, in like manner, places human perfection in an *internal* condition, in the growth and predominance of our humanity proper, as distinguished from our animality. It places it in the ever-increasing efficacy and in the general harmonious expansion of those gifts of thought and feeling, which make the peculiar dignity, wealth, and happiness of human nature. As I have said on a former occasion: "It is in making endless additions to itself, in the endless expansion of its powers, in endless growth in wisdom and beauty, that the spirit of the human race finds its ideal. To reach this ideal, culture is an indispensable aid, and that is the true value of culture." Not a having and a resting, but a growing and a becoming, is the character of perfection as culture conceives it; and here, too, it coincides with religion.

And because men are all members of one great whole, and the sympathy which is in human nature will not allow one member to be indifferent to the rest or to have a perfect welfare independent of the rest, the expansion of our humanity, to suit the idea of perfection which culture forms, must be a *general* expansion. Perfection, as culture conceives it, is not possible while the individual remains isolated. The individual is required, under pain of beng stunted and enfeebled in his own development if he disobeys, to carry others along with him in his march towards perfection, to be continually doing all he can to enlarge and increase the volume of the human stream sweeping thitherward. And, here, once more, culture lays on us the same obligation as religion, which says, as Bishop Wilson has admirably put it, that "to promote the kingdom of God is to increase and hasten one's own happiness."

But, finally, perfection,—as culture from a thorough disinterested study of human nature and human experience learns to conceive it,—is a harmonious expansion of *all* the powers which make the beauty and worth of human nature, and is not consistent with the overdevelopment of any one power at the expense of the rest. Here culture goes beyond religion as religion is generally conceived by us. . . .

The pursuit of perfection, then, is the pursuit of sweetness and light. He who works for sweetness and light, works to make reason and the will of God prevail. He who works for machinery, he who works for hatred, works only for confusion. Culture looks beyond machinery, culture hates hatred; culture has one great passion, the passion for sweetness and light. It has one even yet greater!—the passion for making them *prevail*. It is not satisfied till we *all* come to a perfect man; it knows that the sweetness and light of the few must be imperfect until the raw and unkindled masses of humanity are touched with sweetness and light. If I have not shrunk from saying that we must work for sweetness and light, so neither have I shrunk from saying that we must have a broad basis, must have sweetness and light for as many as possible. Again and again I have insisted how those are the happy moments of humanity, how those are the marking epochs of a people's life, how those are the flowering times for literature and art and all the creative power of genius, when there is a *national* glow of life and thought, when the whole of society is in the fullest measure permeated by thought, sensible to beauty, intelligent and alive. Only it must be *real* thought and *real* beauty; *real* sweetness and *real* light. Plenty of people will try to give the masses, as they call them, an intellectual food prepared and adapted in the way they think proper for the actual condition of the masses. The ordinary popular literature is an example of this way of working on the masses. Plenty of people will try to indoctrinate the masses with the set of ideas and judgments constituting the creed of their own profession or party. Our religious and political organizations give an example of this way of working on the masses. I condemn neither way; but culture works differently. It does not try to teach down to the level of inferior classes; it does not try to win them for this or that sect of its own, with ready-made judgments and watchwords. It seeks to do away with classes; to make the best that has been thought and known in the world current everywhere; to make all men live in an atmosphere of sweetness and light, where they may use ideas, as it uses them itself, freely,—nourished, and not bound by them.

This is the *social idea;* and the men of culture are the true apostles of equality. The great men of culture are those who have had a passion for diffusing, for making prevail, for carrying from one end of society to the other, the best knowledge, the best ideas of their time; who have labored to divest knowledge of all that was harsh, uncouth, difficult, abstract, professional, exclusive; to humanize it, to make it efficient outside the clique of the cultivated and learned, yet still remaining the *best* knowledge and thought of the time, and a true source, therefore, of sweetness and light.

For Discussion

1. This essay attempts to answer the question "Does culture have any value in itself beyond intellectual vanity or class snobbery?" What is the popular notion of culture given in the opening paragraph? What two meanings does Arnold associate with the word "curiosity"?
2. What is Arnold's own definition of culture? How does this definition differ from the popular notion? How does it differ from the diseased curiosity about intellectual matters?
3. What does Arnold mean when he terms culture *"a study of perfection"*? How does he define the relationship between knowing and doing?

4. Arnold says that the "moral and social passion for doing good" requires "times of faith and ardor; times when the intellectual horizon is opening and widening." Did Arnold believe these times existed in Victorian England? What dangers did he see in the intellectual climate of his day?
5. What is the first step in "making reason and the will of God prevail"? What does Arnold say is the relation between religion and culture? What is the ideal of the human race as Arnold defines it? Do you agree with his definition? Discuss.
6. How is the pursuit of culture related to the general welfare? How does this relate to Arnold's definition of perfection?
7. What does Arnold mean by the concept "sweetness and light"? Why must this, in Arnold's plan, be a social doctrine? How does this idea differ from the workings of the "religious and political organizations" who "try to indoctrinate the masses"?
8. Does Arnold offer any norm for judging the value of culture? Can one judge objectively the role of culture in life? Discuss.
9. Analyze the sentence structure in the last two paragraphs of the essay. Find examples of balanced sentences and parallel structure. What do these elements do for the presentation of the argument? What is the effect of Arnold's use of repetition?

For Composition

1. Write a theme in which you explore whether or not the modern mass media "try to indoctrinate the masses with the set of ideas and judgments constituting the creed of their own profession or party."
2. Arnold uses the word "curiosity," defines it and discusses its meaning and application. Reread the sections of the selection in which this is done and note Arnold's technique; then choose another such word and in a brief essay treat it as Arnold might.

John Henry, Cardinal Newman

(1801-1890)

Cardinal Newman was a staunch believer in the values of the traditional liberal education and defended it in the classic *The Idea of a University*. For Newman, the University was a place "to fit men of the world for the world"; it was not there mainly to instill virtue nor to train a student for a particular occupation. He stressed the need for a broad general culture to correct the narrowness that results when a student begins specialization too soon. By being least useful, the liberal arts are most useful because they teach a student to think; thus the man who knows "how to think and to reason and to compare and to analyze" can undertake meaningfully any study.

Newman's writing style has been highly praised as one of the finest in the nineteenth century. A master of the art of revision, he presents his ideas clearly and lucidly. His sentences are carefully constructed and show the keen mind at work. His diction has the grace, elegance, and dignity expected of a trained classicist.

KNOWLEDGE VIEWED IN RELATION TO PROFESSIONAL SKILL

1

... Truth of whatever kind is the proper object of the intellect; its cultivation then lies in fitting it to apprehend and contemplate truth. Now the intellect in its present state, with exceptions which need not here be specified, does not discern truth intuitively, or as a whole. We know, not by a direct and simple vision, not at a glance, but, as it were, by piecemeal and accumulation, by a mental process, by going round an object, by the comparison, the combination, the mutual correction, the continual adaptation, of many partial notions, by the employment, concentration, and joint action of many faculties and exercises of mind. Such a union and concert of the intellectual powers, such an enlargement and development, such a comprehensiveness, is necessarily a matter of training. And again, such a training is a matter of rule; it is not mere application, however exemplary, which introduces the mind to truth, nor the reading many books, nor the getting up many subjects, nor the witnessing many experiments, nor the attending many lectures. All this is short of enough; a man may have done it all, yet be lingering in the vestibule of knowledge:—he may not realize what his mouth utters; he may not see with his mental eye what confronts him; he may have no grasp of things as they are; or at least he may have no power at all of advancing one step forward of himself, in consequence of what he has already acquired, no power of discriminating between truth and falsehood, of sifting out the grains of truth from the mass, of arranging things according to their real value, and, if I may use the phrase, of building up ideas. Such a power is the result of a scientific formation of mind; it is an acquired faculty of judgment, of clear-sightedness, of sagacity, of wisdom, of philosophical reach of mind, and of intellectual self-possession and repose,—qualities which do not come of mere acquirement. The bodily eye, the origin for apprehending material objects, is provided by nature; the eye of the mind, of which the object is truth, is the work of discipline and habit.

This process of training, by which the intellect, instead of being formed or sacrificed to some particular or accidental purpose, some specific trade or profession, or study or science, is disciplined for its own sake, for the perception of its own proper object, and for its own highest culture, is called

Liberal Education; and though there is no one in whom it is carried as far as is conceivable, or whose intellect would be a pattern of what intellects should be made, yet there is scarcely any one but may gain an idea of what real training is, and at least look towards it, and make its true scope and result, not something else, his standard of excellence; and numbers there are who may submit themselves to it, and secure it to themselves in good measure. And to set forth the right standard, and to train according to it, and to help forward all students towards it according to their various capacities, this I conceive to be the business of a University.

In the sections omitted, Newman outlines the debate on educational theory between the scholars of Oxford and the scientists and Utilitarians from Edinburgh University and the *Edinburgh Review*. He pays particular attention to John Locke's [1] concept of utility in education and his attacks on classical education.

5

Now, I am not at present concerned with the specific question of classical education; else, I might reasonably question the justice of calling an intellectual discipline, which embraces the study of Aristotle,[2] Thucydides,[3] and Tacitus,[4] which involves Scholarship and Antiquities, *imaginative;* still so far I readily grant, that the cultivation of the "understanding," of a "talent for speculation and original inquiry," and of "the habit of pushing things up to their first principles," is a principal portion of a *good* or *liberal* education. If then the Reviewers consider such cultivation the characteristic of a *useful* education, as they seem to do [in a section omitted] it follows, that what they mean by "useful"

---

[1] **John Locke:** English philosopher (1632–1704), who was the forerunner of empiricism, a philosophy which has as its roots Locke's idea that the basis of all knowledge is in experience.
[2] **Aristotle:** Greek philosopher (384–322 B.C.).
[3] **Thucydides:** Athenian historian (471?–400? B.C.).
[4] **Tacitus:** Roman historian (55?–117?)

is just what I mean by "good" or "liberal:" and Locke's question becomes a verbal one. Whether youths are to be taught Latin or verse-making will depend on the *fact,* whether these studies tend to mental culture; but, however this is determined, so far is clear, that in that mental culture consists what I have called a liberal or non-professional, and what the Reviewers call a useful education.

This is the obvious answer which may be made to those who urge upon us the claims of Utility in our plans of Education; but I am not going to leave the subject here: I mean to take a wider view of it. Let us take "useful," as Locke takes it, in its proper and popular sense, and then we enter upon a large field of thought, to which I cannot do justice in one Discourse, though to-day's is all the space that I can give to it. I say, let us take "useful" to mean, not what is simply good, but what *tends* to good, or is the *instrument* of good; and in this sense also, Gentlemen, I will show you how a liberal education is truly and fully a useful, though it be not a professional, education. "Good" indeed means one thing, and "useful" means another; but I lay it down as a principle, which will save us a great deal of anxiety, that, though the useful is not always good, the good is always useful. Good is not only good, but reproductive of good; this is one of its attributes; nothing is excellent, beautiful, perfect, desirable for its own sake, but it overflows, and spreads the likeness of itself all around it. Good is prolific; it is not only good to the eye, but to the taste; it not only attracts us, but it communicates itself; it excites first our admiration and love, then our desire and our gratitude, and that, in proportion to its intenseness and fulness in particular instances. A great good will impart great good. If then the intellect is so excellent a portion of us, and its cultivation so excellent, it is not only beautiful, perfect, admirable, and noble in itself, but in a true and high sense it must be useful to the possessor and to all around him; not useful in any low, mechanical, mercantile sense, but as diffusing good, or as a blessing, or a gift, or power, or a treasure, first to the owner, then through him to the world. I say then, if a liberal education be good, it must necessarily be useful too.

6

You will see what I mean by the parallel of bodily health. Health is a good in itself, though nothing came of it, and is especially worth seeking and cherishing; yet, after all, the blessings which attend its presence are so great, while they are so close to it and so redound back upon it and encircle it, that we never think of it except as useful as well as good, and praise and prize it for what it does, as well as for what it is, though at the same time we cannot point out any definite and distinct work or production which it can be said to effect. And so as regards intellectual culture, I am far from denying utility in this large sense as the end of Education, when I lay it down, that the culture of the intellect is a good in itself and its own end; I do not exclude from the idea of intellectual culture what it cannot but be, from the very nature of things; I only deny that we must be able to point out, before we have any right to call it useful, some art, or business, or profession, or trade, or work, as resulting from it, and as its real and complete end. The parallel is exact:—As the body may be sacrificed to some manual or other toil, whether moderate or oppressive, so may the intellect be devoted to some specific profession; and I do not call *this* the culture of the intellect. Again, as some member or organ of the body may be inordinately used and developed, so may memory, or imagination, or the reasoning faculty; and *this* again is not intellectual culture. On the other hand, as the body may be tended, cherished, and exercised with a simple view to its general health, so may the intellect also be generally exercised in order to its perfect state; and this *is* its cultivation.

Again, as health ought to precede labour of the body, and as a man in health can do what an unhealthy man cannot do, and as of this health the properties are strength, energy, agility, graceful carriage and action, manual dexterity, and endurance of fatigue, so in like manner general culture of mind is the best aid to professional and scientific study, and educated men can do what illiterate cannot; and the man who has learned to think and to reason and to compare and to discriminate and to analyze, who has refined his taste, and formed his judgment, and sharpened his mental vision, will not indeed at once be a lawyer, or a pleader, or an orator, or a statesman, or a physician, or a good landlord, or a man of business, or a soldier, or an engineer, or a chemist, or a geologist, or an antiquarian, but he will be placed in that state of intellect in which he can take up any one of the sciences or callings I have referred to, or any other for which he has a taste or special talent, with an ease, a grace, a versatility, and a success, to which another is a stranger. In this sense then, and as yet I have said but a very few words on a large subject, mental culture is emphatically *useful*. . . .

This then is how I should solve the fallacy, for so I must call it, by which Locke and his disciples would frighten us from cultivating the intellect, under the notion that no education is useful which does not teach us some temporal calling, or some mechanical art, or some physical secret. I say that a cultivated intellect, because it is a good in itself, brings with it a power and a grace to every work and occupation which it undertakes, and enables us to be more useful, and to a greater number. There is a duty we owe to human society as such, to the state to which we belong, to the sphere in which we move, to the individuals towards whom we are variously related, and whom we successively encounter in life; and that philosophical or liberal education, as I have called it, which is the proper function of a University, if it refuses the foremost place to professional interests, does but postpone them to the formation of the citizen, and, while it subserves the larger interests of philanthropy, prepares also for the successful prosecution of those merely personal objects, which at first sight it seems to disparage.

In Sections 7, 8, and 9, Newman quotes Dr. Copleston of Oxford and John Davidson to show that a liberal education is of supreme benefit to man as a social being and that it is the means to avoid the narrowness of view of the man who is solely interested in business.

10

. . . . If then a practical end must be assigned to a University course, I say it is that of training good members of society. Its art is the art of social life, and its end is fitness for the world. It neither confines its views to particular professions on the one hand, nor creates heroes or inspires genius on the other. Works indeed of genius fall under no art; heroic minds come under no rule; a University is not a birthplace of poets or of immortal authors, of founders of schools, leaders of colonies, or conquerors of nations. It does not promise a generation of Aristotles or Newtons, of Napoleons or Washingtons, of Raphaels or Shakespeares, though such miracles of nature it has before now contained within its precincts. Nor is it content on the other hand with forming the critic or the experimentalist, the economist or the engineer, though such too it includes within its scope. But a University training is the great ordinary means to a great but ordinary end; it aims at raising the intellectual tone of society, at cultivating the public mind, at purifying the national taste, at supplying true principles to popular enthusiasm and fixed aims to popular aspiration, at giving enlargement and sobriety to the ideas of the age, at facilitating the exercise of political power, and refining the intercourse of private life. It is the education which gives a man a clear conscious view of his own opinions and judgments, a truth in developing them, an eloquence in expressing them, and a force in urging them. It teaches him to see things as they are, to go right to the point, to disentangle a skein of thought, to detect what is sophistical, and to discard what is irrelevant. It prepares him to fill any post with credit, and to master any subject with facility. It shows him how to accommodate himself to others, how to throw himself into their state of mind, how to bring before them his own, how to influence them, how to come to an understanding with them, how to bear with them. He is at home in any society, he has common ground with every class; he knows when to speak and when to be silent; he is able to converse, he is able to listen; he can ask a question pertinently, and gain a lesson seasonably, when he has nothing to impart himself; he is ever ready, yet never in the way; he is a pleasant companion, and a comrade you can depend upon; he knows when to be serious and when to trifle, and he has a sure tact which enables him to trifle with gracefulness and to be serious with effect. He has the repose of a mind which lives in itself, while it lives in the world, and which has resources for its happiness at home when it cannot go abroad. He has a gift which serves him in public, and supports him in retirement, without which good fortune is but vulgar, and with which failure and disappointment have a charm. The art which tends to make a man all this, is in the object which it pursues as useful as the art of wealth or the art of health, though it is less susceptible of method, and less tangible, less certain, less complete in its result.

For Discussion

1. What is the definition of Liberal Education as Newman presents it in the first section of this discourse? How does he relate Liberal Education to the nature of man? What sentences in Section 1 state Newman's fundamental thesis?
2. In Section 4, how does Newman use the words of his opponents to prove his own case? What does he mean when he says "though the useful is not always good, the good is always useful"? How does the analogy of bodily health used in Section 6 develop this point? Is Newman's argument valid? Discuss.
3. Do you agree with Newman that "general culture of mind is the best aid to professional and scientific study"? Discuss.

4. What, according to Newman in Section 10, is the aim of a University? What is the relation between its social and its intellectual aims?
5. How does a University give a man "a clear conscious view of his own opinions and judgments"?
6. What would you say is Newman's definition of an educated man? How does Newman answer the charge, often made in his own time, that Liberal Education tended to class consciousness and snobbery? Do you agree? How does Liberal Education develop both the inner and the outer man?
7. Pick out sections which show Newman's control over the principles of argumentation—his use of examples, his use of the arguments of his opponents, and his orderly presentation of ideas.
8. Newman's prose style is very much that of the educated man. Point out examples of balanced sentences and parallelism. What does the use of these techniques indicate about the writer? For example, is he romantic in his approach to his subject? What is the relationship between the structure of sentences and the argument of the essay?

LITERATURE

9

. . . By Letters or Literature is meant the expression of thought in language, where by "thought" I mean the ideas, feelings, views, reasonings, and other operations of the human mind. And the Art of Letters is the method by which a speaker or writer brings out in words, worthy of his subject, and sufficient for his audience or readers, the thoughts which impress him. Literature, then, is of a personal character; it consists in the enunciations and teachings of those who have a right to speak or representatives of their kind, and in whose words their brethren find an interpretation of their own sentiments, a record of their own experience, and a suggestion for their own judgments. A great author, Gentlemen, is not one who merely has a *copia verborum*,[1] whether in

[1] **copia verborum:** fluency of words

prose or verse, and can, as it were, turn on at his will any number of splendid phrases and swelling sentences; but he is one who has something to say and knows how to say it. I do not claim for him, as such, any great depth of thought, or breadth of view, or philosophy, or sagacity, or knowledge of human nature, or experience of human life, though these additional gifts he may have, and the more he has of them the greater he is; but I ascribe to him, as his characteristic gift, in a large sense the faculty of Expression. He is master of the two-fold Logos, the thought and the word, distinct, but inseparable from each other. He may, if so be, elaborate his compositions, or he may pour out his improvisations, but in either case he has but one aim, which he keeps steadily before him, and is conscientious and single-minded in fulfilling. That aim is to give forth what he has within him; and from his very earnestness it comes to pass that, whatever be the splendour of his diction or the harmony of his periods, he has with him the charm of an incommunicable simplicity. Whatever be his subject, high or low, he treats it suitably and for its own sake. . . .

He writes passionately, because he feels keenly; forcibly, because he conceives vividly, he sees too clearly to be vague; he is too serious to be otiose; he can analyze his subject, and therefore he is rich; he embraces it as a whole and in its parts, and therefore he is consistent; he has a firm hold of it, and therefore he is luminous. When his imagination wells up, it overflows in ornament; when his heart is touched, it thrills along his verse. He always has the right word for the right idea, and never a word too much. If he is brief, it is because few words suffice; when he is lavish of them, still each word has its mark, and aids, not embarrasses, the vigorous march of his elocution. He expresses what all feel, but all cannot say; and his sayings pass into proverbs among his people, and his phrases become household words and idioms of their daily speech, which is tessellated [2] with the rich fragments of his

---
[2] **tessellated:** inlaid

language, as we see in foreign lands the marbles of Roman grandeur worked into the walls and pavements of modern palaces.

Such pre-eminently is Shakespeare among ourselves; such pre-eminently Virgil among the Latins; such in their degree are all those writers who in every nation go by the name of Classics. To particular nations they are necessarily attached from the circumstance of the variety of tongues, and the peculiarities of each; but so far they have a catholic and ecumenical character, that what they express is common to the whole race of man, and they alone are able to express it.

10

If then the power of speech is a gift as great as any that can be named,—if the origin of language is by many philosophers even considered to be nothing short of divine,—if by means of words the secrets of the heart are brought to light, pain of soul is relieved, hidden grief is carried off, sympathy conveyed, counsel imparted, experience recorded, and wisdom perpetuated,—if by great authors the many are drawn up into unity, national character is fixed, a people speaks, the past and the future, the East and the West are brought into communication with each other,—if such men are, in a word, the spokesmen and prophets of the human family,—it will not answer to make light of Literature or to neglect its study; rather we may be sure that, in proportion as we master it in whatever language, and imbibe its spirit, we shall ourselves become in our own measure the ministers of like benefits to others, be they many or few, be they in the obscurer or the more distinguished walks of life,—who are united to us by social ties, and are within the sphere of our personal influence.

For Discussion

1. This selection is taken from one of a series of discourses on the various subjects in the University curriculum. What is

Newman's definition of literature? What does he mean by the "Art of Letters"? Why must literature be fundamentally personal?
2. Newman defines a great author as "one who has something to say and knows how to say it." What is the relationship between thought and style? What should be the aim of the writer?
3. What essential role does literature have in the University curriculum? Does Newman assign a didactic role to the study of literature? Discuss.
4. Discuss the relationship between Arnold's view of literature and Newman's view. How are they alike? How do they differ?

For Composition

1. Choose a work of literature you feel would qualify as great literature according to Newman's definition. Write an essay in which you show how this particular work expresses thoughts, feelings, and ideas "common to the whole race of man."
2. Write an essay in which you try to define the educated man in the twentieth century.

Robert Louis Stevenson

(1850–1894)

Robert Louis Stevenson turned to writing at an early age and became one of the foremost essayists and adventure novelists of the late nineteenth century. With novels such as *Treasure Island* and *Kidnapped*, he emphasized the love for adventure, the lure of exotic places, and the spirit of romance which have a deep appeal for readers.

In addition to the novels for which he was most famous, Stevenson also produced travel books, poetry, letters, essays, and short stories. He cultivated the familiar essay and wrote with the ease and lightness of a lover of words. In these essays, he did what he was best at—talking about himself. In the short story form, which he helped to popularize in England, he used all the elements of suspense and adventure characteristic of his novels. In "Markheim," however, he presents a story which probes psychologically the problem of good and evil in an individual.

MARKHEIM

"Yes," said the dealer, "our windfalls are of various kinds. Some customers are ignorant, and then I touch a dividend on my superior knowledge. Some are dishonest," and here he held up the candle, so that the light fell strongly on his visitor, "and in that case," he continued, "I profit by my virtue."

Markheim had but just entered from the daylight streets, and his eyes had not yet grown familiar with the mingled shine and darkness in the shop. At these pointed words, and before the near presence of the flame, he blinked painfully and looked aside.

The dealer chuckled. "You come to me on Christmas day," he resumed, "when you know that I am alone in my house, put up my shutters, and make a point of refusing business. Well, you will have to pay for that; you will have to pay for my loss of time, when I should be balancing my books; you will have to pay, besides, for a kind of manner that I remark in you today very strongly. I am the essence of discretion, and ask no awkward questions; but when a customer cannot look me in the eye, he has to pay for it." The dealer once more chuckled; and then, changing to his usual business voice, though still with a note of irony, "You can give, as usual, a clear account of how you came into the possession of the object?" he continued. "Still your uncle's cabinet? A remarkable collector, sir!"

And the little pale, round-shouldered dealer stood almost on tip-toe, looking over the top of his gold spectacles, and nodding his head with every mark of disbelief. Markheim returned his gaze with one of infinite pity, and a touch of horror.

"This time," said he, "you are in error. I have not come to sell, but to buy. I have no curios to dispose of; my uncle's cabinet is bare to the wainscot; even were it still intact, I have done well on the Stock Exchange, and should more likely add to it than otherwise, and my errand today is simplicity itself. I seek a Christmas present for a lady," he continued, waxing more fluent as he struck into the speech he had prepared; "and certainly I owe you every excuse for thus disturbing you upon so small a matter. But the thing was neglected yesterday; I must produce my little compliment at dinner; and, as you very well know, a rich marriage is not a thing to be neglected."

There followed a pause, during which the dealer seemed to weigh this statement incredulously. The ticking of many clocks among the curious lumber of the shop, and the faint rushing of the cabs in a near thoroughfare, filled up the interval of silence.

"Well, sir," said the dealer, "be it so. You are an old customer after all; and if, as you say, you have the chance of a good marriage, far be it from me to be an obstacle. Here is a nice thing for a lady now," he went on, "this hand-glass—fifteenth century, warranted; comes from a good collection, too; but I reserve the name, in the interests of my customer, who was, just like yourself, my dear sir, the nephew and sole heir of a remarkable collector."

The dealer, while he thus ran on in his dry and biting voice, had stooped to take the object from its place; and, as he had done so, a shock had passed through Markheim, a start both of hand and foot, a sudden leap of many tumultuous passions to the face. It passed as swiftly as it came, and left no trace beyond a certain trembling of the hand that now received the glass.

"A glass," he said hoarsely, and then paused, and repeated it more clearly. "A glass? For Christmas? Surely not?"

"And why not?" cried the dealer. "Why not a glass?"

Markheim was looking upon him with an indefinable expression. "You ask me why not?" he said, "Why, look here—look in it—look at yourself! Do you like to see it? No! nor I—nor any man."

The little man had jumped back when Markheim had so suddenly confronted him with the mirror; but now, perceiving there was nothing worse on hand, he chuckled. "Your future lady, sir, must be pretty hard favoured." said he.

"I ask you," said Markheim, "for a Christmas present, and you give me this—this damned reminder of years, and sins and follies—this hand-conscience! Did you mean it? Had you a thought in your mind? Tell me. It will be better for you if you do. Come, tell me about yourself. I hazard a guess now, that you are in secret a very charitable man?"

The dealer looked closely at his companion. It was very

odd, Markheim did not appear to be laughing; there was something in his face like an eager sparkle of hope, but nothing of mirth.

"What are you driving at?" the dealer asked.

"Not charitable?" returned the other, gloomily. "Not charitable; not pious; not scrupulous; unloving, unbeloved; a hand to get money, a safe to keep it. Is that all? Dear God, man, is that all?"

"I will tell you what it is," began the dealer, with some sharpness, and then broke off again into a chuckle. "But I see this is a love-match of yours, and you have been drinking the lady's health."

"Ah!" cried Markheim, with a strange curiosity. "Ah, have you been in love? Tell me about that."

"I!" cried the dealer. "I in love! I never had the time, nor have I the time today for all this nonsense. Will you take the glass?"

"Where is the hurry?" returned Markheim. "It is very pleasant to stand here talking; and life is so short and insecure that I would not hurry away from any pleasure—no, not even from so mild a one as this. We should rather cling, cling to what little we can get, like a man at a cliff's edge. Every second is a cliff, if you think upon it—a cliff a mile high—high enough, if we fall, to dash us out of every feature of humanity. Hence it is best to talk pleasantly. Let us talk of each other; why should we wear this mask? Let us be confidential. Who knows, we might become friends?"

"I have just one word to say to you," said the dealer. "Either make your purchase, or walk out of my shop."

"True, true," said Markheim. "Enough fooling. To business. Show me something else."

The dealer stooped once more, this time to replace the glass upon the shelf, his thin blond hair falling over his eyes as he did so. Markheim moved a little nearer, with one hand in the pocket of his great-coat; he drew himself up and filled his lungs; at the same time many different emotions were depicted together on his face—terror, horror, and resolve, fascination and a physical repulsion; and through a haggard lift of his upper lip, his teeth looked out.

"This, perhaps, may suit," observed the dealer; and then, as he began to rearise, Markheim bounded from behind upon his victim. The long, skewerlike dagger flashed and fell. The dealer struggled like a hen, striking his temple on the shelf, and then tumbled on the floor in a heap.

Time had some score of small voices in that shop, some stately and slow as was becoming to their great age; others garrulous and hurried. All these told out the seconds in an intricate chorus of tickings. Then the passage of a lad's feet, heavily running on the pavement, broke in upon these smaller voices and startled Markheim into the consciousness of his surroundings. He looked about him awfully. The candle stood on the counter, its flame solemnly wagging in a draught; and by that inconsiderable movement, the whole room was filled with noiseless bustle and kept heaving like a sea: the tall shadows nodding, the gross blots of darkness swelling and dwindling as with respiration, the faces of the portraits and the china gods changing and wavering like images in water. The inner door stood ajar, and peered into that leaguer of shadows with a long slit of daylight like a pointing finger.

From these fear-stricken rovings, Markheim's eyes returned to the body of his victim, where it lay both humped and sprawling, incredibly small and strangely meaner than in life. In these poor, miserly clothes, in that ungainly attitude, the dealer lay like so much sawdust. Markheim had feared to see it, and, lo! it was nothing. And yet, as he gazed, this bundle of old clothes and pool of blood began to find eloquent voices. There it must lie; there was none to work the cunning hinges or direct the miracle of locomotion—there it must lie till it was found. Found! ay, and then? Then would this dead flesh lift up a cry that would ring over England, and fill the world with the echoes of pursuit. Ay, dead or not, this was still the enemy. "Time was that when the brains were out," [1] he thought; and the first word struck into his mind. Time, now that the deed was accomplished—time, which had closed for the victim, had become instant and momentous for the slayer.

The thought was not yet in his mind, when, first one and then another, with every variety of pace and voice—one deep as the bell from a cathedral turret, another ringing on its treble notes the prelude of a waltz—the clocks began to strike the hour of three in the afternoon.

The sudden outbreak of so many tongues in that dumb chamber staggered him. He began to bestir himself, going to and fro with the candle, beleaguered by moving shadows, and startled to the soul by chance reflections. In many rich mirrors, some of home designs, some from Venice or Amsterdam, he saw his face repeated and repeated, as it were an army of spies; his own eyes met and detected him; and the sound of his own steps, lightly as they fell, vexed the surrounding quiet. And still as he continued to fill his pockets, his mind accused him, with a sickening iteration, of the thousand faults of his design. He should have chosen a more quiet hour; he should have prepared an alibi; he should not have used a knife; he should have been more cautious, and only bound and gagged the dealer, and not killed him; he should have been more bold, and killed the servant also; he should have done all things otherwise; poignant regrets, weary, incessant toiling of the mind to change what was unchangeable, to plan what was now useless, to be the architect of the irrevocable past. Meanwhile, and behind all this activity, brute terrors, like the scurrying of rats in a deserted attic, filled the more remote chambers of his brain with riot; the hand of the constable would fall heavy on his shoulder, and his nerves would jerk like a hooked fish; or he beheld, in galloping defile, the dock, the prison, the gallows, and the black coffin.

Terror of the people in the street sat down before his mind like a besieging army. It was impossible, he thought, but that

[1] **"Time was that when the brains were out"**: from *Macbeth,* Act III, Scene 4

some rumour of the struggle must have reached their ears and set on edge their curiosity; and now, in all the neighbouring houses, he divined them sitting motionless and with uplifted ear—solitary people, condemned to spend Christmas dwelling alone on memories of the past, and now startingly recalled from that tender exercise; happy family parties, struck into silence round the table, the mother still with raised finger: every degree and age and humour, but all, by their own hearths, prying and hearkening and weaving the rope that was to hang him. Sometimes it seemed to him he could not move too softly; the clink of the tall Bohemian goblets rang out loudly like a bell; and alarmed by the bigness of the ticking, he was tempted to stop the clocks. And then, again, with a swift transition of his terrors, the very silence of the place appeared a source of peril, and a thing to strike and freeze the passer-by; and he would step more boldly, and bustle aloud among the contents of the shop, and imitate, with elaborate bravado, the movements of a busy man at ease in his own house.

But he was now so pulled about by different alarms that, while one portion of his mind was still alert and cunning, another trembled on the brink of lunacy. One hallucination in particular took a strong hold on his credulity. The neighbour hearkening with white face beside his window, the passer-by arrested by a horrible surmise on the pavement—these could at worst suspect, they could not know; through the brick walls and shuttered windows only sounds could penetrate. But here, within the house, was he alone? He knew he was; he had watched the servant set forth sweethearting, in her poor best, "out for the day" written in every ribbon and smile. Yes, he was alone, of course; and yet, in the bulk of empty house about him, he could surely hear a stir of delicate footing—he was surely conscious, inexplicably conscious of some presence. Ay, surely; to every room and corner of the house his imagination followed it; and now it was a faceless thing, and yet had eyes to see with; and again it was a shadow of himself; and yet again behold the image of the dead dealer, reinspired with cunning and hatred.

At times, with a strong effort, he would glance at the open door which still seemed to repel his eyes. The house was tall, the skylight small and dirty, the day blind with fog; and the light that filtered down to the ground story was exceedingly faint, and showed dimly on the threshold of the shop. And yet, in that strip of doubtful brightness, did there not hang wavering a shadow?

Suddenly, from the street outside, a very jovial gentleman began to beat with a staff on the shop-door, accompanying his blows with shouts and railleries in which the dealer was continually called upon by name. Markheim, smitten into ice, glanced at the dead man. But no! he lay quite still; he was fled away far beyond ear-shot of these blows and shoutings; he was sunk beneath seas of silence; and his name, which would once have caught his notice above the howling of a storm, had become an empty sound. And presently the jovial gentleman desisted from his knocking and departed.

Here was a broad hint to hurry what remained to be done, to get forth from this accusing neighbourhood, to plunge into a path of London multitudes, and to reach, on the other side of day, that haven of safety and apparent innocence—his bed. One visitor had come: at any moment another might follow and be more obstinate. To have done the deed, and yet not to reap the profit, would be too abhorrent a failure. The money, that was now Markheim's concern; and as a means to that, the keys.

He glanced over his shoulder at the open door, where the shadow was still lingering and shivering; and with no conscious repugnance of the mind, yet with a tremor of the belly, he drew near the body of his victim. The human character had quite departed. Like a suit half-stuffed with bran, the limbs lay scattered, the trunk doubled, on the floor; and yet the thing repelled him. Although so dingy and inconsiderable to the eye, he feared it might have more significance to the touch. He took the body by the shoulders, and turned it on its back. It was strangely light and supple, and the limbs, as if they had been broken, fell into the oddest postures. The face was robbed of all expression; but it was as pale as wax, and shockingly smeared with blood about one temple. That was, for Markheim, the one displeasing circumstance. It carried him back, upon the instant, to a certain fair day in a fishers' village: a gray day, a piping wind, a crowd upon the street, the blare of brasses, the booming of drums, the nasal voice of a ballad-singer; and a boy going to and fro, buried over head in the crowd and divided between interest and fear, until, coming out upon the chief place of concourse, he beheld a booth and a great screen with pictures, dismally designed, garishly coloured: Brownrigg with her apprentice; the Mannings with their murdered guest; Weare in the death-grip of Thurtell; [2] and a score besides of famous crimes. The thing was as clear as an illusion; he was once again the little boy; he was looking once again, and with the same sense of physical revolt, at these vile pictures; he was still stunned by the thumping of the drums. A bar of that day's music returned upon his memory; and at that, for the first time, a qualm came over him, a breath of nausea, a sudden weakness of the joints, which he must instantly resist and conquer.

He judged it more prudent to confront than to flee from these considerations; looking the more hardily in the dead face, bending his mind to realize the nature and greatness of his crime. So little a while ago that face had moved with every change of sentiment, that pale mouth had spoken, that body had been all on fire with governable energies; and now, and by his act, that piece of life had been arrested, as the horologist, with interjected finger, arrests the beating of the clock. So he reasoned in vain; he could rise to no more remorseful consciousness; the same heart which had shuddered before the painted effigies of crime, looked on its reality unmoved. At best, he felt a gleam of pity for one who had been

[2] **Brownrigg, Mannings, Thurtell:** notorious murderers

endowed in vain with all those faculties that can make the world a garden of enchantment, one who had never lived and who was now dead. But of penitence, no, not a tremor.

With that, shaking himself clear of these considerations, he found the keys and advanced towards the open door of the shop. Outside, it had begun to rain smartly; and the sound of the shower upon the roof had banished silence. Like some dripping cavern, the chambers of the house were haunted by an incessant echoing, which filled the ear and mingled with the ticking of the clocks. And, as Markheim approached the door, he seemed to hear, in answer to his own cautious tread, the steps of another foot withdrawing up the stair. The shadow still palpitated loosely on the threshold. He threw a ton's weight of resolve upon his muscles, and drew back the door.

The faint, foggy daylight glimmered dimly on the bare floor and stairs; on the bright suit of armour posted, halbert in hand, upon the landing; and on the dark wood-carvings, and framed pictures that hung against the yellow panels of the wainscot. So loud was the beating of the rain through all the house that, in Markheim's ears, it began to be distinguished into many different sounds. Footsteps and sighs, the tread of regiments marching in the distance, the chink of money in the counting, and the creaking of doors held stealthily ajar, appeared to mingle with the patter of the drops upon the cupola and the gushing of the water in the pipes. The sense that he was not alone grew upon him to the verge of madness. On every side he was haunted and begirt by presences. He heard them moving in the upper chambers; from the shop, he heard the dead man getting to his legs; and as he began with a great effort to mount the stairs, feet fled quietly before him and followed stealthily behind. If he were but deaf, he thought, how tranquilly he would possess his soul! And then again, and hearkening with ever fresh attention, he blessed himself for that unresting sense which held the outposts and stood a trusty sentinel upon his life. His head turned continually on his neck; his eyes, which seemed starting from their orbits, scouted on every side, and on every side were half-rewarded as with the tail of something nameless vanishing. The four-and-twenty steps to the first floor were four-and-twenty agonies.

On that first story, the doors stood ajar, three of them like three ambushes, shaking his nerves like the throats of cannon. He could never again, he felt, be sufficiently immured and fortified from men's observing eyes; he longed to be home, girt in by walls, buried among bedclothes, and invisible to all but God. And at that thought he wondered a little, recollecting tales of other murderers and the fear they were said to entertain of heavenly avengers. It was not so, at least, with him. He feared the laws of nature, lest, in their callous and immutable procedure, they should preserve some damning evidence of his crime. He feared tenfold more, with a slavish, superstitious terror, some scission in the continuity of man's experience, some willful illegality of nature. He played a game of skill, depending on the rules, calculating consequence from cause; and what if nature, as the defeated tyrant overthrew the chess-board, should break the mould of their succession? The like had befallen Napoleon (so writers said) when the winter changed the time of its appearance. The like might befall Markheim: the solid walls might become transparent and reveal his doings like those of bees in a glass hive; the stout planks might yield under his foot like quicksands and detain him in their clutch; ay, and there were soberer accidents that might destroy him: if, for instance, the house should fall and imprison him beside the body of his victim; or the house next door should fly on fire, and the firemen invade him from all sides. These things he feared; and, in a sense, these things might be called the hands of God reached forth against sin. But about God himself he was at ease; his act was doubtless exceptional, but so were his excuses, which God knew; it was there, and not among men, that he felt sure of justice.

When he had got safe into the drawing-room, and shut the door behind him, he was aware of a respite from alarms. The room was quite dismantled, uncarpeted besides, and strewn with packing-cases and incongruous furniture; several great pier-glasses, in which he beheld himself at various angles, like an actor on a stage; many pictures, framed and unframed, standing, with their faces to the wall; a fine Sheraton sideboard, a cabinet of marquetry, and a great old bed, with tapestry hangings. The windows opened to the floor; but by great good fortune the lower part of the shutters had been closed, and this concealed him from the neighbours. Here, then, Markheim drew in a packing-case before the cabinet, and began to search among the keys. It was a long business, for there were many; and it was irksome, beside; for, after all, there might be nothing in the cabinet, and time was on the wing. But the closeness of the occupation sobered him. With the tail of his eye he saw the door—even glanced at it from time to time directly, like a besieged commander pleased to verify the good estate of his defences. But in truth he was at peace. The rain falling in the street sounded natural and pleasant. Presently, on the other side, the notes of a piano were wakened to the music of a hymn, and the voices of many children took up the air and words. How stately, how comfortable was the melody! How fresh the youthful voices! Markheim gave ear to it smilingly, as he sorted out the keys; and his mind was thronged with answerable ideas and images; church-going children and the pealing of the high organ; children afield, bathers by the brookside, ramblers on the brambly common, kite-flyers in the windy and cloud-navigated sky; and then, at another cadence of the hymn, back again to church, and the somnolence of summer Sundays, and the high genteel voice of the parson (which he smiled a little to recall) and the painted Jacobean tombs, and the dim lettering of the Ten Commandments in the chancel.

And as he sat thus, at once busy and absent, he was startled to his feet. A flash of ice, a flash of fire, a bursting gush of blood, went over him, and then he stood transfixed and thrilling. A step mounted the stair slowly and steadily, and presently a hand was laid upon the knob, and the lock clicked, and the door opened.

Fear held Markheim in a vice. What to expect he knew not, whether the dead man walking, or the official ministers of human justice, or some chance witness blindly stumbling in to consign him to the gallows. But when a face was thrust into the aperture, glanced round the room, looked at him, nodded and smiled as if in friendly recognition, and then withdrew again, and the door closed behind it, his fear broke loose from his control in a hoarse cry. At the sound of this the visitant returned.

"Did you call me?" he asked, pleasantly, and with that he entered the room and closed the door behind him.

Markheim stood and gazed at him with all his eyes. Perhaps there was a film upon his sight, but the outlines of the newcomer seemed to change and waver like those of the idols in the wavering candlelight of the shop; and at times he thought he knew him; and at times he thought he bore a likeness to himself; and always, like a lump of living terror, there lay in his bosom the conviction that this thing was not of the earth and not of God.

And yet the creature had a strange air of the commonplace, as he stood looking on Markheim with a smile; and when he added: "You are looking for the money, I believe?" it was in the tones of everyday politeness.

Markheim made no answer.

"I should warn you," resumed the other, "that the maid has left her sweetheart earlier than usual and will soon be here. If Mr. Markheim be found in this house, I need not describe to him the consequences."

"You know me?" cried the murderer.

The visitor smiled. "You have long been a favorite of mine," he said; "and I have long observed and often sought to help you."

"What are you?" cried Markheim: "the devil?"

"What I may be," returned the other, "cannot affect the service I propose to render you."

"It can," cried Markheim; "it does! Be helped by you? No, never; not by you! You do not know me yet; thank God, you do not know me!"

"I know you," replied the visitant, with a sort of kind severity or rather firmness. "I know you to the soul."

"Know me!" cried Markheim. "Who can do so? My life is but a travesty and slander on myself. I have lived to belie my nature. All men do; all men are better than this disguise that grows about and stifles them. You see each dragged away by life, like one whom bravos have seized and muffled in a cloak. If they had their own control—if you could see their faces, they would be altogether different, they would shine out for heroes and saints! I am worse than most; myself is more overlaid; my excuse is known to me and God. But, had I the time, I could disclose myself."

"To me?" inquired the visitant.

"To you before all," returned the murderer. "I supposed you were intelligent. I thought—since you exist—you would prove a reader of the heart. And yet you would propose to judge me by my acts! Think of it; my acts! I was born and I have lived in a land of giants; giants have dragged me by the wrists since I was born out of my mother—the giants of circumstance. And you would judge me by my acts! But can you not look within? Can you not understand that evil is hateful to me? Can you not see within me the clear writing of conscience, never blurred by any wilful sophistry, although too often disregarded? Can you not read me for a thing that surely must be common as humanity—the unwilling sinner?"

"All this is very feelingly expressed," was the reply, "but it regards me not. These points of consistency are beyond my province, and I care not in the least by what compulsion you may have been dragged away, so as you are but carried in the right direction. But time flies; the servant delays, looking in the faces of the crowd and at the pictures on the hoardings, but still she keeps moving nearer; and remember, it is as if the gallows itself were striding towards you through the Christmas streets! Shall I help you; I, who know all? Shall I tell you where to find the money?"

"For what price?" asked Markheim.

"I offer you the service for a Christmas gift," returned the other.

Markheim could not refrain from smiling with a kind of bitter triumph. "No," said he, "I will take nothing at your hands; if I were dying of thirst, and it was your hand that put the pitcher to my lips, I should find the courage to refuse. It may be credulous, but I will do nothing to commit myself to evil."

"I have no objection to a death-bed repentance," observed the visitant.

"Because you disbelieve their efficacy!" Markheim cried.

"I do not say so," returned the other; "but I look on these things from a different side, and when the life is done my interest falls. The man has lived to serve me, to spread black looks under colour of religion, or to sow tares in the wheatfield, as you do, in a course of weak compliance with desire. Now that he draws so near to his deliverance, he can add but one act of service—to repent, to die smiling, and thus to build up in confidence and hope the more timorous of my surviving followers. I am not so hard a master. Try me. Accept my help. Please yourself in life as you have done hitherto; please yourself more amply, spread your elbows at the board; and when the night begins to fall and the curtains to be drawn, I tell you, for your greater comfort, that you will find it even easy to compound your quarrel with your conscience, and to make a truckling peace with God. I came but now from such a death-bed, and the room was full of sincere mourners, listening to the man's last words: and when I looked into that face, which had been set as a flint against mercy, I found it smiling with hope."

"And do you, then, suppose me such a creature?" asked Markheim. "Do you think I have no more generous aspirations than to sin, and sin, and sin, and, at last, sneak into heaven? My heart rises at the thought. Is this, then, your experience of mankind? or is it because you find me with red hands that you presume such baseness? and is this crime of murder indeed so impious as to dry up the very springs of good?"

"Murder is to me no special category," replied the other. "All sins are murder, even as all life is war. I behold your race, like starving mariners on a raft, plucking crusts out of the hands of famine and feeding on each other's lives. I follow sins beyond the moment of their acting; I find in all that the last consequence is death; and to my eyes, the pretty maid who thwarts her mother with such taking graces on a question of a ball, drips no less visibly with human gore than such a murderer as yourself. Do I say that I follow sins? I follow virtues also; they differ not by the thickness of a nail, they are both scythes for the reaping angel of Death. Evil, for which I live, consists not in action, but in character. The bad man is dear to me; not the bad act, whose fruits, if we could follow them far enough down the hurtling cataract of the ages, might yet be found more blessed than those of the rarest virtues. And it is not because you have killed a dealer, but because you are Markheim, that I offered to forward your escape."

"I will lay my heart open to you," answered Markheim. "This crime on which you find me is my last. On my way to it I have learned many lessons; itself is a lesson, a momentous lesson. Hitherto I have been driven with revolt to what I would not; I was a bondslave to poverty, driven and scourged. There are robust virtues that can stand in these temptations; mine was not so: I had a thirst of pleasure. But today, and out of this deed, I pluck both warning and riches—both the power and a fresh resolve to be myself. I become in all things a free actor in the world; I begin to see myself all changed, these hands the agents of good, this heart at peace. Something comes over me out of the past; something of what I have dreamed on Sabbath evenings to the sound of the church organ, of what I forecast when I shed tears over noble books, or talked, an innocent child, with my mother. There lies my life; I have wandered a few years, but now I see once more my city of destination."

"You are to use this money on the Stock Exchange, I think?" remarked the visitor; "and there, if I mistake not, you have already lost some thousands?"

"Ah," said Markheim, "but this time I have a sure thing."

"This time, again, you will lose," replied the visitor quietly.

"Ah, but I keep back the half!" cried Markheim.

"That also you will lose," said the other.

The sweat started upon Markheim's brow. "Well, then, what matter?" he exclaimed. "Say it be lost, say I am plunged again in poverty, shall one part of me, and that the worse, continue until the end to override the better? Evil and good run strong in me, hailing me both ways. I do not love the one thing, I love all. I can conceive great deeds, renunciations, martyrdoms; and though I be fallen to such a crime as murder, pity is no stranger to my thoughts. I pity the poor; who knows their trials better than myself? I pity and help them; I prize love, I love honest laughter; there is no good thing nor true thing on earth but I love it from my heart. And are my vices only to direct my life, and my virtues to lie without effect, like some passive lumber of the mind? Not so; good, also, is a spring of acts."

But the visitant raised his finger. "For six-and-thirty years that you have been in this world," said he, "through many changes of fortune and varieties of humour, I have watched you steadily fall. Fifteen years ago you would have started at a theft. Three years back you would have blenched at the name of murder. Is there any crime, is there any cruelty or meanness, from which you still recoil?—five years from now I shall detect you in the fact! Downward, downward, lies your way; nor can anything but death avail to stop you."

"It is true," Markheim said huskily, "I have in some

degree complied with evil. But it is so with all: the very saints, in the mere exercise of living, grow less dainty, and take on the tone of their surroundings."

"I will propound to you one simple question," said the other; "and as you answer, I shall read to you your moral horoscope. You have grown in many things more lax; possibly you do right to be so; and at any account, it is the same with all men. But granting that, are you in any one particular, however trifling, more difficult to please with your own conduct, or do you go in all things with a looser rein?"

"In any one?" repeated Markheim, with an anguish of consideration. "No," he added, with despair, "in none! I have gone down in all."

"Then," said the visitor, "content yourself with what you are, for you will never change; and the words of your part on this stage are irrevocably written down."

Markheim stood for a long while silent, and indeed it was the visitor who first broke the silence. "That being so," he said, "shall I show you the money?"

"And grace?" cried Markheim.

"Have you not tried it?" returned the other. "Two or three years ago, did I not see you on the platform of revival meetings, and was not your voice the loudest in the hymn?"

"It is true," said Markheim; "and I see clearly what remains for me by way of duty. I thank you for these lessons from my soul; my eyes are opened, and I behold myself at last for what I am."

At this moment, the sharp note of the door-bell rang through the house; and the visitant, as though this were some concerted signal for which he had been waiting, changed at once in his demeanour.

"The maid!" he cried. "She has returned, as I forewarned you, and there is now before you one more difficult passage. Her master, you must say, is ill; you must let her in, with an assured but rather serious countenance—no smiles, no overacting, and I promise you success! Once the girl within, and the door closed, the same dexterity that has already rid you of the dealer will relieve you of this last danger in your path. Thenceforward you have the whole evening—the whole night, if needful—to ransack the treasures of the house and to make good your safety. This is help that comes to you with the mask of danger. Up!" he cried: "up, friend; your life hangs trembling in the scales: up, and act!"

Markheim steadily regarded his counsellor. "If I be condemned to evil acts," he said, "there is still one door of freedom open—I can cease from action. If my life be an ill thing, I can lay it down. Though I be, as you say truly, at the beck of every small temptation, I can yet, by one decisive gesture, place myself beyond the reach of all. My love of good is damned to barrenness; it may, and let it be! But I have still my hatred of evil; and from that, to your galling disappointment, you shall see that I can draw both energy and courage."

The features of the visitor began to undergo a wonderful and lovely change: they brightened and softened with a tender triumph; and, even as they brightened, faded and dislimned. But Markheim did not pause to watch or understand the transformation. He opened the door and went down-stairs very slowly, thinking to himself. His past went soberly before him; he beheld it as it was, ugly and strenuous like a dream, random as chance-medley—a scene of defeat. Life, as he thus reviewed it, tempted him no longer; but on the farther side he perceived a quiet haven for his bark. He paused in the passage, and looked into the shop, where the candle still burned by the dead body. It was strangely silent. Thoughts of the dealer swarmed into his mind, as he stood gazing. And then the bell once more broke out into impatient clamour.

He confronted the maid upon the threshold with something like a smile.

"You had better go for the police," said he: "I have killed your master."

For Discussion

1. This story can be read on many levels. It can be enjoyed as a murder story filled with suspense and terror; it can also be read as a probing of a character who is drawn between good and evil. Study carefully the opening paragraphs of the story. What details of setting set the mood of the story? What details reveal the two characters? What is ironic about the setting and the time?
2. What is the function of the hand-glass? Why does Markheim call it a "hand-conscience"? How is this image developed? What relation does it have to the story's theme?
3. The first section of the story ends with the murder. What is the effect of the references to the clocks and to the outside world? What is Markheim's reaction to the striking of the clocks? What does this tell about his state of mind?
4. How does Markheim's imagination create terror in the second section? Do you think that this is being true to human nature; that is, do we tend to create ourselves more terrors than there are? Point out elements of suspense in this section. What is the effect of the reference to the incident in Markheim's boyhood?
5. As Markheim moves through the house, he overcomes his terror. What is the function of the references to innocence and peace at the end of the second section?
6. The third section of the story begins with the appearance of the "visitant." What is Markheim's reaction to this visitor? Who is the visitor?
7. What excuse does Markheim give for his actions? Why does he call himself an "unwilling sinner"?
8. What technique does the visitant use to achieve his purpose with Markheim? What is the meaning of the visitant's statement "Evil . . . consists not in action, but in character"?
9. What is the meaning of the final description of the visitant? What is Stevenson saying about the struggle between good and evil in man?
10. What is the method of narration used in this story? Is it effective? Discuss.

VICTORIAN POETS

Like the prose of the period, Victorian poetry reflected the conflicting theories of the age. On the one hand, the people regarded the poet as a prophet and looked for instruction in poetry; on the other hand it became apparent that there was a lack of communication between poet and people. Much of the poetry of the period is characterized by a search for certainty or by an escape from the demands of a materialistic society.

The diversity of poetry written during the Victorian Age makes generalizations very difficult. Certainly, it is apparent that the spirit of the Romantic writers is much in evidence, particularly the spirit of Shelley and Keats. This influence seems strongest at the beginning of the period and toward the end of the period. The early Tennyson might be the lyrical Romantic singing songs of melancholy and isolation. Later, poets like Algernon Charles Swinburne, Dante Gabriel Rossetti, and some of the lesser poets were at times like the defiant Romantics who wished to escape from the harsh realities of life. Love, a favorite theme of the Romantics, received lyrical expression in the works of Elizabeth Barrett Browning; but others, like her husband Robert Browning and George Meredith, treated love much more realistically in an age where "respectability" was the watchword. The Victorians kept alive the sense of an imaginative force along with a real concern for form and discipline in writing.

However, the realities of Victorian life, with its multiplicity of problems, gave the poet the obligation not only of showing the wonder of the world but also of being a support for the moral values of life. For many, the poet was the one who could teach his readers the art of living; and poetry assumed a tone of moral earnestness.

Like the prose writers, the poets saw the growth of industrialization as a threat to the human condition. Commercial and mercantile world leadership, they felt, was being paid for by human misery and moral degradation. In their poetry, we see that economic progress had resulted in an exploitation of man, in sharp class distinctions, and, too often, in a lack of concern and feeling for the victims. It is ironic that the lines often chosen to represent the complacent optimism of the times—"God's in His Heaven/All's right with the world"—are said by Pippa as she enjoys the one day in the year when she is freed from work.

The conflict between science and religion was a special concern of the poets. Tennyson and Browning expressed in eloquent verse a spirit of confidence in a God of Love and a sense of the value of progress. But, beset by doubts himself, Matthew Arnold voiced a much more somber and pessimistic attitude. In many of his poems, he attempted to escape from the "sick fatigue, the languid doubt" which life was to him. Francis Thompson pictured the flight of man across the world struggling after human pleasure in a desire to satisfy the craving for God.

The diversity and expansiveness of Victorian poetry mirrored the age itself and were partly caused by the dilemma facing the poet trying to define his role in society. Tennyson gave voice to the declamation of Victorian progress, but he also wrote poems concerned with the role of the artist in society. Arnold believed that the poet was a prophet-seer and that poetry, therefore, was a moral force for the good and the true. Reacting against the oppressive middle-class tastes, the Pre-Raphaelites, a group of artists and writers who banded together in the 1840's, sought in art and poetry to recapture the clarity and directness of the medieval artists in an attempt to be a reforming influence. Browning, and to a much greater extent Gerard Manley Hopkins, experimented with language and syntax to communicate the intensity of feeling and the depths of human experience. Each in his own way was trying to communicate the sense that the poet had something to say to his fellow men, and these attempts stand in the first rank of English literature.

Alfred, Lord Tennyson was the poetic craftsman of his age and stands as the "representative man" among the eminent Victorians. During his own lifetime he had enormous popularity with the masses, both in England and in America, and, as Poet Laureate, became the image of the upstanding, patriotic Englishman, the inheritor and embodiment of his time.

Caught in the struggle of his day between faith and doubt, Tennyson tried to resolve the conflict in his own way. His long elegy, *In Memoriam*, one of the most widely read poems during the Victorian Period, represents most clearly his personal effort to come to terms with this problem. What he reached through his despair and questioning was a faith in a reality which implied a God of Love and individual immortality. Tennyson's was a voice which searched for certainty without the extremes of pessimism or optimism.

Robert Browning responded to the world with a seemingly intuitive optimism and enthusiasm. His poetry abounds in a spirit of cheerful courage and masculine energy based on his concept of aspiration. It is aspiration, the striving for a goal, which is the measure of the man: "A man's reach should exceed his grasp, Or what's a heaven for" is the answer he gave to the doubters of the Victorian Age.

However, this confidence does not mean that Browning was unaware of the great problems of his day or that he merely sidestepped the issues. In his dramatic monologues, he explored through the voices of his characters the sense of evil in the world and the struggle between faith and doubt in man.

Basing his beliefs more on intuition and faith than on reason, Browning was able to maintain his optimism in the face of the disillusionment of the later Victorian years. For him the poet had but one office—that of imparting the gift of seeing to his readers.

Elizabeth Barrett, before she met Robert Browning, was a highly praised writer. Her essays, translations, and poetry had given her a reputation which her future husband did not have at that time. However, with the notable exception of *Sonnets from the Portuguese,* much of her poetry has not stood the test of time. Her early poems like "The Cry of Nature" and "The Cry of the Children," show an ardent concern with liberal causes and social reform. If today we view them as little more than melodramatic hysterics, lacking control both in form and emotion, we must also remember that they helped awaken the conscience of the country to the plight of the child laborers and the poor.

The poetry of Matthew Arnold represents the sober mind of the Victorian Age at mid-century. It is an isolated poetry of wandering, disillusionment, and doubt and pictures concretely the despair of men "wandering between two worlds, one dead/The other powerless to be born."

Poetry, as he said in his *Essays in Criticism,* should have the "power of so dealing with things as to awaken in us a wonderfully full, new, and intimate sense of them, and of our relations with them." It was his hope that poetry, as a "criticism of life" could help to bring an end to class-consciousness. His pessimistic austerity, his doubt, his searching, and his melancholy tone mirror the age and give a preview of the inner search of the modern man.

Francis Thompson defined his role in life when he said: "To be the poet of the return to nature is something, but I would rather be the poet of the return to God." His poems themselves speak of his own experience as an outcast, introspective wanderer and addict and his struggles to return to God.

In his religious mysticism and his delight in rich imagery, Thompson has more in common with the metaphysical poets of the seventeenth century than with the poets of his own time. It has been said that had he lived in the Middle Ages, he might have expressed his visions of heavenly beauty in allegorical poems like those of the Pearl Poet. The dazzling exuberance of a poem like "The Hound of Heaven" attests to the influence of both the metaphysicals and the Romantics and shows the wide variety of poetry produced during the Victorian period.

Thomas Hardy is best known as a novelist who portrayed what he saw as man's helpless fight against nature and against fate. Yet despite Hardy's fatalism, his major characters, like Tess in *Tess of the D'Urbervilles* and Michael Henchard in *The Mayor of Casterbridge,* achieve dignity and dramatic stature by the strength of their humanity and the depths of their struggle.

Coming at the end of the Victorian Age, Hardy's is a stark voice, filled with melancholy and pessimism. In his poetry, too, he illustrated the adversity of coincidence and ironic fate. His poems stand in sharp contrast to the works of Victorian poets who were complacently certain that "all's right with the world."

Alfred, Lord Tennyson

(1809–1892)

Alfred, Lord Tennyson, the "representative man" of the Victorian Age, experimented with many different forms of poetry, exploiting the elements of rhythm and sound to give his work its great intensity and compactness of emotion. His is a lyric voice, and his best poems demonstrate a weaving of words and syntax into melody which was unsurpassed by the other Victorian poets. In a poem like "Ulysses" he uses landscape not only as a background for human characters but also, as did the Romantics, to represent states of mind. Although his poetry is uncomplicated and clear, he did write of the grave moral questions and issues which confronted the Victorians, in a conservative voice echoing the conventional morality of the Victorian middle class.

ULYSSES

It little profits that an idle king,
By this still hearth, among these barren crags,[1]
Matched with an agèd wife,[2] I mete and dole
Unequal laws unto a savage race
That hoard and sleep and feed, and know not me. 5
I cannot rest from travel; I will drink
Life to the lees; all times I have enjoyed
Greatly, have suffered greatly, both with those
That loved me, and alone; on shore, and when

---

[1] **barren crags:** refers to Ulysses' home on the island of Ithaca
[2] **agèd wife:** Penelope

Thro' scudding drifts the rainy Hyades [3] 10
Vext the dim sea; I am become a name;
For always roaming with a hungry heart
Much have I seen and known; cities of men
And manners, climates, councils, governments,
Myself not least, but honored of them all; 15
And drunk delight of battle with my peers,
Far on the ringing plains of windy Troy.
I am a part of all that I have met;
Yet all experience is an arch wherethrough
Gleams that untravelled world, whose margin fades 20
For ever and for ever when I move.
How dull it is to pause, to make an end,
To rust unburnished, not to shine in use!
As though to breathe were life. Life piled on life
Were all too little, and of one to me 25
Little remains; but every hour is saved
From that eternal silence, something more,
A bringer of new things; and vile it were
For some three suns to store and hoard myself,
And this grey spirit yearning in desire 30
To follow knowledge, like a sinking star,
Beyond the utmost bound of human thought.

    This is my son, mine own Telemachus,
To whom I leave the scepter and the isle—
Well-loved of me, discerning to fulfil 35
This labor, by slow prudence to make mild
A rugged people, and through soft degrees
Subdue them to the useful and the good.
Most blameless is he, centered in the sphere
Of common duties, decent not to fail 40
In offices of tenderness, and pay
Meet adoration to my household gods,
When I am gone. He works his work, I mine.

---

[3] **Hyades:** stars in a constellation associated with rain

There lies the port; the vessel puffs her sail;
There gloom the dark broad seas. My mariners, 45
Souls that have toiled, and wrought, and thought with me—
That ever with a frolic welcome took
The thunder and the sunshine, and opposed
Free hearts, free foreheads—you and I are old;
Old age hath yet his honor and his toil; 50
Death closes all; but something ere the end,
Some work of noble note, may yet be done,
Not unbecoming men that strove with gods.
The lights begin to twinkle from the rocks;
The long day wanes; the slow moon climbs; the deep 55
Moans round with many voices. Come, my friends,
'Tis not too late to seek a newer world.
Push off, and sitting well in order smite
The sounding furrows; for my purpose holds
To sail beyond the sunset, and the baths 60
Of all the western stars, until I die.
It may be that the gulfs will wash us down;
It may be we shall touch the Happy Isles,[4]
And see the great Achilles,[5] whom we knew.
Though much is taken, much abides; and though 65
We are not now that strength which in old days
Moved earth and heaven; that which we are, we are;
One equal temper of heroic hearts,
Made weak by time and fate, but strong in will
To strive, to seek, to find, and not to yield. 70

[4] **Happy Isles:** the place where heroes went after their death
[5] **Achilles:** hero in the Trojan War which Ulysses fought in before his long series of adventures on the way home

For Discussion

1. In this dramatic monologue, we see Homer's Ulysses as an old man reflecting on the present, the past, and the future. What is the present as he sees it in the first five lines? What

is the effect of words like "idle," "still," "barren," "aged," "savage"? What does he mean by the statement that the "savage race . . . know not me"?
2. What is the force of the resolution in lines 6 and 7? Why has Ulysses "become a name" (line 11)? What is the ideal of life expressed in lines 18–21 and 24–32? What knowledge is Ulysses seeking "beyond the utmost bound of human thought"?
3. Does Ulysses understand the nature of the work done by Telemachus? Does he, as a man of action, look down on the works of "slow prudence"?
4. In line 44 Ulysses turns toward his ship and addresses his mariners. What is the relationship between Ulysses and his men? What does he propose they do? How does the natural description in lines 54–56 help to represent the state of mind of Ulysses and his men? What is the effect of the change of rhythm in these lines? Does this change help to enrich the meaning?
5. Why do the men sail westward? What is the possible symbolic intent? Is there only positive action in the last six lines of the poem or is there also a sense of awareness of the limitation imposed on men? Is Ulysses only a man in terms of the poem or is he also a symbol of an ideal? Discuss.
6. It has been said that two voices speak in "Ulysses": that of resolution and that of despair. Do you agree? Discuss. What values are put forth in the poem?
7. The poem may be divided into three sections. What idea is developed in each section?
8. What is the verse form used in this poem? Why is this appropriate for the subject? Does the language of the poem seem too much like that of an orator or does it also have the naturalness of speech? What words and phrases help to identify Ulysses as a man of action?

FLOWER IN THE CRANNIED WALL

Flower in the crannied wall,
I pluck you out of the crannies,
I hold you here, root and all, in my hand,
Little flower—but *if* I could understand
What you are, root and all, and all in all, 5
I should know what God and man is.

For Discussion

1. What, according to the poem, are the relationships among the flower, the man, and God? What is the poem saying about life? What Victorian influences are implied in this short poem?
2. What, in effect, is the poet saying about so deep a theme by his choice of such simple diction?

THE LADY OF SHALOTT

Part I

On either side the river lie
Long fields of barley and of rye,
That clothe the wold and meet the sky;
And thro' the field the road runs by
    To many-towered Camelot; 5
And up and down the people go,
Gazing where the lilies blow [1]
Round an island there below,
    The Island of Shalott.

Willows whiten, aspens quiver, 10
Little breezes dusk and shiver
Thro' the wave that runs for ever
By the island in the river
    Flowing down to Camelot.

---
[1] **blow:** bloom

Four grey walls, and four grey towers,
Overlook a space of flowers,
And the silent isle imbowers
          The Lady of Shalott.

By the margin, willow-veiled,
Slide the heavy barges trailed
By slow horses; and unhailed
The shallop flitteth silken-sailed
          Skimming down to Camelot:
But who hath seen her wave her hand?
Or at the casement seen her stand?
Or is she known in all the land,
          The Lady of Shalott?

Only reapers, reaping early
In among the bearded barley,
Hear a song that echoes cheerly
From the river winding clearly,
          Down to towered Camelot:
And by the moon the reaper weary,
Piling sheaves in uplands airy,
Listening, whispers " 'Tis the fairy
          Lady of Shalott."

Part II

There she weaves by night and day
A magic web with colors gay.
She has heard a whisper say,
A curse is on her if she stay
          To look down to Camelot.
She knows not what the curse may be,
And so she weaveth steadily,
And little other care hath she,
          The Lady of Shalott.

And moving thro' a mirror clear
That hangs before her all the year,
Shadows of the world appear.
There she sees the highway near
        Winding down to Camelot:
There the river eddy whirls,
And there the surly village-churls,
And the red cloaks of market girls,
        Pass onward from Shalott.

Sometimes a troop of damsels glad,
An abbot on an ambling pad,[2]
Sometimes a curly shepherd-lad,
Or long-haired page in crimson clad,
        Goes by to towered Camelot;
And sometimes thro' the mirror blue
The knights come riding two and two:
She hath no loyal knight and true,
        The Lady of Shalott.

But in her web she still delights
To weave the mirror's magic sights,
For often thro' the silent nights
A funeral, with plumes and lights
        And music, went to Camelot:
Or when the moon was overhead,
Came two young lovers lately wed;
"I am half sick of shadows," said
        The Lady of Shalott.

Part III

A bow-shot from her bower-eaves,
He rode between the barley-sheaves,
The sun came dazzling thro' the leaves,
And flamed upon the brazen greaves
        Of bold Sir Lancelot.

[2] **pad:** palfrey

A red-cross knight for ever kneeled
To a lady in his shield,
That sparkled on the yellow field,
    Beside remote Shalott.

The gemmy bridle glittered free,
Like to some branch of stars we see
Hung in the golden galaxy.[3]
The bridle bells rang merrily
    As he rode down to Camelot:
And from his blazoned baldric slung
A mighty silver bugle hung;
And as he rode, his armor rung,
    Beside remote Shalott.

All in the blue unclouded weather
Thick-jewelled shone the saddle-leather,
The helmet and the helmet-feather
Burned like one burning flame together,
    As he rode down to Camelot.
As often thro' the purple night,
Below the starry clusters bright,
Some bearded meteor, trailing light,
    Moves over still Shalott.

His broad clear brow in sunlight glowed;
On burnished hooves his war-horse trode;
From underneath his helmet flowed
His coal-black curls as on he rode,
    As he rode down to Camelot.
From the bank and from the river
He flashed into the crystal mirror,
"Tirra lirra," by the river
    Sang Sir Lancelot.

[3] **Galaxy:** the Milky Way

She left the web, she left the loom,
She mades three paces thro' the room,
She saw the water-lily bloom,
She saw the helmet and the plume,
    She looked down to Camelot.
Out flew the web and floated wide;
The mirror cracked from side to side;
"The curse is come upon me," cried
    The Lady of Shalott.

Part IV

In the stormy east-wind straining,
The pale yellow woods were waning,
The broad stream in his banks complaining,
Heavily the low sky raining
    Over towered Camelot;
Down she came and found a boat
Beneath a willow left afloat,
And round about the prow she wrote
    The Lady of Shalott.

And down the river's dim expanse—
Like some bold seër in a trance,
Seeing all his own mischance—
With a glassy countenance
    Did she look to Camelot.
And at the closing of the day
She loosed the chain, and down she lay;
The broad stream bore her far away,
    The Lady of Shalott.

Lying, robed in snowy white
That loosely flew to left and right—
The leaves upon her falling light—
Thro' the noises of the night
    She floated down to Camelot:

And as the boat-head wound along
The willowy hills and fields among,
They heard her singing her last song,
      The Lady of Shalott.

Heard a carol, mournful, holy,   145
Chanted loudly, chanted lowly,
Till her blood was frozen slowly,
And her eyes were darkened wholly,
      Turned to towered Camelot.
For ere she reached upon the tide   150
The first house by the water-side,
Singing in her song she died,
      The Lady of Shalott.

Under tower and balcony,
By garden-wall and gallery,   155
A gleaming shape she floated by,
Dead-pale between the houses high,
      Silent into Camelot.
Out upon the wharfs they came,
Knight and burgher, lord and dame,   160
And round the prow they read her name,
      The Lady of Shalott.

Who is this? and what is here?
And in the lighted palace near
Died the sound of royal cheer;   165
And they crossed themselves for fear,
      All the knights at Camelot:
But Lancelot mused a little space;
He said, "She has a lovely face;
God in his mercy lend her grace,   170
      The Lady of Shalott."

For Discussion

1. What dramatic contrast is there between Camelot and the island of Shalott? How does this contrast help to define not only the island but also the Lady? What is the mood and tone of Part I? How is it achieved?
2. Part II picks up a sense of magic and color. How is this done? Why are the images in the mirror called "shadows of the world"?
3. Tennyson himself said that the key to the symbolic meaning of the poem is to be found in lines 71–72. What has happened to bring the Lady to her statement "I am half sick of shadows"? What might the "shadows" be?
4. Point out the details in Part III which develop Lancelot as an image of vital and intense life. What is the relationship between this vitality and the Lady? What happens when the Lady "looked down to Camelot"?
5. What is the mood of Part IV? What images help to develop this mood? How is the swan image used? What is the reaction of "knight and burgher, lord and dame" to the Lady's death? What is it that they do not understand? What irony is suggested by Lancelot's reaction?
6. Critics have variously interpreted this poem. Some suggest that it is a symbolic presentation of the conflict within a person between isolation from the world and commitment to it; others see it as the symbol of the dedicated artist who is destroyed by a world lacking in understanding. Which interpretation seems more compelling? Discuss, making certain that in your interpretation you account for the various elements in the poem.
7. This poem, which was heavily revised by Tennyson, has the sensuousness which we associate with John Keats. Point out examples of the sensuous appeals to sight and sound and show how they enrich the poem. Are there other Romantic characteristics in the poem?

MORTE D'ARTHUR

So all day long the noise of battle rolled
Among the mountains by the winter sea,
Until King Arthur's table, man by man,
Had fallen in Lyonnesse [1] about their lord,
King Arthur; then, because his wound was deep, 5
The bold Sir Bedivere uplifted him,
Sir Bedivere, the last of all his knights,
And bore him to a chapel nigh the field,
A broken chancel [2] with a broken cross,
That stood on a dark strait of barren land. 10
On one side lay the ocean and on one
Lay a great water, and the moon was full

    Then spake King Arthur to Sir Bedivere:
"The sequel of today unsolders all
The goodliest fellowship of famous knights 15
Whereof this world holds record. Such a sleep
They sleep—the men I loved. I think that we
Shall never more, at any future time,
Delight our souls with talk of knightly deeds,
Walking about the gardens and the halls 20
Of Camelot,[3] as in the days that were.
I perish by this people which I made,—
Though Merlin sware that I should come again
To rule once more—but let what will be, be.
I am so deeply smitten through the helm 25
That without help I cannot last till morn.
Thou therefore take my brand Excalibur,
Which was my pride; for thou rememberest how
In those old days, one summer noon, an arm
Rose up from out the bosom of the lake, 30

---
[1] **Lyonnesse:** Arthur was believed to have come from this legendary land, south of Cornwall
[2] **chancel:** sanctuary
[3] **Camelot:** seat of King Arthur's court

Clothed in white samite,[4] mystic, wonderful,
Holding the sword—and how I rowed across
And took it, and have worn it, like a king;
And, wheresoever I am sung or told
In aftertime, this also shall be known.
But now delay not; take Excalibur,
And fling him far into the middle mere;[5]
Watch what thou seest, and lightly bring me word."

    To him replied the bold Sir Bedivere:
"It is not meet, Sir King, to leave thee thus,
Aidless, alone, and smitten through the helm.
A little thing may harm a wounded man.
Yet I thy hest will all perform at full,
Watch what I see, and lightly bring thee word."

    So saying, from the ruined shrine he stepped
And in the moon athwart the place of tombs,
Where lay the mighty bones of ancient men,
Old knights, and over them the sea-wind sang
Shrill, chill, with flakes of foam. He, stepping down
By zigzag paths, and juts of pointed rock,
Came on the shining levels of the lake.

    There drew he forth the brand Excalibur,
And o'er him, drawing it, the winter moon,
Brightening the skirts of a long cloud, ran forth
And sparkled keen with frost against the hilt;
For all the haft twinkled with diamond sparks,
Myriads of topaz-lights, and jacinth-work
Of subtlest jewelry. He gazed so long
That both his eyes were dazzled, as he stood,
This way and that dividing the swift mind,
In act to throw; but at the last it seemed
Better to leave Excalibur concealed
There in the many-knotted water-flags,
That whistled stiff and dry about the marge.

---

[4] **samite:** silken fabric
[5] **mere:** lake

So strode he back slow to the wounded king.
   Then spake King Arthur to Sir Bedivere:
"Hast thou performed my mission which I gave?
What is it thou hast seen? or what hast heard?"
   And answer made the bold Sir Bedivere:
"I heard the ripple washing in the reeds,
And the wild water lapping on the crag."
   To whom replied King Arthur, faint and pale:
"Thou hast betrayed thy nature and thy name,
Not rendering true answer, as beseemed
Thy fealty, nor like a noble knight;
For surer sign had followed, either hand,
Or voice, or else a motion of the mere.
This is a shameful thing for men to lie.
Yet now, I charge thee, quickly go again
As thou art lief and dear, and do the thing
I bade thee, watch, and lightly bring me word."
   Then went Sir Bedivere the second time
Across the ridge, and paced beside the mere,
Counting the dewy pebbles, fixed in thought;
But when he saw the wonder of the hilt,
How curiously and strangely chased, he smote
His palms together, and he cried aloud:
   "And if indeed I cast the brand away,
Surely a precious thing, one worthy note,
Should thus be lost forever from the earth,
Which might have pleased the eyes of many men.
What good should follow this, if this were done?
What harm, undone? deep harm to disobey,
Seeing obedience is the bond of rule.
Were it well to obey then, if a king demand
An act unprofitable, against himself?
The King is sick, and knows not what he does.
What record, or what relic of my lord
Should be to aftertime, but empty breath
And rumors of a doubt? but were this kept,
Stored in some treasure-house of mighty kings,

Some one might show it at a joust of arms,
Saying, 'King Arthur's sword, Excalibur,
Wrought by the lonely maiden of the lake;
Nine years she wrought it, sitting in the deeps 105
Upon the hidden bases of the hills.'
So might some old man speak in the aftertime
To all the people, winning reverence;
But now much honor and much fame were lost."
    So spake he, clouded with his own conceit, 110
And hid Excalibur the second time,
And so strode back slow to the wounded king.
    Then spoke King Arthur, breathing heavily:
"What is it thou has seen? or what hast heard?"
    And answer made the bold Sir Bedivere: 115
"I heard the water lapping on the crag,
And the long ripple washing in the reeds."
    To whom replied King Arthur, much in wrath:
"Ah, miserable and unkind, untrue,
Unknightly, traitor-hearted! Woe is me! 120
Authority forgets a dying king,
Laid widowed of the power in his eye
That bowed the will. I see thee what thou art,
For thou, the latest-left of all my knights,
In whom should meet the offices of all, 125
Thou wouldst betray me for the precious hilt;
Either from lust of gold, or like a girl
Valuing the giddy pleasure of the eyes.
Yet, for a man may fail in duty twice,
And the third time may prosper, get thee hence; 130
But, if thou spare to fling Excalibur,
I will arise and slay thee with my hands."
    Then quickly rose Sir Bedivere, and ran,
And, leaping down the ridges lightly, plunged
Among the bulrush-beds, and clutched the sword, 135
And strongly wheeled and threw it. The great brand
Made lightnings in the splendor of the moon,

And flashing round and round, and whirled in an arch,
Shot like a streamer of the northern morn.[6]
Seen where the moving isles of winter shock 140
By night, with noises of the northern sea.
So flashed and fell the brand Excalibur;
But ere he dipped the surface, rose an arm
Clothed in white samite, mystic, wonderful,
And caught him by the hilt, and brandished him 145
Three times, and drew him under in the mere.
And lightly went the other to the king
    Then spoke King Arthur, drawing thicker breath:
"Now see I by thine eyes that this is done.
Speak out; what is it thou hast heard, or seen?" 150
    And answer made the bold Sir Bedivere:
"Sir King, I closed mine eyelids, lest the gems
Should blind my purpose, for I never saw,
Nor shall see, here or elsewhere, till I die,
Not though I live three lives of mortal men, 155
So great a miracle as yonder hilt.
Then with both hands I flung him, wheeling him;
But when I looked again, behold an arm,
Clothed in white samite, mystic, wonderful,
That caught him by the hilt, and brandished him 160
Three times, and drew him under in the mere."
    And answer made King Arthur, breathing hard:
"My end draws nigh; 'tis time that I were gone.
Make broad thy shoulders to receive my weight,
And bear me to the margin; yet I fear 165
My wound hath taken cold, and I shall die."
    So saying, from the pavement he half rose,
Slowly, with pain, reclining on his arm,
And looking wistfully with wide blue eyes
As in a picture. Him Sir Bedivere 170
Remorsefully regarded through his tears,
And would have spoken, but he found not words,

---

[6] Refers to the northern lights.

Then took with care, and kneeling on one knee,
O'er both his shoulders drew the languid hands,
And rising bore him through the place of tombs.   175
    But, as he walked, King Arthur panted hard,
Like one that feels a nightmare on his bed
When all the house is mute. So sighed the king,
Muttering and murmuring at his ear, "Quick, quick!
I fear it is too late, and I shall die."   180
But the other swiftly strode from ridge to ridge,
Clothed with his breath, and looking, as he walked,
Larger than human on the frozen hills.
He heard the deep behind him, and a cry
Before. His own thought drove him like a goad.   185
Dry clashed his harness in the icy caves
And barren chasms, and all to left and right
The bare black cliff clanged round him, as he based
His feet on juts of slippery crag that rang
Sharp-smitten with the dint of arméd heels—   190
And on a sudden, lo! the level lake,
And the long glories of the winter moon.
    Then saw they how there hove a dusky barge,
Dark as a funeral scarf from stem to stem,
Beneath them; and descending they were ware   195
That all the decks were dense with stately forms
Black-stoled, black-hooded, like a dream—by these
Three queens with crowns of gold—and from them rose
A cry that shivered to the tingling stars,
And, as it were one voice, an agony   200
Of lamentation, like a wind that shrills
All night in a waste land, where no one comes,
Or hath come, since the making of the world.
    Then murmured Arthur, "Place me in the barge,"
And to the barge they came. There those three queens   205
Put forth their hands, and took the king, and wept.
But she, that rose the tallest of them all
And fairest, laid his head upon her lap,

And loosed the shattered casque, and chafed his hands,
And called him by his name, complaining [7] loud, 210
And dropping bitter tears against his brow
Striped with dark blood; for all his face was white
And colorless, and like the withered moon
Smote by the fresh beam of the springing east;
And all his greaves and cuisses dashed with drops 215
Of onset; and the light and lustrous curls—
That made his forehead like a rising sun
High from the dais-throne—were parched with dust;
Or, clotted into points and hanging loose,
Mixed with the knightly growth that fringed his lips. 220
So like a shattered column lay the king;
Not like that Arthur who, with lance in rest,
From spur to plume a star of tournament,
Shot through the lists at Camelot, and charged
Before the eyes of ladies and of kings. 225

    Then loudly cried the bold Sir Bedivere:
"Ah! my Lord Arthur, whither shall I go?
Where shall I hide my forehead and my eyes?
For now I see the true old times are dead,
When every morning brought a noble chance, 230
And every chance brought out a noble knight.
Such times have been not since the light that led
The holy Elders with the gift of myrrh.[8]
But now the whole *Round Table* is dissolved
Which was an image of the mighty world; 235
And I, the last, go forth companionless,
And the days darken round me, and the years,
Among new men, strange faces, other minds."

    And slowly answered Arthur from the barge:
"The old order changeth, yielding place to new, 240
And God fulfills himself in many ways,
Lest one good custom should corrupt the world.

---
[7] **complaining:** wailing
[8] Refers to the star that led the three kings to the Christ child.

"Comfort thyself: what comfort is in me?
I have lived my life, and that which I have done
May He within himself make pure! but thou, 245
If thou shouldst never see my face again,
Pray for my soul. More things are wrought by prayer
Than this world dreams of. Wherefore, let thy voice
Rise like a fountain for me night and day.
For what are men better than sheep or goats 250
That nourish a blind life within the brain,
If, knowing God, they lift not hands of prayer
Both for themselves and those who call them friend?
For so the whole round earth is every way
Bound by gold chains about the feet of God. 255
But now farewell. I am going a long way
With these thou seest—if indeed I go—
(For all my mind is clouded with a doubt)
To the island-valley of Avilion; [9]
Where falls not hail, or rain, or any snow, 260
Nor ever wind blows loudly; but it lies
Deep-meadowed, happy, fair with orchard lawns
And bowery hollows crowned with summer sea,
Where I will heal me of my grievous wound."

So said he, and the barge with oar and sail 265
Moved from the brink, like some full-breasted swan
That, fluting a wild carol ere her death,
Ruffles her pure cold plume, and takes the flood
With swarthy webs. Long stood Sir Bedivere
Revolving many memories, till the hull 270
Looked one black dot against the verge of dawn,
And on the mere the wailing died away. . . .

[9] **Avilion:** Avalon, the paradise of Arthurian legend

For Discussion

1. This section was written before Tennyson had developed his plan for *The Idylls of the King*. It was later incorpo-

rated into "The Passing of Arthur," the last of *The Idylls.* Outline the events of the last hours of Arthur. What is the significance of lines 21–24?
2. Why does Sir Bedivere not do King Arthur's bidding? What were Arthur's reactions to Bedivere's two failures? What does Bedivere see when he throws Excalibur into the lake?
3. Who are the "three queens with crowns of gold"? Do they have symbolic value? What is the effect of the contrast between the dying Arthur and the Arthur of former times? Point out the use of figurative language which makes this contrast so telling.
4. How, according to Bedivere, was the Round Table "an image of the mighty world"?
5. What possible interpretations can you give for Arthur's answer in lines 240–243? Are these lines and the didactic lines which follow more suitable for the Victorian Age than for the situation at the time of Arthur? Discuss.
6. In what meter is this poem written? What poetic form is used? Why are these appropriate for the subject and tone of the poem?
7. Do you think Tennyson was attracted to medieval themes as a means of escaping from his own times or as a means of seeing Victorian England more clearly? Discuss, pointing out passages from this poem to support your answer.

CROSSING THE BAR

Sunset and evening star,
    And one clear call for me!
And may there be no moaning of the bar,
    When I put out to sea,

But such a tide as moving seems asleep,   5
    Too full for sound and foam,
When that which drew from out the boundless deep
    Turns again home.

> Twilight and evening bell,
>   And after that the dark!
> And may there be no sadness of farewell,
>   When I embark;
>
> For tho' from out our bourne of time and place
>   The flood may bear me far,
> I hope to see my Pilot face to face
>   When I have crossed the bar.

For Discussion

1. Tennyson asked that this poem be placed at the end of all editions of his poetry. What is the basic metaphor of the poem? How do the images of light and dark develop the basic metaphor?
2. What is symbolized by the tide in line 5? What is the dark in line 10? Who is the Pilot in line 15?
3. What is the effect of the irregular length of line in this poem? Does it follow a pattern?
4. What is the mood of this poem? How would you characterize its tone? Is there certainty here or is it a firm hope? Discuss.

For Composition

1. Using these lines of Ulysses as your starting point, write a theme in which you explore the necessity for action as a part of life:

   > How dull it is to pause, to make an end,
   > To rust unburnished, not to shine in use!
   > As though to breathe were life!

2. Write a critical paper comparing "The Lady of Shalott" with Keats's "La Belle Dame Sans Merci" as to imagery and the use of the medieval setting.

Robert Browning

(1812–1889)

Robert Browning's poetry underscores the value he places on action and endurance. Much more than the attainment of the goal itself is the power and strength to be gained in the struggle. The "apparent failure" shows a deep sense of the imperfection of man; but, more important, it leads Browning to a sense of the infinite perfection of Heaven. In poems like "Prospice" the image of the joyful contest of life is mirrored in the final fight which comes to all men, a fight which Browning would have men accept wholeheartedly.

However joyous was Browning's optimism, he did explore the dark and twisted side of man's nature, particularly in his dramatic monologues. Although he was not the first to use this form, he made it his own by adding a subtle interplay between the speaker and the audience. In a work like "My Last Duchess," he ironically exposes the Duke through the tone and diction of his own statements.

Perhaps the finest contribution Browning made to poetry is his use of the colloquial idiom, often harsh and prosaic, but always vital and real. This ability, together with his keen insight into the psychological states of mind of his imaginary characters, has made Browning one of the most popular Victorian poets in the twentieth century.

CAVALIER TUNES

1. Marching Along

Kentish Sir Byng [1] stood for his King,
Bidding the crop-headed Parliament [2] swing:
And, pressing [3] a troop unable to stoop
And see the rogues flourish and honest folk droop,
Marched them along, fifty-score strong,
Great-hearted gentlemen, singing this song.

God for King Charles! Pym [4] and such carles [5]
To the Devil that prompts 'em their treasonous parles! [6]
Cavaliers, up! Lips from the cup,
Hands from the pasty, nor bite take nor sup,
Till you're—

> *Chorus.* Marching along, fifty-score strong,
> Great-hearted gentlemen, singing this song!

Hampden [7] to hell, and his obsequies' knell
Serve Hazelrig, Fiennes, and young Harry [8] as well!
England, good cheer! Rupert is near!
Kentish and loyalists, keep we not here,

> *Chorus.* Marching along, fifty-score strong,
> Great-hearted gentlemen, singing this song!

Then, God for King Charles! Pym and his snarls
To the Devil that pricks on such pestilent carles!

---

[1] **Sir Byng:** an imaginary person
[2] **crop-headed Parliament:** In 1640 the British Parliament was dominated by Puritans who cut their hair short as a symbol of their convictions.
[3] **pressing:** enlisting
[4] **Pym:** a Puritan opponent of King Charles I
[5] **carles:** rude persons
[6] **parles:** conspirings
[7] **Hampden:** another Puritan opponent of the king
[8] **Hazelrig, Fiennes, Harry:** three Puritans

Hold by the right, you double your might;
So, onward to Nottingham,[9] fresh for the fight,

> *Chorus.* March we along, fifty-score strong,
> Great-hearted gentlemen, singing this song!

2. Give a Rouse

King Charles, and who'll do him right now?
King Charles, and who's ripe for fight now?
Give a rouse: here's, in hell's despite now,
King Charles!

Who gave me the goods that went since?
Who raised me the house that sank once?
Who helped me to gold I spent since?
Who found me in wine you drank once?

> *Chorus.* King Charles, and who'll do him right now?
> King Charles, and who's ripe for fight now?
> Give a rouse: here's, in hell's despite now,
> King Charles!

To whom used my boy George quaff else,
By the old fool's side that begot him?
For whom did he cheer and laugh else,
While Noll's [10] damned troopers shot him?

> *Chorus.* King Charles, and who'll do him right now? . . .

3. Boot and Saddle

Boot, saddle, to horse, and away!
Rescue my castle before the hot day
Brightens to blue from its silvery grey.
> *Chorus.* Boot, saddle, to horse, and away!

Ride past the suburbs, asleep as you'd say;
Many's the friend there, will listen and pray,

---
[9] **Nottingham:** where the Cavaliers attacked the Puritan army in 1642
[10] **Noll:** term of contempt for Oliver Cromwell

"God's luck to gallants that strike up the lay—
Chorus. Boot, saddle, to horse, and away!"

Forty miles off, like a roebuck at bay,
Flouts Castle Brancepeth the Roundheads' array:
Who laughs, "Good fellows ere this, by my fay,
Chorus. Boot, saddle, to horse, and away!"

Who? My wife Gertrude; that, honest and gay,
Laughs when you talk of surrendering, "Nay!
I've better counsellors; what counsel they?
Chorus. Boot, saddle, to horse, and away!"

For Discussion

1. These rousing songs display the attitude of the Cavaliers, those loyal to King Charles I, toward the Puritans. Show how in each poem it is this loyalist spirit which is the source of the emotion. What is the attitude toward the Puritans expressed in each song?
2. The second of these songs is an open-hearted cheer for the King. What has the King done for these men? Examine the first line in the third song. How does the blend of rhythm and use of words convey the sense of action?
3. What qualities of the ballad and drinking song are displayed in these poems? What is the function of the chorus in these drinking songs? What is the rhythm in each song? What rhythms help to convey the galloping sense of the songs?

"HOW THEY BROUGHT THE GOOD NEWS FROM GHENT [1] TO AIX"

I sprang to the stirrup, and Joris, and he;
I galloped, Dirck galloped, we galloped all three;
"Good speed!" cried the watch, as the gate-bolts undrew;
"Speed!" echoed the wall to us galloping through;

[1] **Ghent:** city in Belgium 100 miles from Aix, a city in Germany

"How They Brought the Good News from Ghent to Aix"

Behind shut the postern,[2] the lights sank to rest, 5
And into the midnight we galloped abreast.

Not a word to each other; we kept the great pace
Neck by neck, stride by stride, never changing our place;
I turned in my saddle and made its girths tight
Then shortened each stirrup, and set the pique [3] right, 10
Rebuckled the cheek-strap, chained slacker the bit,
Nor galloped less steadily Roland a whit.

'Twas moonset at starting; but while we drew near
Lokeren, the cocks crew and twilight dawned clear;
At Boom, a great yellow star came out to see; 15
At Düffeld, 'twas morning as plain as could be;
And from Mecheln church-steeple we heard the half-chime,
So Joris broke silence with, "Yet there is time!"

At Aershot, up leaped of a sudden the sun,
And against him the cattle stood black every one, 20
To stare through the mist at us galloping past,
And I saw my stout galloper Roland at last,
With resolute shoulders, each butting away
The haze, as some bluff river headland its spray;

And his low head and crest, just one sharp ear bent back 25
For my voice, and the other pricked out on his track;
And one eye's black intelligence—ever that glance
O'er its white edge at me, his own master, askance!
And the thick heavy spume-flakes which aye and anon
His fierce lips shook upwards in galloping on. 30

By Hasselt, Dirck groaned; and cried Joris, "Stay spur!
Your Roos galloped bravely, the fault's not in her,
We'll remember at Aix"—for one heard the quick wheeze
Of her chest, saw the stretched neck and staggering knees,

---

[2] **postern:** a side or back door
[3] **pique:** pommel

And sunk tail, and horrible heave of the flank, 35
As down on her haunches she shuddered and sank.

So we were left galloping, Joris and I,
Past Looz and past Tongres, no cloud in the sky;
The broad sun above laughed a pitiless laugh,
'Neath our feet broke the brittle bright stubble like chaff; 40
Till over by Dalhem a dome-spire sprang white,
And "Gallop," gasped Joris, "for Aix is in sight!"

"How they'll greet us!"—and all in a moment his roan
Rolled neck and croup over, lay dead as a stone;
And there was my Roland to bear the whole weight 45
Of the news which alone could save Aix from her fate,
With his nostrils like pits full of blood to the brim,
And with circles of red for his eye-sockets' rim.

Then I cast loose my buffcoat, each holster let fall,
Shook off both my jack-boots, let go belt and all. 50
Stood up in the stirrup, leaned, patted his ear,
Called my Roland his pet-name, my horse without peer;
Clapped my hands, laughed and sang, any noise, bad or good,
Till at length into Aix Roland galloped and stood.

And all I remember is, friends flocking round 55
As I sat with his head 'twixt my knees on the ground;
And no voice but was praising this Roland of mine,
As I poured down his throat our last measure of wine,
Which (the burgesses voted by common consent)
Was no more than his due who brought good news from
   Ghent. 60

For Discussion

   1. Who is the speaker in the poem? How does the use of verbs
     help to give the sense of speed, strain, and urgency that is

so evident? What is the predominant meter of the poem? Is this appropriate for the subject?
2. Browning takes particular care to let the reader know the time element. When did the riders leave? Point out the passages which denote time and which help to plot the journey. What forces were fighting against the men and the horses. What is suggested by the description of the horses?
3. How does this poem capture the spirit of masculine striving so valued by Browning?

THE LAST RIDE TOGETHER

1

I said—Then, dearest, since 'tis so,
Since now at length my fate I know,
Since nothing all my love avails,
Since all, my life seemed meant for, fails,
    Since this was written and needs must be—   5
My whole heart rises up to bless
Your name in pride and thankfulness!
Take back the hope you gave,—I claim
Only a memory of the same,
—And this beside, if you will not blame,   10
    Your leave for one more last ride with me.

2

My mistress bent that brow of hers;
Those deep dark eyes where pride demurs
When pity would be softening through,
Fixed me a breathing-while or two   15
    With life or death in the balance: right!
The blood replenished me again;
My last thought was at least not vain:
I and my mistress, side by side
Shall be together, breathe and ride,   20
So, one day more am I deified.
    Who knows but the world may end tonight?

3

Hush! if you saw some western cloud
All billowy-bosomed, over-bowed
By many benedictions—sun's
And moon's and evening-star's at once—
    And so, you, looking and loving best,
Conscious grew, your passion drew
Cloud, sunset, moonrise, star-shine too,
Down on you, near and yet more near,
Till flesh must fade for heaven was here!—
Thus leant she and lingered—joy and fear!
    Thus lay she a moment on my breast.

4

Then we began to ride. My soul
Smoothed itself out, a long-cramped scroll
Freshening and fluttering in the wind.
Past hopes already lay behind.
    What need to strive with a life awry?
Had I said that, had I done this,
So might I gain, so might I miss.
Might she have loved me? just as well
She might have hated, who can tell!
Where had I been now if the worst befell?
    And here we are riding, she and I.

5

Fail I alone, in words and deeds?
Why, all men strive, and who succeeds?
We rode; it seemed my spirit flew,
Saw other regions, cities new,
    As the world rushed by on either side.
I thought,—All labour, yet no less
Bear up beneath their unsuccess.
Look at the end of work, contrast

The petty done, the undone vast,
This present of theirs with the hopeful past!
I hoped she would love me; here we ride.

6

What hand and brain went ever paired?
What heart alike conceived and dared?
What act proved all its thought had been?
What will but felt the fleshly screen?
We ride and I see her bosom heave.
There's many a crown for who can reach.
Ten lines, a statesman's life in each!
The flag stuck on a heap of bones,
A soldier's doing! what atones?
They scratch his name on the Abbey-stones.
My riding is better, by their leave.

7

What does it all mean, poet? Well,
Your brains beat into rhythm, you tell
What we felt only; you expressed
You hold things beautiful the best,
And place them in rhyme so, side by side.
'Tis something, nay 'tis much: but then,
Have you yourself what's best for men?
Are you—poor, sick, old ere your time—
Nearer one whit your own sublime
Than we who never have turned a rhyme?
Sing, riding's a joy! For me, I ride.

8

And you, great sculptor—so, you gave
A score of years to Art, her slave,
And that's your Venus, whence we turn
To yonder girl that fords the burn!

You acquiesce, and shall I repine?
What, man of music, you grown grey
With notes and nothing else to say,
Is this your sole praise from a friend, 85
"Greatly his opera's strains intend,
But in music we know how fashions end!"
 I gave my youth; but we ride, in fine.

9

Who knows what's fit for us? Had fate
Proposed bliss here should sublimate 90
My being—had I signed the bond—
Still one must lead some life beyond,
 Have a bliss to die with, dim-descried.

This foot once planted on the goal,
This glory-garland round my soul, 95
Could I descry such? Try and test!
I sink back shuddering from the quest.
Earth being so good, would heaven seem best?
 Now, heaven and she are beyond this ride.

10

And yet—she has not spoke so long! 100
What if heaven be that, fair and strong
At life's best, with our eyes upturned
Whither life's flower is first discerned,
 We, fixed so, ever should so abide?
What if we still ride on, we two 105
With life for ever old, yet new,
Changed not in kind but in degree,
The instant made eternity,—
And heaven just prove that I and she
 Ride, ride together, for ever ride? 110

For Discussion

1. This is another of Browning's "riding" poems, but this ride is far different from the ride to Ghent. Pay careful attention to the voice of the speaker. What is the dramatic situation given in the opening stanza? What is the speaker feeling for the lady? What does he mean by line 21, "one day more am I deified"?
2. What is his attitude toward the past? How has the past influenced the future? What are the feelings expressed in stanzas 4 and 5? Do you think that the speaker's comparison of his own failures to the failures of other men is an example of a human weakness? What is his attitude toward hope? What is the meaning of line 55?
3. What does stanza 6 tell of his attitude toward human achievement? What is the meaning of line 66, "My riding is better, by their leave" in the light of the preceding stanzas?
4. Stanzas 7 and 8 compare poetry, sculpture, and music to love and life. Does the speaker see these as rivals to love or as ways of expressing the feelings of love more objectively? Discuss.
5. In stanzas 9 and 10 the poem moves with certainty toward a symbolic meaning for the ride. What does the ride symbolize? Do you think that the poem suggests the impossibility of man's achieving perfect happiness? Or is the poem saying that such moments are short-lived periods amid a life filled with frustration and failure? What is the meaning and significance of lines 105–110?
6. Chart the rhythmic pattern and the rhyme scheme of the first stanza. How does Browning succeed in making rhythm suggest ordinary speech?

MY LAST DUCHESS

Ferrara

That's my last duchess painted on the wall,
Looking as if she were alive. I call
That piece a wonder, now: Frà Pandolf's [1] hands
Worked busily a day, and there she stands.
Will't please you sit and look at her? I said   5
"Frà Pandolf" by design, for never read
Strangers like you that pictured countenance,
The depth and passion of its earnest glance,
But to myself they turned (since none puts by
The curtain I have drawn for you, but I)   10
And seemed as they would ask me, if they durst,
How such a glance came there; so, not the first
Are you to turn and ask thus. Sir, 'twas not
Her husband's presence only, called that spot
Of joy into the duchess' cheek: perhaps   15
Frà Pandolf chanced to say, "Her mantle laps
Over my lady's wrist too much," or "Paint
Must never hope to reproduce the faint
Half-flush that dies along her throat"; such stuff
Was courtesy, she thought, and cause enough   20
For calling up that spot of joy. She had
A heart—how shall I say?—too soon made glad,
Too easily impressed; she liked whate'er
She looked on, and her looks went everywhere.
Sir, 'twas all one! My favor at her breast,   25
The dropping of the daylight in the west,
The bough of cherries some officious fool
Broke in the orchard for her, the white mule
She rode with round the terrace—all and each
Would draw from her alike the approving speech,   30
Or blush, at least. She thanked men,—good; but thanked

---

[1] **Frà Pandolf:** imaginary artist

Somehow—I know not how—as if she ranked
My gift of a nine-hundred-years-old name
With anybody's gift. Who'd stoop to blame
This sort of trifling? Even had you skill   35
In speech (which I have not) to make your will
Quite clear to such an one, and say, "Just this
Or that in you disgusts me; here you miss,
Or there exceed the mark"—and if she let
Herself be lessoned so, nor plainly set   40
Her wits to yours, forsooth, and made excuse,—
E'en then would be some stooping, and I choose
Never to stoop. Oh, sir, she smiled, no doubt,
Whene'er I passed her; but who passed without
Much the same smile? This grew; I gave commands;   45
Then all smiles stopped together. There she stands
As if alive. Will't please you rise? We'll meet
The company below, then. I repeat,
The count your master's known munificence
Is ample warrant that no just pretense   50
Of mine for dowry will be disallowed;
Though his fair daughter's self, as I avowed
At starting, is my object. Nay, we'll go
Together down, sir! Notice Neptune,[2] though,
Taming a sea-horse, thought a rarity,   55
Which Claus of Innsbruck [3] cast in bronze for me.

[2] **Neptune:** god of the sea
[3] **Claus of Innsbruck:** imaginary sculptor

For Discussion

1. In the dramatic monologue, the speaker reveals himself and we, as readers and viewers of this drama, work out our own judgments about his values and ideals. In this monologue, the Duke of Ferrara is speaking to an emissary. What is the situation at the beginning of the poem? What is the Duke's attitude toward the painting?
2. What is the character of the Duchess as given by the Duke? The Duke's annoyance with the Duchess is revealed in sev-

eral ways. What actions of the Duchess annoy him? What do these comments tell us about the Duke? Is your evaluation of the Duchess's character the same as his? If not, how does it differ?
3. What is your evaluation of the Duke's character? What phrases and remarks most reveal his character? Do you think he intended to give this impression? Discuss.
4. Who is the emissary? What is the relationship between the emissary's reason for visiting the Duke and the incidents about the Duchess which the Duke tells? What is the effect of the word "self" (line 52) referring to the Duke's future bride?
5. The poem begins and ends with references to art. Compare the sensitive and intelligent feeling for art with the Duke's attitude toward human relationships. What is the artistic function of the poet's using rhymed couplets in a poem of conversation?

PROSPICE [1]

Fear death?—to feel the fog in my throat,
    The mist in my face,
When the snows begin, and the blasts denote
    I am nearing the place,
The power of the night, the press of the storm,   5
    The post of the foe;
Where he stands, the Arch Fear [2] in a visible form,
    Yet the strong man must go:
For the journey is done and the summit attained,
    And the barriers fall,   10
Though a battle's to fight ere the guerdon be gained,
    The reward of it all.
I was ever a fighter, so—one fight more,
    The best and the last!
I would hate that death bandaged my eyes, and forbore,   15
    And bade me creep past.

[1] **Prospice:** derived from the Latin word meaning "look forward"
[2] **Arch Fear:** Death

No! let me taste the whole of it, fare like my peers
    The heroes of old,
Bear the brunt, in a minute pay glad life's arrears
    Of pain, darkness and cold.
For sudden the worst turns the best to the brave,
    The black minute's at end,
And the elements' rage, the fiend-voices that rave,
    Shall dwindle, shall blend,
Shall change, shall become first a peace out of pain,
    Then a light, then thy breast,
O thou soul of my soul! I shall clasp thee again,
    And with God be the rest!

For Discussion

1. This poem is about death, but it is also about love. What is the basic metaphor underlying the poem? Enumerate the details used to develop this metaphor.
2. What is the effect of "No!" (line 17)? To what is this the answer? What one fate does the speaker fear? How does the reference to "the heroes of old" widen the scope of the concept?
3. How do the last seven lines show that the "worst turns the best to the brave"? Who is the "soul of my soul"?
4. Show how Browning's use of sound and rhythm in the poem aid the meaning.

For Composition

1. Imagine that you are the emissary visiting the Duke of Ferrara. Write a letter to your master giving your impressions of the character of the Duke and making your recommendations concerning the marriage.
2. Write a theme contrasting the spirit of war reflected in the "Cavalier Tunes" or "How They Brought the Good News from Ghent to Aix" with attitudes toward war at the present time. Try to use specific references to develop your generalizations.

Elizabeth Barrett Browning

(1806–1861)

The sonnet sequence, *Sonnets from the Portuguese,* which Elizabeth Barrett Browning presented to her husband, stands among the finest love poems written during the nineteenth century. In these poems, she expressed the warmth of love and affection with intensity and vibrancy. Within the controlled sonnet form she found the discipline which allowed her to express profound emotion without the excesses of unrestrained feeling.

from SONNETS FROM THE PORTUGUESE

1

I thought once how Theocritus [1] had sung
Of the sweet years, the dear and wished-for years,
Who each one in a gracious hand appears
To bear a gift for mortals, old or young;
And, as I mused it in his antique tongue, 5
I saw, in gradual vision through my tears,
The sweet, sad years, the melancholy years,
Those of my own life, who by turns had flung
A shadow across me. Straightway I was 'ware,
So weeping, how a mystic Shape did move 10
Behind me, and drew me backward by the hair;
And a voice said in mastery, while I strove,
"Guess now who holds thee?"—"Death," [2] I said. But, there,
The silver answer rang—"Not Death, but Love."

[1] **Theocritus:** a famous Greek poet of the third century B.C.
[2] **Death:** Miss Barrett, an invalid, had expected to die soon

For Discussion

1. What is the contrast between the songs of Theocritus and the years of the life of the narrator? Why does she call her years "sweet, sad" (line 7)? What is the "shadow" (line 9)?
2. Is there a change in mood in the sestet of the sonnet? What words help to determine the mood? What is the "mystic Shape"? Why is the answer the voice gives called "silver"?

6

Go from me. Yet I feel that I shall stand
Henceforward in thy shadow. Nevermore
Alone upon the threshold of my door
Of individual life, I shall command
The uses of my soul, nor lift my hand   5
Serenely in the sunshine as before,
Without the sense of that which I forbore—
Thy touch upon the palm. The widest land
Doom takes to part us, leaves thy heart in mine
With pulses that beat double. What I do   10
And what I dream include thee, as the wine
Must taste of its own grapes. And when I sue
God for myself, He hears that name of thine,
And sees within my eyes the tears of two.

For Discussion

1. What is the effect of the imperative "Go from me"? Judging from the tone of the next four lines, with what emotion are these words said?
2. Discuss the images of light and dark as they are used in the octave. What feelings do these images convey? What is the meaning of "Thy touch upon the palm" (line 8)?
3. What contrast is afforded by the sestet to the sense of separation presented in the octave? What does the poet mean by the image of wine and grapes?

14

If thou must love me, let it be for naught
Except for love's sake only. Do not say
"I love her for her smile—her look—her way
Of speaking gently—for a trick of thought
That falls in well with mine, and certes brought   5
A sense of pleasant ease on such a day"—
For these things in themselves, Belovéd, may
Be changed, or change for thee—and love, so wrought,
May be unwrought so. Neither love me for
Thine own dear pity's wiping my cheeks dry—   10
A creature might forget to weep, who bore
Thy comfort long, and lose thy love thereby!
But love me for love's sake, that evermore
Thou mayst love on, through love's eternity.

For Discussion

1. Why do you think the poet says she wants to be loved for love's sake alone? Does she imply that the things usually associated with love are merely the externals and not the reality of love?
2. Compare lines 7–9 with these lines from Shakespeare's Sonnet 116: "Love is not love/ Which alters when it alteration finds." What is the attitude toward reality in these excerpts?
3. What relationship is the basic image in the sestet? What is the meaning of lines 11–12? How do these lines prepare for the last two lines? What is "love" in this sonnet?
4. This sonnet has a conversational tone. How do the structure of sentences and the run-on lines help to achieve this effect?
5. Chart the rhyme scheme of this sonnet. Is it Shakespearean or Petrarchan? What is the relation between the sonnet structure and the meaning?

26

I lived with visions for my company [1]
Instead of men and women, years ago,
And found them gentle mates, nor thought to know
A sweeter music than they played to me.
But soon their trailing purple was not free   5
Of this world's dust, their lutes did silent grow,
And I myself grew faint and blind below
Their vanishing eyes. Then THOU didst come—to be,
Belovéd, what they seemed. Their shining fronts,
Their songs, their splendors (better, yet the same,   10
As river-water hallowed into fonts),
Met in thee, and from out thee overcame
My soul with satisfaction of all wants:
Because God's gifts put man's best dreams to shame.

[1] Refers to the years when she was an invalid before her marriage.

For Discussion

1. This sonnet deals with dreams and reality. What "visions" were the speaker's company? Why did she not think to know "A sweeter music than they played to me"?
2. What does the poet mean by her statement that her visions were "not free/ Of this world's dust"? What is her reaction to this?
3. The present reality of THOU is given in the sestet. How does this reality contrast with the "visions"? What is the effect of the word "hallowed" (line 11)?
4. What is the distinction the speaker makes between "God's gift" and "man's best dreams"? What does this say about love and its place in human life?

43

How do I love thee? Let me count the ways.
I love thee to the depth and breadth and height
My soul can reach, when feeling out of sight
For the ends of Being and ideal Grace.
I love thee to the level of every day's   5
Most quiet need, by sun and candle-light.
I love thee freely, as men strive for Right;
I love thee purely, as they turn from Praise.
I love thee with the passion put to use
In my old griefs, and with my childhood's faith.   10
I love thee with a love I seemed to lose
With my lost saints—I love thee with the breath,
Smiles, tears, of all my life!—and, if God choose,
I shall but love thee better after death.

For Discussion

1. This is the most famous of all the *Sonnets from the Portuguese*. What qualities make it a classic expression of love of woman for man?
2. Discuss the "ways." Do the individual expressions of love encompass the whole of life? Discuss the imagery which develops each way.
3. The resonance of this poem is created by the use of open vowels. How do the sounds in "depth, and breadth and height" echo the meaning? How does the simplicity of diction help the poem to achieve the depth of feeling that it has?

For Composition

1. Write a critical paper comparing the diction used in Sonnet 1 with that used in Sonnet 43. How do the differences in diction account for the differences in effect, resonance, and communication of feeling?
2. In Sonnet 26, the poet talks about dreams and reality. Write a short theme in which you discuss the relationship between dreams and reality in your own life.

Matthew Arnold

(1822–1888)

In a letter to his mother, Matthew Arnold assessed his poetry as representing "the main movement of mind of the last quarter of a century." In his poetry, he presented the divided soul of the thoughtful, sensitive man seeking to reconcile the opposing forces in himself and in Victorian life—doubt and faith; emotion and firm control; Romantic imagination and moral earnestness.

At the same time that he expressed this doubt, he showed what he saw with beauty, power, and technical skill. Most of the poetry has an underlying note of sadness, which is expressed with classical plainness of style and structure and calm restraint. Arnold's was a meditative voice which echoed the spiritual problems of his age. His "Dover Beach" stands as a poem which bespeaks the problem of the age and is one of the finest expressions of religious doubt in English.

SELF-DEPENDENCE

Weary of myself, and sick of asking
What I am, and what I ought to be,
At this vessel's prow I stand, which bears me
Forwards, forwards, o'er the starlit sea.

And a look of passionate desire 5
O'er the sea and to the stars I send:
"Ye who from my childhood up have calmed me,
Calm me, ah, compose me to the end!

"Ah, once more," I cried, "ye stars, ye waters,
On my heart your mighty charm renew;   10
Still, still let me, as I gaze upon you,
Feel my soul becoming vast like you!"

From the intense, clear, star-sown vault of heaven,
Over the lit sea's unquiet way,
In the rustling night-air came the answer: 15
"Wouldst thou *be* as these are? *Live* as they.

"Unaffrighted by the silence round them,
Undistracted by the sights they see,
These demand not that the things without them
Yield them love, amusement, sympathy.   20

"And with joy the stars perform their shining,
And the sea its long moon-silvered roll;
For self-poised they live, nor pine with noting
All the fever of some differing soul.

"Bounded by themselves, and unregardful   25
In what state God's other works may be,
In their own tasks all their powers pouring,
These attain the mighty life you see."

O air-born voice! long since, severely clear,
A cry like thine in mine own heart I hear: 30
"Resolve to be thyself; and know that he
Who finds himself loses his misery!"

For Discussion

1. What is the dramatic situation of this poem? What is the attitude of the man? What does he ask of nature? What is the meaning of line 12?
2. What is the meaning of line 16, the first words spoken by

the second voice in the poem? What, according to this speaker, is the way of life of the stars and the sea? How are they "self-poised" (line 23)?
3. What does the second voice say about human relationships? Would you say that lines 25 and 26 indicate the means for the first speaker to find the calm he is seeking?
4. How do the last two lines of the poem relate to the message of the "air-born voice"? Discuss the significance of these two lines.
5. Except for the last stanza, the poet usually rhymes the second and fourth lines of each stanza. What is the change in the last stanza? What effect is achieved by the change?

REQUIESCAT [1]

Strew on her roses, roses,
    And never a spray of yew!
In quiet she reposes;
    Ah! would that I did too!

Her mirth the world required;   5
    She bathed it in smiles of glee.
But her heart was tired, tired,
    And now they let her be.

Her life was turning, turning,
    In mazes of heat and sound;   10
But for peace her soul was yearning,
    And now peace laps her round.

Her cabined, ample spirit,
    It fluttered and failed for breath.
Tonight it doth inherit   15
    The vasty hall of death.

---

[1] **Requiescat:** let her rest in peace

For Discussion

1. The speaker asks that roses be strewn on the grave of the woman. Why roses and not yew? What might these symbolize?
2. What was the character of the woman? What contradictions of her life are described in the poem? Who are the "they" in line 8?
3. What do lines 9–10 tell us about the life of the woman? What is the effect of calling her spirit both "cabined" and "ample"? What is the function of "vasty" in line 16?
4. What is the tone of this poem? How does the structure help to define the tone?

SHAKESPEARE

Others abide our question.[1] Thou art free.[2]
We ask and ask—Thou smilest and art still,
Out-topping knowledge. For the loftiest hill
That to the stars uncrowns his majesty,
Planting his steadfast footsteps in the sea,   5
Making the heaven of heavens his dwelling-place,
Spares but the cloudy border of his base
To the foiled searching of mortality;[3]
And thou, who didst the stars and sunbeams know,
Self-schooled, self-scanned, self-honored, self-secure,   10
Didst tread on earth unguessed at.—Better so!
All pains the immortal spirit must endure,
All weakness which impairs, all griefs which bow,
Find their sole speech in that victorious brow.

[1] **abide our question:** are easily understood
[2] **free:** too deep for our understanding
[3] **mortality:** humanity

For Discussion

1. What is the essential question being asked of Shakespeare? What is the answer?
2. How is the image of the hill which begins in line 3 developed in the remaining lines of the octave? What is the "cloudy border of his base"?
3. Discuss the contrast between the first three lines of the sestet and the last three lines. What is the effect of "Better so!"? Why is Shakespeare's brow "victorious"?
4. Arnold said that poetry should "animate," bring to life. Does this sonnet indicate that Shakespeare had the gift of animating "mortality"? Discuss.

THE BURIED LIFE

Light flows our war of mocking words, and yet,
Behold, with tears mine eyes are wet!
I feel a nameless sadness o'er me roll.
Yes, yes, we know that we can jest,
We know, we know that we can smile!   5
But there's a something in this breast,
To which thy light words bring no rest,
And thy gay smiles no anodyne.[1]
Give me thy hand, and hush awhile,
And turn those limpid eyes on mine,   10
And let me read there, love! thy inmost soul.

Alas! is even love too weak
To unlock the heart, and let it speak?
Are even lovers powerless to reveal
To one another what indeed they feel?   15
I knew the mass of men concealed
Their thoughts, for fear that if revealed
They would by other men be met
With blank indifference, or with blame reproved;

[1] **anodyne:** pain-relieving drug

I knew they lived and moved   20
Tricked in disguises, alien to the rest
Of men, and alien to themselves—and yet
The same heart beats in every human breast!

But we, my love!—doth a like spell benumb
Our hearts, our voices?—must we too be dumb?   25
Ah! well for us, if even we,
Even for a moment, can get free
Our heart, and have our lips unchained;
For that which seals them hath been deep-ordained!

Fate, which foresaw   30
How frivolous a baby man would be—
By what distractions he would be possessed,
How he would pour himself in every strife,
And well-nigh change his own identity—
That it might keep from his capricious play   35
His genuine self, and force him to obey
Even in his own despite his being's law,
Bade through the deep recesses of our breast
The unregarded river of our life
Pursue with indiscernible flow its way;   40
And that we should not see
The buried stream, and seem to be
Eddying at large in blind uncertainty,
Though driving on with it eternally.

But often, in the world's most crowded streets,   45
But often, in the din of strife,
There rises an unspeakable desire
After the knowledge of our buried life;
A thirst to spend our fire and restless force
In tracking out our true, original course;   50
A longing to inquire
Into the mystery of this heart which beats

The Buried Life

So wild, so deep in us—to know
Whence our lives come and where they go.
And many a man in his own breast then delves,
But deep enough, alas! none ever mines.
And we have been on many thousand lines,
And we have shown, on each, spirit and power;
But hardly have we, for one little hour,
Been on our own line, have we been ourselves—
Hardly had skill to utter one of all
The nameless feelings that course through our breast,
But they course on forever unexpressed.
And long we try in vain to speak and act
Our hidden self, and what we say and do
Is eloquent, is well—but 'tis not true!
And then we will no more be racked
With inward striving, and demand
Of all the thousand nothings of the hour
Their stupefying power;
Ah, yes, and they benumb us at our call!
Yet still, from time to time, vague and forlorn,
From the soul's subterranean depth upborne
As from an infinitely distant land,
Come airs, and floating echoes, and convey
A melancholy into all our day.

Only—but this is rare—
When a belovéd hand is laid in ours,
When, jaded with the rush and glare
Of the interminable hours,
Our eyes can in another's eyes read clear,
When our world-deafened ear
Is by the tones of a loved voice caressed—
A bolt is shot back somewhere in our breast,
And a lost pulse of feeling stirs again:
The eye sinks inward, and the heart lies plain,
And what we mean, we say, and what we would, we know.

A man becomes aware of his life's flow.
And hears its winding murmur; and he sees
The meadows where it glides, the sun, the breeze. 90

And there arrives a lull in the hot race
Wherein he doth forever chase
That flying and elusive shadow, rest.
An air of coolness plays upon his face,
And an unwonted calm pervades his breast. 95
And then he thinks he knows
The hills where his life rose,
And the sea where it goes.

For Discussion

1. The buried life which this poem talks about may be considered the real man, the genuine self we bury that we may not meet the indifference of the world. In a way it is a self-deception. What incident has brought the speaker to question his buried life? The words "mocking" and "jest" suggest a lightness of tone. Is the tone of the opening lines light and bantering? Discuss.
2. To whom is the speaker talking? What had he hoped to find in love? What effects do the words "benumb" (line 24) and "dumb" (line 25) have?
3. What image conveys the sense of the buried life? How effective is this image? What is the speaker's attitude toward role-playing and deception, the "putting on a face" to meet the world?
4. What, according to the speaker, happens to the man who continually buries his self? What is the significance of lines 65 and 66? Why are the "thousand nothings of the hour" said to have a "stupefying power"?
5. When, according to the speaker, does a person really become alive? What happens to the world at this moment?
6. How does the ending of the poem complete the basic image of the buried life? What, according to the speaker, is the answer to the problem of self-deception?

DOVER BEACH

The sea is calm tonight,
The tide is full, the moon lies fair
Upon the straits; on the French coast, the light
Gleams and is gone; the cliffs of England stand,
Glimmering and vast, out in the tranquil bay.   5
Come to the window, sweet is the night-air!
Only, from the long line of spray
Where the sea meets the moon-blanched land,
Listen! you hear the grating roar
Of pebbles which the waves draw back, and fling,   10
At their return, up the high strand,
Begin and cease, and then again begin,
With tremulous cadence slow, and bring
The eternal note of sadness in.

Sophocles [1] long ago   15
Heard it on the Aegean,[2] and it brought
Into his mind the turbid ebb and flow
Of human misery; we
Find also in the sound a thought,
Hearing it by this distant northern sea.   20

The sea of faith
Was once, too, at the full, and round earth's shore
Lay like the folds of a bright girdle furled.
But now I only hear
Its melancholy, long, withdrawing roar,   25
Retreating, to the breath
Of the night-wind, down the vast edges drear
And naked shingles [3] of the world.

---

[1] **Sophocles:** great ancient Greek writer of tragedies in the fifth century B.C.
[2] **Aegean:** sea between Greece and Asia Minor
[3] **shingles:** pebbled shores

>   Ah, love, let us be true
>   To one another! for the world, which seems   30
>   To lie before us like a land of dreams,
>   So various, so beautiful, so new,
>   Hath really neither joy, nor love, nor light,
>   Nor certitude, nor peace, nor help for pain;
>   And we are here as on a darkling plain   35
>   Swept with confused alarms of struggle and flight,
>   Where ignorant armies clash by night.

For Discussion

1. This dramatic monologue is perhaps the finest expression of the problem of belief found in Victorian literature. It proceeds from a definite and carefully defined setting to an eternity of man's search for belief. What is the dramatic situation in the first stanza? How do you know the speaker is not alone? Are the descriptive details in the first fourteen lines literal or metaphorical?
2. "Sophocles" begins the second stanza. How does this name develop "the eternal note of sadness"? Is the sea image in the second stanza literal or metaphorical?
3. "The sea of faith" is, of course, metaphorical. Explain the basis of this metaphor. How is the sense of the decline of religious faith echoed in the construction of lines 24–28? How does the irregular rhyme scheme achieve the effect of disorder? What is the significance of the word "retreating" (line 26)?
4. The fourth stanza begins with an exhortation and returns to the initial scene. How does the speaker hope to realize the values to which the world is opposed?
5. What is the effect of the negatives in lines 33 and 34? Contrast these lines with lines 31–32. What is the effect of this juxtaposition? What is the impact of "darkling," "ignorant," and "night"?
6. In the third stanza, Arnold uses an irregular rhyme scheme to develop the sense of disorder brought about by the loss

of religious faith. How does he use sound and meter to give the effect of movement, particularly in the development of the sea image? Point out specific lines for discussion.

For Composition

1. In writing about Arnold's poetry, his sister said "I felt . . . that it showed a knowledge of life and conflict which was *strangely like experience.*" Write a critical paper in which you discuss the sense of human experience in "Dover Beach."
2. The themes expressed in "The Buried Life" are similar to those expressed in "Self-Dependence" and "Dover Beach." In a short paper, discuss these themes, their significant similarities and differences. How valid do you feel Arnold's conclusions are?

Francis Thompson

(1859–1907)

Francis Thompson's poetry shows the influence of the Romantics, particularly Shelley, and the seventeenth-century Metaphysical poets. In his love of nature and the very sweep of his poetry, he continued in the vein of the Romantics. His poems of childhood are rich with the innocent joy of the young, their delight in the world and in nature. Like the Metaphysicals, he used startling and arresting conceits and intricate poetic structure with exuberance and abandon.

The critic Arthur Symons has said of him: "Francis Thompson was one of the few poets . . . in whom there was some trace of that divine essence which we best symbolize by fire. Emptiness he had and extravagances, but he was a poet, and he had made of many influences a new beauty. . . ." His major poem, "The Hound of Heaven," which abounds in rich and luxuriant imagery, occupies a unique position among the imaginative works which depict the search of the sensitive, tormented soul for God.

ENVOY

Go, songs, for ended is our brief, sweet play;
    Go, children of swift joy and tardy sorrow;
And some are sung, and that was yesterday,
    And some unsung, and that may be tomorrow.

Go forth; and if it be o'er stony way,   5
    Old joy can lend what newer grief must borrow;
And it was sweet, and that was yesterday,
    And sweet is sweet, though puchaséd with sorrow.

Go, songs, and come not back from your far way;
    And if men ask you why ye smile and sorrow,   10
Tell them ye grieve, for your hearts know Today,
    Tell them ye smile, for your eyes know Tomorrow.

For Discussion

1. This poem is modeled on the lyrics of the seventeenth century. What are the "songs" which are being sent forth? What do these "songs" say to people? What is it that these songs convey?
2. Examine the diction used in this poem. What is the relationship between the simplicity of diction and structure and the theme which the songs bring?
3. How are both metaphor and personification used in describing the songs?

THE HOUND OF HEAVEN

I fled Him, down the nights and down the days;
    I fled Him, down the arches of the years;
I fled Him, down the labyrinthine ways
    Of my own mind; and in the mist of tears
I hid from Him, and under running laughter.   5
        Up vistaed hopes I sped;
        And shot, precipitated,
Adown Titanic glooms of chasméd fears,
    From those strong Feet that followed, followed after.
        But with unhurrying chase,   10
        And unperturbéd pace,
    Deliberate speed, majestic instancy,
        They beat—and a Voice beat
        More instant than the Feet—
    "All things betray thee, who betrayest Me."   15

        I pleaded, outlaw-wise,
By many a hearted casement, curtained red.

    Trellised with intertwining charities
(For, though I knew His love Who followéd,
        Yet was I sore adread   20
Lest, having Him, I must have naught beside)
But, if one little casement parted wide,
    The gust of His approach would clash it to.
Fear wist not to evade, as Love wist to pursue.
Across the margent of the world I fled,   25
    And troubled the gold gateways of the stars,
        Smiting for shelter on their clangéd bars;
            Fretted to dulcet jars
And silvern chatter the pale ports o' the moon.
I said to dawn, Be sudden; to eve, Be soon;   30
    With thy young skyey blossoms heap me over
        From this tremendous Lover!
Float thy vague veil about me, lest He see!
    I tempted all His servitors, but to find
My own betrayal in their constancy,   35
In faith to Him their fickleness to me,
    Their traitorous trueness, and their loyal deceit.
To all swift things for swiftness did I sue;
    Clung to the whistling mane of every wind.
        But whether they swept, smoothly fleet,   40
    The long savannahs of the blue;
        Or whether, Thunder-driven,
    They clanged his chariot 'thwart a heaven
Plashy with flying lightnings round the spurn o' their feet—
    Fear wist not to evade as Love wist to pursue.   45
        Still with unhurrying chase,
        And unperturbéd pace,
    Deliberate speed, majestic instancy,
        Came on the following Feet,
        And a Voice above their beat—   50
    "Naught shelters thee, who wilt not shelter Me."

I sought no more that after which I strayed
    In face of man or maid;

But still within the little children's eyes
    Seems something, something that replies;
They at least are for me, surely for me!
I turned me to them very wistfully;
But, just as their young eyes grew sudden fair
    With dawning answers there,
Their angel plucked them from me by the hair.
"Come then, ye other children, Nature's—share
With me" (said I) "your delicate fellowship;
    Let me greet you lip to lip,
    Let me twine with you caresses,
        Wantoning
    With our Lady-Mother's vagrant tresses,
        Banqueting
    With her in her wind-walled palace,
    Underneath her azured dais,
    Quaffing, as your taintless way is,
        From a chalice
Lucent-weeping out of the dayspring."
    So it was done:
I in their delicate fellowship was one—
Drew the bolt of Nature's secrecies.
    I knew all the swift importings
    On the willful face of skies;
    I knew how the clouds arise
    Spuméd of the wild sea-snortings;
    All that's born or dies
    Rose and drooped with—made them shapers
Of mine own moods, or wailful or divine—
    With them joyed and was bereaven.
    I was heavy with the even,
    When she lit her glimmering tapers
    Round the day's dead sanctities.
    I laughed in the morning's eyes.
I triumphed and I saddened with all weather,
    Heaven and I wept together,
And its sweet tears were salt with mortal mine;

Against the red throb of its sunset heart
      I laid my own to beat,
      And share commingling heat;
But not by that, by that, was eased my human smart.
In vain my tears were wet on Heaven's gray cheek.
For ah! we know not what each other says,
      These things and I; in sound *I* speak—
Their sound is but their stir, they speak by silences.
Nature, poor stepdame, cannot slake my drouth;
      Let her, if she would owe me,
Drop yon blue bosom-veil of sky, and show me
      The breasts o' her tenderness;
Never did any milk of hers once bless
      My thirsting mouth.
         Nigh and nigh draws the chase,
         With unperturbéd pace,
     Deliberate speed, majestic instancy;
         And past those noiséd Feet
         A voice comes yet more fleet—
"Lo! naught contents thee, who content'st not Me."

Naked I wait Thy love's uplifted stroke!
My harness piece by piece Thou hast hewn from me,
      And smitten me to my knee;
    I am defenseless utterly.
     I slept, methinks, and woke,
And, slowly gazing, find me stripped in sleep.
In the rash lustihead of my young powers,
     I shook the pillaring hours
And pulled my life upon me; grinned with smears,
I stand amid the dust o' the mounded years—
My mangled youth lies dead beneath the heap,
My days have crackled and gone up in smoke,
Have puffed and burst as sun-starts on a stream.
     Yea, faileth now even dream
The dreamer, and the lute the lutanist;

Even the linked fantasies, in whose blossomy twist
I swung the earth a trinket at my wrist,
Are yielding; cords of all too weak account
For earth, with heavy griefs so overplussed.
    Ah! is Thy love indeed
A weed, albeit an amaranthine weed,
Suffering no flowers except its own to mount?
    Ah! must—
    Designer infinite!—
Ah! must Thou char the wood ere Thou canst limn with it?
My freshness spent its wavering shower i' the dust;
And now my heart is as a broken fount,
Wherein tear-drippings stagnate, spilt down ever
    From the dank thoughts that shiver
Upon the sighful branches of my mind.
    Such is; what is to be?
The pulp so bitter, how shall taste the rind?
I dimly guess what Time in mists confounds;
Yet ever and anon a trumpet sounds
From the hid battlements of Eternity;
Those shaken mists a space unsettle, then
Round the half glimpsèd turrets slowly wash again,
    But not ere him who summoneth
    I first have seen, enwound
With glooming robes purpureal, cypress-crowned;
His name I know, and what his trumpet saith.
Whether man's heart or life it be which yields
    Thee harvest, must Thy harvest fields
    Be dunged with rotten death?

    Now of that long pursuit
    Comes on at hand the bruit;
That Voice is round me like a bursting sea:
    "And is thy earth so marred,
    Shattered in shard on shard?
Lo, all things fly thee, for thou fliest Me!

        Strange, piteous, futile thing!
Wherefore should any set thee love apart?
Seeing none but I makes much of naught" (He said),
"And human love needs human meriting:
    How hast thou merited—   165
Of all man's clotted clay the dingiest clot?
    Alack, thou knowest not
How little worthy of any love thou art!
Whom wilt thou find to love ignoble thee
    Save Me, save only Me?   170
All which I took from thee I did but take,
    Not for thy harms,

But just that thou might'st seek it in My arms.
    All which thy child's mistake
Fancies as lost, I have stored for thee at home;   175
    Rise, clasp My hand, and come!"
        Halts by me that footfall;
     Is my gloom, after all,
  Shade of His hand, outstretched caressingly?
        "Ah, fondest, blindest, weakest,   180
      I am He Whom thou seekest!
Thou dravest love from thee, who dravest Me."

For Discussion

1. This poem is dominated by a single conceit, the metaphor of God as Hound pursuing man. Do you think it is accurate and effective? Why or why not?
2. The poem opens in flight. What words does Thompson use to achieve the effect of great speed in the first nine lines? What dramatic contrast is given in lines 10–15? What is the effect of the combination of opposites in these lines?
3. In fleeing from God, this sinner seeks refuge first in family life and human love. Why does he conceive of himself as an "outlaw" (line 16)? What image is given by "hearted casement," "curtained red," "intertwining charities"?

4. Where does the sinner flee in lines 25–45? Why can he not find solace? Why does the sinner turn to children for solace (line 54)?
5. What imagery does the poet use to describe nature in lines 61–72? Is his attitude toward nature reminiscent of that of the Romantic poets? Why cannot "Nature, poor stepdame, slake [his] drouth"?
6. The climax of the poem comes in line 111. What has happened? What words pick up the image of a new birth? Is this a complete renewal? What very human question does the sinner ask in lines 130–132? What does the sinner fear? How close is fear to belief?
7. What images are used to develop the thoughts expressed in lines 130–132? How do these images show the true complexity of religious experience?
8. The last section of the ode has the Pursuer answering the question. What essential paradox is expressed in these lines? What is the meaning of lines 171–173?
9. The usual image of man's search for God is the quest—the knight seeking the Holy Grail. Is Thompson's inverted quest particularly appropriate for the Victorian period? Is it more in keeping with the human condition? Discuss.
10. What would have happened to the poem if it had ended at line 111? Much of this poem is autobiographical. How does Thompson succeed in making the poem universal?

For Composition

1. Write a critical paper discussing the diction in "The Hound of Heaven." In the course of the paper, you might need to consider not only the individual words but also the way they are combined with other words in the sentences.
2. Write a critical paper comparing, as religious poems, "The Hound of Heaven" and Matthew Arnold's "Dover Beach."

Thomas Hardy

(1840–1928)

Both in his novels and his poetry, Thomas Hardy reveals despair in a universe where imaginative man is incongruously trapped by blind fate. His poetry, rising now in critical esteem, is enhanced by a rugged simplicity of diction which reveals the influences of the Bible and Shakespeare, as well as the humble speech of the countryfolk among whom he lived.

Deep emotions became for Hardy, as for most poets, associated with specific events, and he described these directly, with stern clarity. Most of his poems are best read as dramatic moments, carefully "staged" with setting and characters. "The Darkling Thrush," such a poem, stands at the threshold of the twentieth century, ushering in the new era in tones grave, stark, and deeply pessimistic, but with a sense of "Some blessèd Hope, whereof he knew / And I was unaware."

SUMMER SCHEMES

When friendly summer calls again,
    Calls again
Her little fifers to these hills,
We'll go—we two—to that arched fame
Of leafage where they prime their bills   5
Before they start to flood the plain
With quavers, minims, shakes, and trills.
    "—We'll go," I sing; but who shall say
    What may not chance before that day!

And we shall see the waters spring,   10
    Waters spring

From chinks the scrubby copses crown;
And we shall trace their oncreeping
To where the cascade tumbles down
And sends the bobbing growths aswing,   15
And ferns not quite but almost drown.
   "—We shall," I say; but who may sing
Of what another moon will bring!

For Discussion

1. What is the tone of this poem? How do the near-repetitions help to develop this tone?
2. Who are the summer "fifers"? What do these fifers do?
3. Discuss the language of the poem, paying particular attention to the nouns and verbs. What is the effect of words and phrases like "quavers, minims, shakes, and trills" (line 7), "oncreeping" (line 13), and "bobbing growths aswing" (line 15)?
4. What point of view, typical of Hardy, is expressed in this poem? How would the poem be changed if the last line of the first stanza read "What else we'll see on that fine day" and the last line of the second stanza read "Of love so sweet and hills that ring"?

IN TIME OF "THE BREAKING OF NATIONS" [1]

Only a man harrowing clods
   In a slow silent walk
With an old horse that stumbles and nods
   Half asleep as they stalk.

Only thin smoke without flame   5
   From the heaps of couch-grass;
Yet this will go onward the same
   Though Dynasties pass.

[1] Jeremiah 51:20

>   Yonder a maid and her wight
>   Come whispering by:
>   War's annals will fade into night
>   Ere their story die.

For Discussion

1. In this poem the speaker presents three vignettes of human experience. What aspects of life does each vignette describe? Are these experiences universal in meaning? What is the speaker's attitude toward these experiences?
2. Discuss the use of contrast in this poem as the means for developing both feeling and meaning. What, perhaps, is the poem saying about natural simplicity and the great works of man?
3. Compare the attitude toward war in this poem to that of Browning's "Cavalier Tunes" (page 310) and "How They Brought the Good News from Ghent to Aix" (page 312).

THE MAN HE KILLED

>   'Had he and I but met
>   By some old ancient inn,
>   We should have sat us down to wet
>   Right many a nipperkin!
>
>   'But ranged as infantry,
>   And staring face to face,
>   I shot at him as he at me,
>   And killed him in his place.
>
>   'I shot him dead because—
>   Because he was my foe,
>   Just so: my foe of course he was;
>   That's clear enough; although

> 'He thought he'd 'list, perhaps,
>   Off-hand like—just as I—
> Was out of work—had sold his traps— 15
>   No other reason why.
>
> 'Yes; quaint and curious war is!
>   You shoot a fellow down
> You'd treat if met where any bar is,
>   Or help to half-a-crown.' 20

For Discussion

1. What has happened to the speaker in this poem? Why does this lead him to question what has occurred? Characterize as definitely as you can the speaker, using language clues to indicate his background.
2. What is the function of the contrast between stanzas 1 and 2? How does the repetition of "because" and "my foe" in stanza 3 help to develop the meaning of the poem? the feeling of the speaker?
3. What exactly is this poem saying about the lot of the individual man in the face of war?

DRUMMER HODGE

> They throw in Drummer Hodge, to rest
>   Uncoffined—just as found:
> His landmark is a kopje-crest [1]
>   That breaks the veldt around;
> And foreign constellations west 5
>   Each night above his mound.
>
> Young Hodge the Drummer never knew—
>   Fresh from his Wessex home—

---
[1] **kopje-crest:** a hillock

The meaning of the broad Karoo,[2]
    The Bush, the dusty loam,   10
And why uprose to nightly view
    Strange stars amid the gloam.

Yet portion of that unknown plain
    Will Hodge forever be;
His homely Northern breast and brain   15
    Grow to some Southern tree,
And strange-eyed constellations reign
    His stars eternally.

[2] **Karoo:** a dry plateau in South Africa

For Discussion

1. What is the situation described in this poem? Who are the "they" of line 1? What is the effect of the word "throw" in that same line? of "west" in line 5? of "homely" in line 15? Who might the speaker be? Discuss.
2. At what point, or points, in this poem is irony most apparent? Explain.
3. What symbols does Hardy use to describe the fate of Drummer Hodge? Why are they particularly appropriate? Note especially the words used as adjectives.
4. Chart the rhyme scheme of the poem. What is the dominant meter? How do the rhyme scheme and the meter reinforce the meaning of the poem? Find and discuss the means Hardy used to tie the parts of the poem together. Note the parallels in form and content.

THE DARKLING THRUSH

I leant upon a coppice gate
    When Frost was specter-gray,
And Winter's dregs made desolate
    The weakening eye of day.
The tangled bine-stems scored the sky   5
    Like strings of broken lyres,

And all mankind that haunted nigh
    Had sought their household fires.

The land's sharp features seemed to be
    The Century's corpse outleant,
His crypt the cloudy canopy,
    The wind his death lament.
The ancient pulse of germ and birth
    Was shrunken hard and dry,
And every spirit upon earth
    Seemed fervourless as I.

At once a voice arose among
    The bleak twigs overhead
In a full-hearted evensong
    Of joy illimited;
An aged thrush, frail, gaunt, and small,
    In blast-beruffled plume,
Had chosen thus to fling his soul
    Upon the growing gloom.

So little cause for carolings
    Of such ecstatic sound
Was written on terrestrial things
    Afar or nigh around,
That I could think there trembled through
    His happy good-night air
Some blessèd Hope, whereof he knew
    And I was unaware.

For Discussion

1. This poem was written on December 31, 1900, at the end of one era and the beginning of another. What is the dramatic setting of the opening stanza? What is the effect of the de-

scriptive words "dregs," "weakening," "broken lyres," and "haunted"? What mood is evoked by the details given?
2. What attitude toward the nineteenth century is shown by the images in the second stanza? What is the meaning of the phrase "The ancient pulse of germ and birth"? Why is the speaker "fervourless"?
3. What dramatic contrast is presented in the third stanza? What is the significance of the phrase "to fling his soul"? Is the "growing gloom" merely the coming of night or does it have a wider significance?
4. Why is there "little cause for carolings"? What does the thrush symbolize for the speaker? What is the meaning of "darkling" in the title?
5. What is the tone of this poem? With what attitude does the speaker view the coming century? Is this a Victorian poem? Discuss.
6. Characterize the speaker, the "I" of the poem. Does he come to a firm sense of confidence as a result of the carol of the bird?

For Composition

1. Write a critical paper comparing the thrush in "The Darkling Thrush" with the skylark in Shelley's "To a Skylark" (page 159). What are the significant similarities and differences in the symbolic uses of the birds?
2. In both "The Man He Killed" and "In Time of 'The Breaking of Nations'" Hardy uses contrast to develop his meaning. Write a short paragraph in which you use contrast as a means of dramatizing a situation. Attempt to present the situation you are describing but avoid making a judgment on it.

ABOUT THE AUTHORS

Matthew Arnold (1822–1888) was a member of an intellectual upper-class family, the son of Dr. Thomas Arnold, famous headmaster of Rugby. He was educated at Rugby and at Balliol College, Oxford, where he won the Newdigate Prize for Poetry. Intellectual, cultured, and urbane, Arnold moved in the most aristocratic circles of English life.

In 1851, he accepted a post as Inspector of Schools, a position which enabled him to marry, and for thirty-five years performed the duties of school inspector with scrupulous fidelity.

In 1857, he was appointed Professor of Poetry at Oxford, a post he held until 1867. In this position he lectured not only on literary subjects but also on the critical social and cultural problems of his day. From 1867 on he devoted himself almost entirely to prose criticism of literary and social problems. His attempt to spread the humane ideals of culture to the complacent "Philistines" was the work of a public man who lived in the center of the great movements of his time, a man who wrote what was perhaps the most important literary and social criticism of that time.

William Blake (1757–1827) received no formal education except in art. Apprenticed to an engraver at fourteen, he later studied art under Sir Joshua Reynolds at the Royal Academy. But Blake's erratic genius could not stand the traditional discipline of the Academy, and he left to open his own print shop. In 1782, he married Catherine Boucher, an almost illiterate girl who had the good sense to recognize her husband's genius and who provided him with a steadying influence.

The ordinary nature of Blake's life does not parallel the turbulence and mystical life of his poetry and engravings. His graphic habit of mind is evident in his first work, *Poetical Sketches* (1783), and even more in the companion volumes, *Songs of Innocence* (1789) and *Songs of Experience* (1794), works which were enhanced by the engravings which he made and colored by hand.

Unappreciated as a poet in his lifetime, Blake made a precarious living as an engraver. Late in his life he attracted a group of young painters, and his old age proved more serene than his early days.

Elizabeth Barrett Browning (1806–1861) was considered the foremost woman poet of her time. Invalided after a spinal injury caused by a fall from a horse, she spent most of her time at 50 Wimpole Street translating Greek, reading Hebrew, and writing fervent and impassioned poetry under the selfishly solicitous care of her father.

Her love for the then little known poet Robert Browning is part of the legend of literature. Against the wishes of her father, they were married in 1846 and then traveled to Italy, where they lived thirteen years of almost idyllic married life. Although never reconciled with her father, Elizabeth had the complete happiness of her husband's love and the love of their son, Pen, in their house in Florence, "Casa Guidi."

Mrs. Browning's greatest achievement is *Sonnets from the Portuguese,* a sequence which describes the stages of her love for her husband.

She died in Florence on June 30, 1861, and is buried there in the Protestant Cemetery.

Robert Browning (1812–1889) took full advantage of the private education given him by his artistic parents, an education that went into the bypaths of knowledge as well as the main roads of art, music, and literature.

His early poems were literary rather than popular successes, and on the strength of this reputation, Browning wrote several dramas, none of which had more than moderate success. Between 1841 and 1846, he printed at his own expense *Bells and Pomegranates,* which won him popular acclaim.

Following his marriage to Elizabeth Barrett, he moved to Italy, where he spent the most productive years of his literary life. The influence of his wife is seen not only in the work of the period but also in *Dramatis Personae* (1864) and *The Ring and the Book* (1868).

Browning died in Venice in 1889 on the day of the publication of his last volume, *Asolando.* He is buried in the Poet's Corner in Westminster Abbey.

Robert Burns (1759–1796) was essentially a man of contradictions. He had fewer than three years of formal schooling, but he was widely read in Shakespeare, Milton, Dryden, and in history and theology. Never a singer himself—he seemed almost tone deaf as a child—he wrote songs that have won the hearts of the most intellectual of men and the simple peasant.

The publication of the famous Kilmarnock Edition in 1786 brought Burns to the attention of the literati of Edinburgh. The adulation he received from them went to the head of this young man, saddened by the death of his betrothed, Mary Campbell. Their sudden lack of interest deeply disappointed him.

He married Jean Armour in 1788 and moved to the farming district near Dumfries. Beset by ill health and constantly plagued by financial difficulties, he was still able to write some of his finest lyrics, "Auld Lang Syne" and "A Man's a Man for a' That." His sympathy with the ideals of the French Revolution is evident in his humanitarian poems which speak of the brotherhood of man. He died in Dumfries at the age of 37.

George Gordon, Lord Byron (1788–1824) was the son of a violent, colorful, and dissolute family and, in the traditions of the aristocracy, was educated at Harrow and at Trinity College, Cambridge, from which he received a Master of Arts degree. A deformed foot aggravated by inept medical treatment made him determined to excel at sports; he became an expert boxer, fencer, horseman, and swimmer.

A short career in the House of Lords came to an end when the first two cantos of *Childe Harold's Pilgrimage* appeared in 1812. This was an immediate literary and social success; and Byron, with his dashing good looks, became the center of London society. After a series of notorious love affairs, he married Anna Isabella Milbanke, an intellectual, straight-laced woman. The marriage lasted one year and ended in legal separation. Subsequent scandal turned society against him, and he left England in 1816, never to return.

In Italy with Shelley and the other members of the "Pisan Circle," he completed *Childe Harold's Pilgrimage* and worked diligently on what he considered to be his masterpiece, *Don Juan*. A lover of freedom, he organized an expedition to assist the Greeks in their war for independence. In the marshy town of Missolonghi where he was training soldiers, he contracted a fever and died there on April 19, 1824. For his work in their struggle for independence, the Greeks still honor Byron as a national hero.

Thomas Carlyle (1795–1881), born in the same year as John Keats, was a Victorian, not a Romantic—a Victorian who saw in his own day problems which still vex mankind. The son of a sometime stone mason, Carlyle studied at the University of Edinburgh but left without taking a degree. He abandoned study for the ministry, tutored for a time, and from 1824 to his death supported himself and his wife, the intelligent and spirited Jane Welsh, whom he married in 1826, by writing and lecturing.

In Craigenputtock he wrote *Sartor Resartus,* which was but moderately successful when published. The *History of the French Revolution* was written at 24 Cheyne Row, the house where the Carlyles were to live for forty-seven years. It was this book that led to Carlyle's being hailed both in England and in America as a strong, original writer.

As the "Sage of Chelsea," he lived the life of a literary man, commenting on the sociological, economic, and philosophical problems which faced England, proclaiming his doctrine of the strong leader or hero as the means to save the world from disaster. In 1866 he was named Lord Rector of Edinburgh University. He died in 1881 and was buried in Ecclefechan, Scotland. A truculent, irascible man, he remained opposed to the claims of democracy until his death.

Samuel Taylor Coleridge (1772–1834), under the alias of Silas Tomkyn Comberbacke, was probably the worst soldier in the history of the British Army. Fortunately, his army career was short-lived and he was sent back to Cambridge. He left Cambridge in 1794 without a degree.

This pattern of unfulfilled plans holds true for much of Coleridge's life and for his work. With Robert Southey, he formed plans for a Utopian community, "Pantisocracy," to be founded on the banks of the Susquehanna River. The only tangible result of this scheme was Coleridge's unhappy marriage to Sara Fricker.

In 1796 he met William Wordsworth, and the almost constant communication between the two men resulted in the *Lyrical Ballads* (1798). It was during these years that Coleridge's poetic power was at its height.

Following the writing of "Dejection, An Ode" (1802), Coleridge's power as a practicing poet waned, but his critical ability, seen particularly in *Biographia Literaria* (1817) and in his lectures delivered between 1807–1818, set a high standard for the writing of literary criticism.

Never a robust person, Coleridge became addicted to opium, which had been prescribed to give him relief from ill health. He spent the last years of his life in the home of Dr. Gillman where, in brilliant conversation, he showed to his friends and admirers more of his ability than he was able to offer the world in published form.

Thomas De Quincey (1785–1859), the son of a wealthy merchant family, was a precocious child who never fulfilled the great promise he showed. He was to study the classics at Oxford, but spent most of his time reading English and German literature. He left Oxford without completing the oral examinations for the Honors A.B.

During his stay at Oxford, he was given laudanum by a druggist for the relief of an attack of rheumatism and toothache. His resulting addiction is memorably recorded in *The Confessions of an English Opium Eater.*

An early admirer of Wordsworth and Coleridge, he leased Wordsworth's house in Glasmere and became an intimate friend of the poet. As a man of letters he contributed to the leading magazines, *London Magazine, Blackwood's* and *Edinburgh Literary Gazette.* His intuitive criticism and his highly romantic prose shine through in the 150 articles which have been identified as his.

Recklessness with the small amount of money he had forced him to work constantly to keep his large family above the level of abject poverty. Almost constant ill-health, relieved only by doses of narcotics, is responsible in no small measure for the discursive nature of his work and the many stylistic faults. That he was a perceptive, subtle, and keen man is seen in his writings, which are examples of an excellence of a special type.

Thomas Gray (1716–1771) was a shy, retiring, learned man who spent the greater part of his life as a scholar at Cambridge, going in the summer to visit his mother in the village of Stoke Poges. His was an intellectual life, centering on pre-Elizabethan poetry, Old Welsh literature, painting, music, and nature study. Except for a Grand Tour of France and Italy taken as a young man with Horace Walpole, Gray was content to remain in the British Isles where, in the Lake District, he went in search of the beautiful in nature.

Considering himself an amateur at poetry, he worked slowly and carefully. "The Elegy Written in a Country Churchyard" was the product of several years' careful and painstaking work. The projection of the melancholy figure stands as a unique achievement in language, cadence, allusion, and tone.

The witty, warm, intellectually curious Gray is to be found in the letters which he wrote to his friends from his study in Cambridge. These are the means to discover the man who, as Professor of Modern History, did not deliver a single lecture.

Thomas Hardy (1840–1928) as a boy served as fiddler for local dances in Dorset, a rural section of southern England that became the "Wessex" of his novels. Apprenticed to a church architect when he was fifteen, he later went to London for further study. He was an avid reader, and completed his education through books and through night study at King's College. More and more he felt himself being drawn to writing as a profession.

Hardy's early poems were rejected by publishers; as a result he turned to fiction to make a living. With the success of *Under the Greenwood Tree*, his second novel, he abandoned architecture in 1872 and until 1896 wrote the novels which brought him his greatest fame. Hardy fought the battle of the censors over several of his books. *The Return of the Native*, now a standard in high school English courses was successful, but the outcry over *Tess of the D'Urbervilles* and *Jude the Obscure* ended his career as a novelist. From 1896 to his death he again wrote poetry, his first love. His lyrics and *The Dynasts*, a verse-epic of the Napoleonic era, stand high in the estimate of modern critics, who now praise the poet as often as the novelist.

During his last years, Hardy was honored as the dean of living English authors. When he died in 1928, his heart was buried in Dorset in the grave of his first wife; his ashes were placed in Westminster Abbey in the Poet's Corner.

William Hazlitt (1778–1830) took up in succession the ministry, painting, and philosophy before he centered on a literary career. The son of an ultra-liberal Unitarian minister, Hazlitt was of a quarrelsome, difficult temperament.

Hazlitt was 36 before he discovered that his vocation was writing. His reading and his varied interests had made him ready and able to do his work as a literary critic, essayist, and lecturer. Particularly interested in the drama of the sixteenth and seventeenth centuries, Hazlitt brought Shakespeare to the attention of his contemporaries. The best of this work is to be found in his "Characteristics of Shakespeare's Plays" (1817–1818), *English Comic Writers* (1819), and *Table Talk* (1821–1822), works which contain perceptive and engaging criticism.

Although his own life was on the surface disastrous—his frequent quarrels with close friends, his two unhappy marriages, his own personal moodiness, and his radical political views which brought him many enemies—he demonstrated a supreme honesty, integrity, and sincerity in his writings. His last words were "Well, I've had a happy life."

John Keats (1795–1821) was another of the English poets who died before he was able to glean his "teeming brain." The son of the manager of a London livery stable, he was educated at Edmonton. Orphaned at fifteen, he was apprenticed to an apothecary and surgeon and later studied surgery at Guy's and St. Thomas's Hospitals in London.

However, the influence of his reading, particularly the poetry of Edmund Spenser, and his friendship with Leigh Hunt, Hazlitt, and

Lamb led him to poetry. "Endymion," published in 1818, was severely criticized by the critics, but that the severity of the criticism was responsible for his death is not borne out by the facts of his later poetic output.

The year 1819 was a pivotal one for Keats. During this time he recognized in himself the signs of tuberculosis, which had killed his mother and his brother. To regain his health, he went to Hampstead to live. Here in his loneliness he fell in love with Fanny Brawne and became engaged. However, because of poverty and illness they never married. It was during this year that Keats wrote his greatest poetry, later published in 1820.

In 1820 he left England for a trip to Italy on the advice of a doctor who had wrongly diagnosed his illness. His last weeks were spent in the mood of knowing that what he had said in his sonnet "When I Have Fears" was to come true. He died in Rome in 1821 and is buried there in the Protestant Cemetery. His epitaph, which he himself wrote, "Here lies one whose name was writ in water," belies the beauty which he has left to the world in his letters and in his poetry.

Charles Lamb (1775–1834), the epitome of the witty, convivial man, lived a life of sacrifice and simple heroism. The youngest of seven children of a lawyer's clerk, he was educated at Christ's Hospital, where he began a lasting friendship with Coleridge. His formal education ended when he was fifteen, and in 1792 he began his thirty-three year career with the East India Company.

The surface life belied his great personal tragedy. When he was twenty-two, his beloved sister Mary, in a fit of insanity, stabbed her mother to death. Lamb himself, as he says in a letter to Coleridge, arrived to snatch the knife out of her hand. For the rest of his life, he uncomplainingly cared for her, except for the brief periods when she was confined to an asylum.

Lamb's earliest writing was in fiction and drama, neither of which proved to be his forte. In 1807, he and Mary wrote *Tales from Shakespeare*. His own interest in Elizabethan drama is seen both in his letters and in his essays, and he was a force in reviving interest in these dramas.

However, Lamb's major contribution is the familiar essay; those warm, chatty conversations on a wide variety of subjects written under the pen name "Elia." In these, as in his letters, he revealed a warm, kindly person who had let his difficulties pass away and who was a lover of the city, old books, and people.

About the Authors

Thomas Babington Macaulay (1800–1859), journalist, lawyer, politician, historian, is in large part responsible for popularizing the art of history. Born into an upper class family, he showed early signs of precocity with his habit of voracious reading and his retentive memory. While at Trinity College, Cambridge, he won the Chancellor's Medal for English Verse twice and a prize for Latin Declamation. When he was twenty-five, he contributed literary essays to the influential *Edinburgh Review*.

As a lawyer and a Whig member of Parliament, he spoke in behalf of the liberal causes of political and social reform. As an advisor for legal affairs in India, he helped to set up a revised penal system and introduced necessary reforms in public education. Gaining financial independence, he was able to devote himself to writing and public service. In 1839, he served as Secretary for War under Lord Melbourne.

The first two volumes of his *History of England* were published in 1848 and he spent the rest of his life working on this project, which he considered his major contribution to the world.

The success of his history brought him not only fame and fortune but also a baronetcy in 1857. During the last years of his life he was also a contributor to the *Encyclopaedia Britannica*. On his death in 1859, he was buried in the Poet's Corner in Westminster Abbey.

John Henry Newman (1801–1890), the son of a banker, was destined to be a leading figure in the religious controversy which shook Victorian England. Newman attended Oxford and was later a teacher at Oriel College and vicar at the Anglican church of St. Mary's in Oxford. He attracted a following of students by the eloquence and intellectual integrity of his sermons. In the 1830's together with other zealous Anglicans at Oxford, he set out to arouse the languishing religious spirit of the English people. He became the chief leader of the Oxford Movement, writing tracts and thoroughly investigating the historical claim of the Anglican Church. The famous *Tract 90* shows him convinced that the Anglican Church had no real connection with the Church founded by Christ. In 1845 at the age of forty-four, he became a Roman Catholic.

After his conversion, Newman became a priest and for the remaining forty years of his life was busy as director of the Oratorians. For a long time, Newman's motives for conversion were questioned both by Anglicans and Catholics. His *Apologia pro Vita Sua* is a moving defense of his own spiritual life and his conversion.

His work on the proposed Catholic university in Dublin resulted in the brilliant essays on education now known as *The Idea of a Uni-*

versity. Newman was named a Cardinal of the Catholic Church by Leo XIII in 1879.

Percy Bysshe Shelley (1792-1822), the embodiment of the heretic and nonconformist, was the son of wealthy and ultra-conservative parents. As a student, both at Eton and at University College, Oxford, he rebelled against the restrictiveness of authoritarianism and petty student tyranny. His expulsion from Oxford following the publication of "On the Necessity of Atheism" further estranged him from his family.

Moving to London, Shelley became a joiner of causes working for social justice. At eighteen he eloped to Scotland with sixteen-year-old Harriet Westbrook, and the two eked out a wandering existence for the next few years. Returning to London he met and was influenced by the radical social philosopher William Godwin. Shelley fell in love with Godwin's daughter Mary and eloped with her to France. Following the death of Harriet in 1818, Shelley married Mary. However, these actions outraged public decency and Shelley left England to live as an alien and exile in Italy.

In Italy he formed a close friendship with Byron and the other members of the "Pisan Circle"; but difficulties of health, the deaths of two of his children, and constant worries over financial matters darkened his world. Yet it was during this period that he completed some of his finest works, among them *Prometheus Unbound* and "Adonais." On July 8, 1822, on a sailing trip with a friend, he was drowned in a sudden squall. His body, washed up later, was identified by his copies of the works of Sophocles and Keats which he had with him. He was eulogized by Byron as "the most gentle, the most amiable, least worldly-minded person I ever met."

Robert Louis Stevenson (1850-1894) suffered most of his life from ill health, constantly struggling against tuberculosis. As a sickly boy, he received an irregular education but later attended the University of Edinburgh. To escape the ravages of his long troubles, he went on walking tours in Scotland and on the Continent. The latter resulted in the amiable book of travel essays, *Travels with a Donkey*.

In France he met Mrs. Fanny Osbourne, whom he married in California after her divorce. For a time they lived in New York State, but Stevenson's health forced them finally to move to Samoa, where they lived in an almost regal state in their home *Vailima*, a Samoan word meaning "Five Waters."

In addition to his famous adventure novels, Stevenson wrote *A Child's Garden of Verses* and *Virginibus Puerisque*, a collection of essays. He is the master storyteller, the "Tusitala" of his natives. A charming and engaging man, he died in the Samoa he learned to love and is buried facing Mt. Vaea. On his tombstone is engraved the epitaph he wrote: "Here he lies where he longed to be:/ Home is the sailor, home from the sea,/ And the hunter home from the hill."

Alfred, Lord Tennyson (1809–1892) was the fourth of a family of twelve born to a country clergyman. In the calm, rural atmosphere, Tennyson read avidly the classical writers and the Romantic poets. Later, at Trinity College, Cambridge, he won the Newdigate Prize for poetry and the respect and friendship of "The Apostles," a group of young writers and critics.

In 1827 he and his brother Charles published *Poems by Two Brothers* and, more important, *Poems, Chiefly Lyrical,* published in 1830. These and an edition published in 1833, were severely criticized by the reviewers as "dismal drivel." However, volumes published in 1842 gave Tennyson the great popularity which he was to enjoy until his death.

The death of his close friend Arthur Hallam in 1833 brought Tennyson to a spiritual crisis. This crisis and his coming to terms with life is recorded in the great elegy *In Memoriam A.H.H.,* published in 1850. The same year he was named Poet Laureate and was married to Emily Sellwood.

The rest of his life was both happy and poetically fruitful. Pilgrims from England and America came to his homes in Surrey and on the Isle of Wight. In 1884, Queen Victoria raised him to the peerage, and on his death he was granted burial in the Poet's Corner in Westminster Abbey.

Francis Thompson (1859–1907) was the son of pious converts to Roman Catholicism. During his teens he studied for the priesthood, but his strange indolence and impractical nature was against him and he left at the request of his superiors. Following the wishes of his physician father, he studied medicine at Owens College, Manchester. Failing this, he went to London where he lived a life of extreme poverty, suffering not only from hunger and want but also from an addiction to narcotics.

In 1888 he was befriended by Wilfred Meynell, the editor of *Merry England,* and his wife Alice, the poet. Regaining his health, although never really robust, he spent several years living at Storrington Priory, where he wrote some of his finest poetry.

Although Thompson did not produce a large volume of work, he did write some of the most impressive poems in the English language. His first volume, *Poems,* published in 1893, contained the magnificent ode

"The Hound of Heaven." In his other poems, particularly those about nature and children, he shows his own innocent and childlike nature. He died of tuberculosis on November 13, 1907.

William Wordsworth (1770–1850) was born in the lake region of Cumberland. Orphaned before his teens, he was brought up by his uncles. In 1787, he entered St. John's College, Cambridge, and graduated with an A.B. During these years, he spent one summer in the Lake District and another in France, two important and lasting influences on his life.

He returned to France in 1791–1792 and became an ardent and enthusiastic supporter of the French Revolution. However, the excesses of the Reign of Terror brought disillusionment and shattered faith. Eventually, the help and companionship of his sister Dorothy, and the friendship of Coleridge enabled him to bring balance back into his life.

Out of his friendship with Coleridge came the *Lyrical Ballads* in 1798, the literary beginning of the Romantic Movement. The three traveled to Germany, absorbing German philosophy along with the scenery. In 1802, Wordsworth married Mary Hutchinson and later received a sinecure as Distributor of Stamps for Westmoreland.

With the exception of *The Prelude,* most of Wordsworth's best poetry was written during his early years. In 1842, he was named Poet Laureate. On his death he was buried in Glasmere in his beloved Lake District.

GLOSSARY OF LITERARY TERMS

A

action: what takes place during the course of a novel, drama, or narrative poem.

aestheticism: a literary movement in the latter half of the nineteenth century, which revered beauty above all things and whose motto was *art for art's sake*.

aesthetics: the science or study of the beautiful.

alliteration: the repetition of a consonant sound, usually at the beginning of two or more words in a line of verse or in a sentence:
> "Doom is darker and deeper than any sea-dingle."
> —W. H. Auden

allusion: a reference to some person, place, or event with literary, historical, or geographical significance.

analogy: a comparison of ideas or objects which are essentially different but which are alike in one significant way; for example, the analogy between the grasshopper and the man who lives only for the moment.

antagonist: the force (usually a person) that opposes the main character (the protagonist) in his attempt to solve a problem and thus resolve the conflict in which he is involved.

anticlimax: an outcome of a situation or series of events that, by contrast with what was anticipated, is ludicrous or disappointing. The anticlimax can often create a humorous effect.

aphorism: a brief statement of a general truth, such as "The devil finds work for idle hands." In present-day usage an aphorism is synonymous with a maxim or proverb.

apostrophe: a figure of speech in which words are addressed to a person or thing—absent or present—or to a personified idea, such as death, truth, or nature:
> "Hail, Holy Light, offspring of Heaven firstborn!"
> —John Milton

archaism: a word or phrase no longer used in actual speech.
> "*Eftsoons* his hand dropped he!"
> —Samuel Taylor Coleridge

assonance: the repetition in lines of verse of the same vowel sound accompanied by unlike consonant sounds, sometimes used in place of rhyme:
> "Or sinking as the light wind lives or dies . . ."
> —John Keats

atmosphere: the general over-all feeling of a literary work conveyed in large part by the setting and the mood.

B

ballad: a narrative that has sprung from unknown sources, has been transmitted by word of mouth (often altered in the process), and was intended to be sung.

    ballad, folk: a ballad which originated with the "folk" or common people. Its authorship is unknown.

    ballad, literary: a ballad composed by a known author who consciously imitated the stanza form, rhythm pattern, and rhyme scheme of the folk ballad. The story told may have originated with the "folk" and have been previously transmitted by word of mouth.

blank verse: unrhymed verse that is generally written in iambic pentameter:

> "Was this the face that launched a thousand ships
> And burnt the topless towers of Ilium?"
> —Christopher Marlowe

C

cadence: the effect created by the rise and fall of the voice and by the emphasis and pause required by the meaning. In other words, the rhythm is not determined by a carefully planned combination of accented and unaccented syllables, as in traditional verse.

caesura: the main pause within a line of verse to indicate both the rhythm and the sense:

> "To be or not to be: that is the question . . ."
> —William Shakespeare

character: a person in a poem, play, or work of fiction; sometimes an animal or object.

characterization: the portrayal in a literary work of an imaginary person by what he says or does, by what others say about him or how they react to him, and by what the author reveals directly or through a narrator.

cliché: an expression used so often that it has lost its freshness and effectiveness.

climax: the point of highest interest or dramatic intensity. Usually it marks a turning point in the action, since the reader is no longer in doubt about the outcome.

conceit: a fanciful image, especially an elaborate or startling analogy.

conflict: the struggle between two opposing forces, ideas, or beliefs, which forms the basis of the plot. The conflict is resolved when one force—usually the protagonist—succeeds or fails in overcoming the opposing force or gives up trying.

connotation: the implied or suggested meaning of a word or expression.

consonance: the close repetition of the same consonant sounds before and after different vowels, such as *splish—splash*.

contrast: the bringing together of ideas, images, or characters to show how they differ.

couplet: two consecutive lines of verse, usually of equal length and rhyming together:

> "Had we but world enough, and time,
> This coyness, Lady, were no crime."
> —Andrew Marvell

D

denotation: the precise, literal meaning of a word or expression.

denouement: the unraveling of the plot, following the climax, in which the writer explains how and why everything turned out as it did.

dialect: the speech that is characteristic of a particular region or of a class or group of people.

dialogue: the printed conversation between two or more characters in fiction, drama, or poetry.

didactic: morally instructive or intended to be so.

dissonance: the juxtaposition of harsh and jarring sounds or rhythmical patterns.

dramatic monologue: a poem in which a single character reveals his own nature as well as the details (time, place, other characters, etc.) of the dramatic situation.

E

elegy: a poem of subjective or meditative nature, especially one of grief.

epigram: any witty or pointed saying tersely expressed:

> "Man is a rational animal who always loses his temper when he is called upon to act in accordance with the dictates of reason."   —Oscar Wilde

episode: a related group of incidents, or a major event, that comprises all or part of the main plot or, in a long work, is related to the main plot.

essay: a fairly short nonfiction piece in which the author expresses his thoughts and feelings on any subject he chooses to discuss.

>**essay, formal:** an essay in which the primary purpose of the author is to make clear the subject being discussed and, at times, its particular meaning or significance. The style is serious and dignified.

essay, informal: an essay in which the primary purpose of the author is to reveal himself through his reactions to, and treatment of, his subject. The style of writing is usually casual and conversational.

euphemism: a mild, inoffensive word or expression used in place of one that is harsh or unpleasant; for example, "to pass away" is a euphemism for "to die."

exposition: the background information that reveals what occurred prior to the time covered in a story, play, or narrative poem; who the main characters are (sometimes before they appear); and what situation has arisen that will lead to a problem requiring a solution.

F

figure of speech: the general term for a number of literary and poetic devices in which words or groups of words are used to create images in the mind or to make a comparison:

". . . she [England] is a fen
Of stagnant waters . . ."
—William Wordsworth

foot: a combination of accented and unaccented syllables which make up a metrical unit. A foot may incorporate syllables from different words, and the foot divisions may cut across words, thus:

"The cúr/tains dráwn/ upón/ unfriénd/ly níght."

foot, anapestic: a metrical unit consisting of two unaccented syllables followed by one accented syllable (interrúpt).

foot, dactylic: a metrical unit consisting of one accented syllable followed by two unaccented syllables (dífferent).

foot, iambic: a metrical unit consisting of one unaccented syllable followed by one accented syllable (abóve).

foot, spondaic: a metrical unit consisting of two accented syllables in succession:

"Bréak, bréak, bréak,
On thy cold gráy stónes, O sea!"
—Alfred Tennyson

foot, trochaic: a metrical unit consisting of one accented syllable followed by one unaccented syllable (prómise).

foreshadowing: the dropping of important hints by the author to prepare the reader for what is to come and to help him to anticipate the outcome.

form: a fixed metrical arrangement, such as the ballade, the sonnet, etc.

free verse: verse which does not conform to any fixed pattern. Such poetic devices as rhyme and regular rhythm occur only incidentally.

H

hyperbole: a figure of speech employing obvious exaggeration; for example, "His mind was a million miles away."

I

idiom: the language or manner of speaking that is typical of a particular region or group of people.

idyll: a poem or prose piece describing the simple pleasures of rural life.

illusion: a quality of belief evoked by a narrative or drama.

image: a general term for any representation of a particular thing with its attendant and evocative detail. It may be a metaphor, a simile, or a straightforward description. An image may also have symbolic meaning.

irony: a mode of expression in which the author says one thing and means the opposite. The term also applies to a situation, or the outcome of an event (or series of events), that is contrary to what is naturally hoped for or expected.

L

legend: a story that has come down from the past and that may have some basis in history.

locale: the particular place in which the action in a work of fiction occurs.

lyric: any short poem that seems to be especially musical and expresses, in most instances, the poet's clearly revealed thoughts and feelings.

M

metaphor: a figure of speech in which two things are compared without the use of *like* or *as*:

> "Life's but a walking shadow, a poor player
> That struts and frets his hour upon the stage
> And then is heard no more."
> —William Shakespeare

meter: the pattern of rhythm determined by the relationship between the accented and unaccented syllables in a line of poetry. Meter is established by the repetition of a dominant foot; for example, iambic pentameter, a line of verse consisting of five iambs:

> "If music be the food of love, play on."
> —William Shakespeare

metonymy: a figure of speech in which one word is used in place of another word that it suggests, as the cause for the effect, the effect for the cause, the sign for the thing signified, the container for the thing contained, etc.; for example, John Milton used metonymy in the line "When I consider how my light is spent," where he substituted *light* for the related word *vision*.

metrical line: a line of verse composed of one or more feet. The following names are used to identify the most common lines:

> **monometer:** one foot
> **dimeter:** two feet
> **trimeter:** three feet
> **tetrameter:** four feet
> **pentameter:** five feet
> **hexameter:** six feet
> **heptameter:** seven feet
> **octameter:** eight feet

monologue: a poem, or a passage in a drama, in which a single character or actor speaks alone and, usually, at some length.

mood: the frame of mind or state of feeling created by a piece of writing; for example, a skeptical mood or a sentimental mood.

moral: the lesson taught by a literary work.

motivation: the cause or reason that compels a character to act as he does.

movement: a literary trend or development.

N

narration: an account or story of an event, or series of events, true or imaginary. Also the act of narrating such an account or story.

narrative poem: a story told in verse form.

O

octave: an eight-line poem or stanza, especially the first eight lines of a sonnet.

ode: a lengthy, dignified lyric poem expressing exalted or enthusiastic emotion, often about some person or occasion worthy of esteem.

onomatopoeia: the use of a word in which the sound suggests what the word designates *(splash, buzz, murmur)*. This device enables the writer to express sense through sound.

P

paradox: a statement which, on the surface, seems contradictory, yet if interpreted figuratively, involves an element of truth:
"The child is father of the man."
—William Wordsworth

parody: a humorous imitation or burlesque of a serious piece of literature or writing.

pathetic fallacy: the ascribing of human traits to nature or to inanimate objects; for example, "a stubborn door."

pathos: that quality in prose or poetry that evokes in the reader a feeling of pity and compassion.

personification: a figure of speech in which places, things, animals, or ideas are endowed with human qualities:

> "These shall the fury Passions tear,
> The vultures of the mind . . ."
> —Thomas Gray

Q

quatrain: a four-line stanza.

R

realistic: the faithful portrayal of people, scenes, and events as they are, not as the writer or artist would like them to be.

resolution: the events following the climax of a work of fiction; it is sometimes called *falling action*.

rhetorical question: a question that is asked for its dramatic effect and to which no answer is expected.

rhyme: the identity of sounds in accented syllables and of all vowel and consonant sounds following (*beautiful, dutiful*). The term *rhyme* is ordinarily used in the sense of end rhyme, the identity of sounds in words occurring at the end of matching lines of poetry.

   rhyme, eye: the appearance, in close proximity, of two words which, because of their similar spellings, look alike but when pronounced do not sound alike (*heath* and *death*).

   rhyme, feminine: a rhyming of matching lines of poetry in which the accented syllable is followed by one or more unaccented syllables which also rhyme:

> "Lord, confound this surly sister,
> Blight her brow and blotch and blister . . ."
> —J. M. Synge

   rhyme, internal: the rhyming of a word in the middle of a line of poetry with another word or words in the line, usually at the end.

> "I sift the snow on the mountains below."
> —Percy Bysshe Shelley

   rhyme, near: an approximate or imperfect rhyme.

rhyme scheme: a fixed pattern of rhymes and also a fixed pattern of lines (stanza form).

rhythm: in poetry, the recurrence of accented and unaccented syllables in a regular, or nearly regular, pattern.

rhythm pattern: the basic movement of a line, stanza, or poem resulting from the choice and arrangement of the metrical units (feet). The rhythm pattern of a line containing five iambic feet is iambic pentameter, thus:

"Blame not my cheeks, though pale with love they be."
—Dylan Thomas

romantic: the portrayal of poeple, scenes, and events as they impress the writer or artist or as he imagines them to be. A romantic work has one or more of the following characteristics: an emphasis on feeling and imagination; a love of nature; a belief in the individual and the common man; an interest in the past, the unusual, the unfamiliar, the bizarre or picturesque; a revolt against authority or tradition.

S

satire: Any piece of writing which criticizes manners, individuals, or political and social institutions by holding them up to ridicule.

scansion: the analysis of the metrical structure of poetry.

sentimentality: a superabundance of emotion in a play, poem, or novel.

sestet: a six-line poem or stanza, especially the last six lines of a sonnet.

setting: the time and place in which the events in a narrative (prose or poetry) take place.

simile: a figure of speech in which a comparison is made between two objects essentially unlike but resembling each other in one or more respects. The comparison is indicated by *like* or *as*:

"O, my love is like a red, red rose . . ."
—Robert Burns

sonnet: a poem consisting of fourteen lines, usually written in iambic pentameter and dealing with a single idea or emotion.

  sonnet, Italian or Petrarchan: a sonnet composed of an octave (eight lines) followed by a sestet (six lines). The rhyme scheme of the octave is *abba abba;* that of the sestet is *cdc, dcd.* Poets frequently vary the scheme of the sestet.

  sonnet, Shakespearean: a sonnet composed of three quatrains and a couplet. The rhyme scheme is generally *abab cdcd efef gg.*

sonnet sequence: a group of sonnets by a single author, generally having a common purpose or thematic link.

stanza: a group of lines of verse treated as a unit and separated from other units by a space.

Spenserian stanza: a stanza form devised by Edmund Spencer, and consisting of nine lines rhymed *ababbcbcc.* The first eight lines are iambic pentameter; the last line, called the Alexandrine, is iambic hexameter. The form connotes a leisurely moving, richly sensuous poem.

stanza, tail-rhyme: a unit of verse in which a short line, following a group of longer ones, rhymes with a preceding short line.

stereotype: a character who conforms to certain widely accepted ideas of how such a person should look, think, or act.

style: the distinctive manner in which the writer uses language: his choice and arrangement of words.

suspense: a feeling of excitement, curiosity, or expectation about the outcome of a narrative (prose or poetry).

symbol: an object that stands for, or represents, an idea, belief, superstition, social or political institution, etc. A pair of scales, for example, is often a symbol for justice.

T

tercet: a three-line stanza.

terza rima: a series of tercets in which the second line of each tercet rhymes with the first and third lines of the following tercet: *aba, bcb, cdc, ded,* etc.

theme: the idea, general truth, or commentary on life or people brought out through a literary work.

tone: the feeling conveyed by the author's attitude toward his subject and the particular way in which he writes about it.